THE ARCHIVE THIEF

THE ARCHIVE THIEF

The Man Who Salvaged
French Jewish History in the
Wake of the Holocaust

LISA MOSES LEFF

OXFORD
UNIVERSITY PRESS

OXFORD
UNIVERSITY PRESS

Oxford University Press is a department of the University of
Oxford. It furthers the University's objective of excellence in research,
scholarship, and education by publishing worldwide.

Oxford   New York
Auckland   Cape Town   Dar es Salaam   Hong Kong   Karachi
Kuala Lumpur   Madrid   Melbourne   Mexico City   Nairobi
New Delhi   Shanghai   Taipei   Toronto

With offices in
Argentina   Austria   Brazil   Chile   Czech Republic   France   Greece
Guatemala   Hungary   Italy   Japan   Poland   Portugal   Singapore
South Korea   Switzerland   Thailand   Turkey   Ukraine   Vietnam

Oxford is a registered trademark of Oxford University Press
in the UK and certain other countries.

Published in the United States of America by
Oxford University Press
198 Madison Avenue, New York, NY 10016

Library of Congress Cataloging-in-Publication Data
Leff, Lisa Moses
The archive thief : the man who salvaged French Jewish history in the wake of
the Holocaust / Lisa Moses Leff.
pages cm
Includes bibliographical references.
ISBN 978-0-19-938095-4 (alk. paper)
1. Szajkowski, Zosa, 1911–   2. Jews—Europe—History—Archival resources.
3. Jews—France—Strasbourg—Archival resources.   4. Archival materials—France—Strasbourg.
5. Theft—France—Strasbourg—History—20th century.   6. Manuscripts—Mutilation,
defacement, etc.—France—Strasbourg—History—20th century.   7. Jewish historians—Biography.
I. Title.
DS135.E83L36 2015
940.53'1807202—dc23
2014043507

1 3 5 7 9 8 6 4 2
Printed in the United States of America
on acid-free paper

*To Ben and
to Adam and Meyer*

CONTENTS

———❖———

ACKNOWLEDGMENTS

IT IS A PLEASURE TO thank the many people who helped me with my research for this book. This project was built on conversations I had with people kind enough to share their memories with me: fellow Jewish historians; archivists and librarians in France, Israel, and the United States; and other people who crossed paths with Szajkowski or other parts of this story in one way or another. In many cases, they provided me with documentation from their personal collections that proved to be essential in putting together this story. Ironically, considering that this is a history of archives, my best "finds" were not archival at all, but rather things that people handed to me, sent me, or told me. Thank you to Phyllis Cohen Albert, Hadassah Assouline, Mordechai Altshuler, Zachary Baker, Solon Beinfeld, Victor Berch, Jay Berkovitz, René Bravmann, Gilbert Cahen, Vicki Caron, Richard I. Cohen, Claire Dienstag, Judith Endelman, Todd Endelman, Simon Epstein, Joshua Fishman z"l, Joel and Rivka Duker Fishman, Shaindel Fogelman, Leonard Gold, Norman Gechlik, Nancy Green, Jonathan Helfand, Paula Hyman z"l, Roger Kohn, Monique Lévy, Yvonne Lévyne, Hans Loeser, Frances Malino, Emmanuel Mark, Michael Marrus, William Meyers and Nahma Sandrow, Chana Mlotek z"l, Albert Moldovan z"l, Gérard Nahon, Pierre Nora, Julia Rosenthal, Jonathan Sarna, Menahem Schmelzer, Jerry Schwarzbard, Simon Schwarzfuchs, Judith Schlanger, Michael Terry, Marek Web, Georges Weill, David Weinberg, Gabriel Weinreich, and Steven Zipperstein.

I would also like to thank the staff of the archives where I conducted research for this project. Their expertise was indispensible, particularly in cases when materials were not catalogued. In many cases, archivists' and librarians' insightful comments about the workings of their institutions in particular and archives in general pushed my thinking in new directions. In France: the Archives de la Ville et de la Communauté Urbaine de Strasbourg; the Archives Départementales du Bas-Rhin; the library of the Alliance Israélite Universelle (particularly Ariel Danan, Jean-Claude Kuperminc, and Rose Lévyne); the Mémorial de la Shoah-Centre de Documentation Juive Contemporaine (particularly Diane Afoumado and Karen Taïeb); the Archives Nationales; and the Bibliothèque Nationale; in Israel: the Central Archives for the History of the Jewish People (where Yochai ben Ghedalia provided invaluable help); and in the United States: the American Jewish Archives (thanks especially to Dana Herman, Kevin Proffitt, and Gary Zola); Brandeis University Library (thanks especially to Surella Seelig); the Klau Library at Hebrew Union College; the library of the Jewish Theological Seminary of America (where Ellen Kastel helped locate hard-to-find materials); Harvard University Library; the Leo Baeck Institute; and the YIVO Institute for Jewish Research (special thanks to Gunnar Berg, Krysia Fisher, Ettie Goldwasser, Leo Greenbaum, Fruma Mohrer, and Vital Zajka).

Thanks also to the colleagues who helped me with research. A few took precious time from their own research to send me copies of documents of great interest from the archives. For this, many thanks to Richard Breitman, Katherine Eade, Christine Haynes, Miriam Intrator, Joshua Karlip, Daniel Lee, Nguyet Nguyen, Nancy Sinkoff, Barry Trachtenberg, and Nick Underwood. Laura Jockusch repeatedly shared her expertise in our shared area of interest. Judith Surkis helped shape my approach. My advisors from graduate school, Leora Auslander, Jan Goldstein, and Bill Sewell were as supportive and generous as ever. Harriet Jackson, Peter Honigmann, and Brad Sabin Hill gave invaluable research advice at numerous points over the years. Judy Fixler helped me navigate the Tcherikower collection the first time I used it, leading to the most valuable find of all. I first sought out translators Iosif Lakhman and Lillian Leavitt when I realized what I was up against with Szajkowski's Yiddish handwriting. What I found with them was more than I could ever have hoped for, as they not only deciphered his handwriting but rendered his words so beautifully into English.

Beyond those thanked above, many other friends and colleagues generously discussed this project with me over the years, and I hope they recognize the mark those conversations left. I am especially grateful to those among them who, at one time or another, read parts of what has become this book and offered their thoughts: Masha Belenky, Richard Breitman, Judy Coffin, Mo Healy, Ethan Katz, James Loeffler, Maud Mandel, Helene Meyers, Johanna Neuman, Simon Perego, Erica Peters, Jessica Roland, Sarah Abrevaya Stein, and Barry Trachtenberg. Warm thanks are also due to the members of my writing group in Washington, DC, and to my fellow participants in the United States Holocaust Memorial Museum's 2011 summer workshop on Jews and the Law in Modern Europe, who read draft chapters and offered many useful suggestions. Alexandra Garbarini helped with this project in innumerable ways from beginning to end, reading the manuscript in its entirety twice over. I am deeply grateful for that, and also for her friendship and wise counsel.

Financial support for this project came from a number of sources. Southwestern University supported my work generously with Cullen grants, a sabbatical, and an extended leave that allowed me to complete most of the research for this book; thanks to Provost James Hunt, History Department Chair Thomas McClendon, and my colleagues in the department for making it possible. American University's International Travel grant and Mellon grants also supported my research, and Dean Peter Starr and History Department Chair Pamela Nadell allowed a flexible teaching arrangement that facilitated the writing. I am also grateful for the fellowships I received from the Memorial Foundation for Jewish Culture, the United Methodist Higher Education Board for its Sam Taylor Fellowship, and the American Jewish Archives for its Vining-Davis Fellowship. I had wonderful experiences as a fellow at Columbia University's Reid Hall in Paris, the University of Chicago's Paris Center, and Harvard University's Minda de Gunzburg Center for European Studies; thanks to all who made those fellowships possible.

Versions of this work were presented in a number of academic settings over the years, and I am grateful to those who organized those wonderful talks, workshops, and conferences, as well as for those who offered feedback on my work at Boston College (2009); Rhodes College (2009); the annual meeting of the Society for French Historical Studies (2010); New York University's Institute for French Studies (2010); the University of Chicago's Jewish Studies Workshop (2010); the annual meeting of the Association for Jewish Studies (2010); the University of Cape Town's conference on the Archive and Jewish Migration (2011); the University of Kentucky (2011); George Washington University's Judaic Studies Workshop (2011); the University of Delaware (2012); the University of Cincinnati (2012); the Central Archives for the History of the Jewish People and Hebrew University (2013); Oxford University (2014); the Center for Jewish History's Seminar on Archival Research (2014); the Washington History Seminar (2014); and Texas A&M University-Corpus Christi (2014).

My family, Claire Moses, Arnold Moses, Susan Leff, Edward Davis, Leslie Moses, David Herring, and Joseph Leff z"l, provided the warm and unconditional support that makes a project like this possible. My mother also lent her seasoned editor's hand to a final round of revisions; the book is much the better for it. The warm hospitality of Barbara Honigmann in Strasbourg and Freddy Rokem in Jerusalem made research travel much more enjoyable. Becky Roiphe and Ben Gruenstein provided a home away from home on my many trips to New York. Finally, I want to express my gratitude to my sons Adam and Meyer, who were always up for the adventures that eventually resulted in this book, and to my husband Ben, for all that and more.

Finally, many thanks to the excellent team at Oxford University Press, especially Nancy Toff and Rebecca Hecht, for all their support and help, and to Beth Hanlon and Peter Bakel, for pointing me in their direction.

THE ARCHIVE THIEF

INTRODUCTION

———⟨∘∘∘⟩———

THE ARCHIVAL SOURCES HISTORIANS USE to write the history of Jews in modern France are scattered across three continents, a veritable diaspora of documents. The pattern they form is curious. Unlike the documentary diaspora of German Jewish archives, which are also spread across the globe, it does not follow the paths of their owners' flight from persecution and their resettlement on safer shores.[1] That would be impossible; Jews have not emigrated en masse from France since these documents were created. Indeed, even after the devastating loss of a quarter of their population in the Holocaust, France's Jews stayed. Their numbers grew, and with new waves of immigration quickly exceeded prewar levels. In spite of the difficulties involved, they managed to rebuild their vibrant communal life. Furthermore, many of the largest French Jewish institutions survived the period of Nazi occupation with their papers intact, and the largest of the libraries looted by the Nazis were found and returned to France after the war.

And yet, across the network of state archives in France—the nation's pride, a treasure trove of government and private papers—troubling gaps are visible in the papers in which Jews are mentioned. A few important French synagogue collections seem riddled with holes as well. At the same time, surprisingly large collections of rare French

Judaica turn up in the special collections departments of university libraries such as Brandeis University (Waltham, Massachusetts), Harvard University (Cambridge, Massachusetts), Hebrew Union College (Cincinnati, Ohio), the Jewish Theological Seminary of America (New York), and Yeshiva University (New York), as well as in the archives of the YIVO Institute for Jewish Research (New York) and the Central Archives for the History of the Jewish People (Jerusalem). Why are these documents no longer in France if French Jews largely opted to remain in France after the Holocaust? How did they wind up dispersed so widely across the globe?

The answer is an open secret. If you ask one of the more seasoned archivists, librarians, or researchers working in any one of these institutions, you are likely to hear some talk of international intrigue. At the center of the intrigue is a peculiar individual: the historian Zosa Szajkowski (Shy-KOV-ski, 1911–1978), a pioneer in the field of French Jewish history. Szajkowski wrote scores of articles in the field, most on topics no one had ever researched before and many of which are still considered indispensible decades after they were written. Beyond his scholarly work, Szajkowski was also a devoted collector of French Judaica. He began his collecting in the late 1930s when, impassioned by Jewish history, he solicited donations from French Jews who had materials of historical interest among their family papers. In the aftermath of the Holocaust, wracked by grief and determined to facilitate the writing of an objective history of catastrophe, he gathered evidence of the persecution from Jewish leaders in Paris and from the wreckage of bombed-out buildings in Berlin. Many Jews in France and the United States saw his collecting of those papers as a heroic effort to preserve the evidence for posterity.

But in time, this rescuer became a thief. Most of the documents he acquired in the 1950s—mostly pertaining to Jewish history in France since the seventeenth century—he stole from the archives. Some were taken from state archives, where he stealthily evaded the gaze of the archivist in the "panoptical" reading room, often cutting old documents out of bound volumes to evade detection.[2] Others were stolen from the private collections of synagogues and private Jewish libraries, institutions that had only recently begun to recover from what had happened in the years of Nazi occupation. In both types of institutions, archivists were betrayed by someone they had come to trust as a professional scholar and, in many of these cases, as a fellow Jew. After Szajkowski's betrayal, they took steps to protect their collections from further losses, but they were only ever able to recover a tiny fraction of what had been taken.

The results of Szajkowski's collecting, particularly if we count the legal together with the illegal, are staggering. Between 1940 and 1961, Szajkowski acquired tens of thousands of documents about Jews from various sources in France and brought them to New York. After he finished his own work with the documents—they were used as evidence in his articles—he sold them to the American and Israeli research libraries and archives where they are now housed. Although few acquisitions records remain, many of these documents bear marks of Szajkowski's handling, including notations made in his handwriting. To the degree that it is possible to trace the collections of French Judaica held outside of France, most of them appear to have been purchased from Szajkowski in the 1950s and 1960s.[3]

Given France's checkered history with regard to the Jews, it is hard to know how to evaluate Szajkowski's collecting overall. Was he simply a thief who destroyed the integrity of the French archives, preying on the disorder the Nazis had left in their wake? Or was he a hero who rescued Jewish papers from a country where on more than one occasion in the past two hundred years, calls for the expulsion of the Jews rang loudly across the land, and in even more recent times, French officials facilitated the deportation of more than 76,000 Jews to Nazi death camps?

However we make sense of them, it is clear that the thefts and sales have had a significant impact on the historiography. The documents in the American and Israeli institutions have been used by dozens of scholars, including the first university-based historians to work on French Jewish history. In fact, a number of the students who helped to create this academic subfield wrote their dissertations right around the time of the sales in the 1960s at some of the very institutions that acquired French Jewish documents from Szajkowski. These include Arthur Hertzberg and Paula Hyman (Columbia University), Phyllis Cohen Albert and Frances Malino (Brandeis University), and Jonathan Helfand (Yeshiva University). Although these scholars and those who followed in their footsteps also did extensive research in France for their work, the existence of source material in American institutions was an important factor in raising their interest in what was, at that time, a topic no scholar working in academia—in the United States, Israel, or France—had yet explored.[4]

My interest in Szajkowski's story began in the 1990s when I was conducting research for my Ph.D. dissertation on Jews in nineteenth-century France. Initially, the tales I was hearing in the archives were just a distraction from the tedium of my research on the "real" history of French Jews. But in time, I grew increasingly aware of Szajkowski's impact on the kinds of questions historians ask in my field, including the ones I myself was asking. The footnotes and bibliographies of works in the field are a testament to Szajkowski's lasting impact as a scholar, but also as a shaper of archives. By stealing what interested him, Szajkowski created holes in French archives and new holdings in American and Israeli ones. What's more, in France, the disappearances led horrified French archivists to catalogue, for the first time, the collections from which Szajkowski had taken materials, thereby making those particular collections accessible in a new way. In the United States, the acquisitions of these documents created entire collections based on his interests. Those actions led in both places to heightened interest in the kinds of questions he pursued and the collections he used. The writing of the "real" history of French Jews on both sides of the Atlantic has been facilitated by Szajkowski as a historian, collector, and thief.

Szajkowski has not only had an impact on what documents we can access, but also, to some extent, the ways in which we read them. By stealing documents about Jews from France and selling them in the United States, Szajkowski re-contextualized important materials and shaped the very way we conceive of the history we are writing when we use them. For the most part, the American and Israeli institutions to which he sold documents identify these materials as "Jewish" because most of them are housed in private Jewish institutions. There, the documents are generally identified as "French materials," alongside other collections of, say, "German" or "Italian" Judaica. This means that in these collections, you will find eighteenth-century tax records from Metz in the same series with nineteenth-century Bordeaux synagogue records and World War II-era Parisian Jewish resistance documents.[5]

In contrast, many related documents that you might see in France are held in the state archives that first collected them, and there, they are organized along with the records of other French institutions, grouped by provenance (i.e., by the agency that created them). For example, in the French National Archives, the records of synagogues built with state support in the nineteenth century are in the same series as the records of Protestant and Catholic churches, since they were regulated by the same state agency. In short, while the records in French archives are organized to reflect the organization of the French state, the records in the American and Israeli documentary collections are organized to reflect the history of the Jews in diaspora, a veritable "ingathering of the exiled documents."[6] As historians, our access to the documentary record of the French Jewish past is thus constructed through institutions with very different conceptions of the place of Jews in France. One makes Jews an integral, if sometimes invisible, part of French history, and another makes France one location among many in the story of dislocated Jewish history. The organization of the archives thus also reflects a key tension in the historiography: Is the story of Jews in France part of French history or part of Jewish history? Here too, Szajkowski has left his mark on the way we understand the past.

Szajkowski's story takes place in what historian Antoinette Burton has called "the backstage of archives," the staging area that we are trained to ignore as we go about our research into the "real" history we are reconstructing based on the documents themselves.[7] Although we rarely examine them as such, archives are themselves historical artifacts. Investigating their history sheds light on the worldviews of their builders and the contexts in which they were built. As Burton writes, archives "arrive at our sightlines as if they were shrink-wrapped, that is, with very little trace of how they were compiled."[8] Yet in reality, their content and organization are not as fixed as we generally assume them to be. If we look carefully, some of the materials they contain bear the marks of their handlers. Learning about the history of the documents we use is as useful as it is interesting, because the web of commitments that built the archives continues to have an impact on our conception of the past.

The history of Jewish archives taken out of Europe during and after World War II is somewhat better known than the history of other archival collections. This is because the looting of European Judaica by the Nazis has been understood in the popular imagination as part of the tragedy of the Holocaust, and the postwar recuperation of these materials has been understood as part of the work of reconstruction and memorialization. But as such, even among scholars, the postwar movement of European Judaica to new homes in the United States and Israel has largely been celebrated as a successful rescue effort in ways that obscure the disputes, illegalities, and ambiguities involved. In the process, they also artificially make the history of Jewish archives an exclusively Jewish tale, sealed off from broader historical developments and practices.[9]

Szajkowski's work with the archives is far more ambiguous than those better known stories of heroism. Some of what he did was celebrated as heroic acts of Judaica rescue, but other transfers were clearly thefts. The ambiguity at the heart of his story provides an interesting vantage point from which to rethink certain assumptions we still have about Jewish resistance in the Holocaust and Jewish reconstruction in its wake, because it unfolds in the same context and was shaped in large part by the same cultural, political, and economic factors. A number of scholars have recently begun to complicate traditional narratives of Jewish reconstruction, giving us a richer picture of Jewish responses to the Holocaust.[10] Placing Szajkowski's story alongside and within the more widely celebrated tales of postwar Judaica "rescue" forces us to see the larger moral complexities in the enterprise as a whole. In so doing, it also normalizes Jewish history, enabling us to draw links between the history of Jewish archives and the history of archives more generally.

Researching the backstage of archives is no easy task. Archives and libraries rarely make their internal records available to researchers, and some do not even keep them for more than a few years. To my surprise, in most of the institutions I consulted in the United States, even records of such basic transactions as purchases had been discarded long ago or were never created in the first place. As for the institutions in France, with only a few notable exceptions, it has been hard to determine what Szajkowski took from their collections illicitly, for his success as a thief depended on being able to accomplish the task without being detected. Only in the small number of places where thefts were actually investigated was I able to find a solid paper trail. As for the collecting he

did more legitimately, the only traces that remain are his own tantaliz-
ingly vague descriptions of these acquisitions in the letters he wrote
to friends, rarely mentioning the names of the individuals or shops
where he found his treasures. This means that we cannot know with
much certainty exactly which documents now held in institutions in
the United States and Israel were stolen, and which were acquired
more legitimately. It is equally difficult to know what exactly is missing
from French collections or the circumstances under which they went
missing. As any archivist or librarian knows, losses are an unfortunate
part of business-as-usual in such institutions, and any thief worth his
salt leaves no trace.

So I have had to work with the traces that do remain: penciled
scribbles in the margins of old French documents found in American
and Israeli archives; missing pages in bound volumes found in French
archives; interviews with archivists and historians who knew Szajkowski
in France, Israel, and the United States. Then there were Szajkowski's
own writings: his scholarly publications in five languages, numbering
almost two hundred, and an amazing cache of lengthy letters he wrote
to a friend in the years of his military service. Out of such evidence, it
has been possible to piece together this story, one that is in many ways
unique, at least in its scope.

But the larger factors that shaped Szajkowski's actions and how they
were seen are far from unique. Only when we understand the issues at
the heart of his story, in all their ambiguity and complexity, can we begin
to address the larger questions of the rightful ownership of archives that
are still so important today, not just with regard to French Jewish documents, but also for other contested archives. Examples are particularly
abundant in the Jewish press in recent years. One such case involves the
papers known as the Iraqi Jewish archive, seized by Saddam Hussein's
intelligence forces from the synagogue where they were left after Iraqi
Jews were forced into exile in the early 1950s. The papers were found
by U.S. troops during the invasion of Baghdad in 2003 and removed
to Washington for restoration work. The removal led to a bitter ownership dispute in which the new Iraqi state claimed its legal right to the
papers while outraged Jews in Israel and the United States advanced a
moral claim against their return to Iraq, arguing that a nation without
Jews is no place for a Jewish archive. Another recent example involves

the library of the sixth Lubavitcher Rebbe, seized by the Soviets in 1918, recovered in part by the family in 1927, seized by the Germans in World War II, seized again by the Soviets in 1945, and now once again the subject of international dispute, this time between the United States and Russia.[11] The problem is not a uniquely Jewish one, but given Jews' history of persecution and mass migration, they have been affected more frequently than most.

In a multicultural world in which victimized groups are frequently on the move, where are the remnants of their past best kept? Who has the right to make such decisions? We still live in an era in which nation-states reign supreme. For minority groups interested in preserving the evidence of their historical experience, the questions remain of the utmost importance.

I

Szajkowski's Passion

ON APRIL 13, 1961, THE Jewish historian Zosa Szajkowski was caught red-handed stealing rare documents from the city archives in Strasbourg, France. His method was rather crude: he was ripping pages out of bound volumes and sliding them surreptitiously into his brief-case. The written confession he penned that night, in words surely dictated by the chief archivist, highlighted the violence of the act in stark terms: "I admit to having lacerated volumes belonging to the Strasbourg Municipal Library," he wrote, signing the damning words not with his historian's nom de plume but with his legal name, Szajko (SHY-ko) Frydman.[1]

The archivist, Philippe Dollinger, initially judged Szajkowski to be "a scholar impassioned by his research" whose crime was motivated by his "excess of interest in his subject."[2] As a historian himself, Dollinger knew this kind of thing sometimes happened in his profession. Who knows, he may have felt the lure of the documents himself at one time or another. Certainly he would have talked about that passion with other historians; ever since archival research became the sine qua non of professional historical practice in the nineteenth century, it has been commonplace for historians to talk about documents in terms of "love, obsession, and more particularly fetishism."[3] And so, surveying the situation that night, Dollinger took pity on the man before him.

Demanding only that Szajkowski write the confession, return the stolen papers, and offer a donation to the archives upon his return to New York, he let the scholar go and waited until morning to file a police report, giving the historian ample time to hop a train to Paris and from there, a plane to London, thereby escaping arrest.[4]

This incident occurred at the height of Szajkowski's unusual career as a historian. Although he had never received a Ph.D.—or any degree, for that matter—by 1961, he was widely regarded as a leading expert in modern Jewish history, a member of the prestigious American Academy for Jewish Research. Born in Russian Poland in 1911, he had immigrated to Paris in 1927 to escape the poverty into which his hometown had sunk. Then, after France fell to the Nazis, he fled to New York, where he remained until his death in 1978. Szajkowski was remarkably productive, and by the time he was caught stealing in the Strasbourg archives, he had published well over a hundred academic articles and eleven books, most of which were based on archival documents and treated subjects that had never before been researched. He would go on to publish almost a hundred more studies.

The historian was known in scholarly circles around the world. His publications had appeared in Yiddish and English, and with the help of translators, a few had appeared in Italian and Hebrew as well. Yet except for a brief engagement as an adjunct instructor at Brandeis University years later, he never held a university position. His lack of credentials made that all but impossible. But since many Jewish studies scholars in the 1950s and 1960s were, like Szajkowski, working outside of academia, it did not keep him from getting his work published in top journals or from earning the respect of his colleagues. To support himself, Szajkowski relied on the modest salary he received from YIVO, the academic institute in New York that was devoted to the study of Jewish life generally and Yiddish culture specifically, where he worked as an archivist and research associate from 1946 until his death.

To catch such a well-respected historian in the act of stealing precious documents must have been quite a blow to the chief archivist at the Strasbourg Municipal Library. The members of his staff had done much to accommodate Szajkowski's tight schedule in the city that week in April 1961, and to be repaid this way was a betrayal of their trust. Such trust was not granted to just anyone who wandered into

French state archives, even smaller ones like this one. But Szajkowski was a scholar, and he had been there before on research trips in 1950 and 1955. Moreover, the studies he had published in American scholarly journals on the basis of his findings there were impressive in their rich documentation, and he had been good about sending offprints to the archives and libraries where he had conducted research. The fact that he was known to be one of the world's experts on the history of Jews in France with a special interest in the local region was good reason to trust him, and so while he was in town that week, Dollinger's staff in the municipal archives had treated him with due respect. That Thursday night, they had even let him stay late with the materials he was reading after the archives closed and the staff had gone home. Knowing his time in the city was running out, they moved the materials he was working on across the hall from the archives to the municipal library, where the reading room stayed open late.[5]

That evening, in the library reading room and not in the more relaxed atmosphere of the archives, a watchful librarian, Madame Solveen, caught the historian in the act and demanded to look inside his briefcase. When he stubbornly refused to open it, she rang the alarm, had the concierge bolt the door, and detained him while she phoned Dollinger. Arriving on the scene, Dollinger persuaded Szajkowski, man to man and historian to historian, to open his briefcase, where they found additional documents—including a fourteenth-century parchment—that had clearly been ripped from the bindings of archival registers. At that point, they must all have known something serious was afoot. Leaving Madame Solveen behind, Dollinger and the concierge, Monsieur Sommer, accompanied Szajkowski back to his room at the Hotel Royal, near the train station.

There they found sixty-nine other documents ripped from the bound registers that Szajkowski had ordered up and consulted that week in the municipal archives, along with twenty-one other documents of unknown origin, which appeared to have come from archives in the south of France. They could not be exactly sure where those other documents originated because, like the documents that they recognized from their own collection, they bore no ownership stamps. Inspecting all those documents in the hotel room with his own eyes, Dollinger saw that Szajkowski had sorted them into folders marked in Yiddish,

French, and English. One folder said "Bibliothèque de New York" (New York Library); another said "To Make Notes"; still others were marked with numbers: 2a, 7, 8, and 9a.[6] Szajkowski had not only stolen these papers, he had also been reorganizing and reimagining them as he went, each extraction a calculated addition to a Jewish-centered collection. Dollinger did not see that, at least not at the time. Taking stock of Szajkowski's theft that night, Dollinger decided that the return of the documents, a signed confession, and a promise to make a donation to the archives was sufficient punishment. He and the concierge headed back to the archives with the documents, leaving Szajkowski in the hotel room alone.

Historians are often passionate about old and rare things, and these stolen papers were old and rare indeed. Moreover, they were clearly related to Szajkowski's research. The document Madame Solveen had seen him "lacerating" concerned, somewhat ironically, the expulsion of Jews without a fixed address from Alsace in September 1784, based on the fear that Jewish migrants were vagabonds destined to become thieves. In Szajkowski's briefcase, Dollinger had found five more documents: two copies of a 1728 document forbidding residents of Strasbourg to trade with Jews, except for horses; a 1648 ruling that forbade Jews to trade with the residents of Strasbourg, except for horses; a 1539 regulation on Jewish usury; and an *ordonnance* from 1530, before Strasbourg was even part of France, by the Magistrat of the free city of Strasbourg forbidding the inhabitants of the town to contract for loans from Jews. The other documents found back in the hotel room were of a similar sort, the bulk of them eighteenth-century regulations pertaining to the Jews. In the archives, they had been organized in bound volumes according to the sovereign body that had issued them, including a 1765 regulation forbidding the insulting of Jews and a 1731 order from the royal *intendant* to the Alsatian *magistrat* to take a census of the Jews in his jurisdiction. The oldest document in the room was a letter, written on parchment in 1357, from the magistrate of Speyer to the magistrate of Strasbourg about the burning of Speyer's Jews.[7]

The documents Szajkowski stole in April 1961 were exactly the kind of thing he had been writing about in his history articles for years. Indeed, for more than a decade, Szajkowski had grappled with the meaning that lay on the pages he was to tear from their bindings, and he stewed over the questions of why such regulations were issued and what their implications were. He had written no fewer than five major studies using documents much like these, and several more on the Jews in the same region during the slightly later era of the Revolution.[8]

These documents depicted the Jews of Alsace living in an era of insecurity. On the one hand, restrictions on their work kept them concentrated in commerce and moneylending, which led to frequent conflicts with non-Jewish neighbors and the perception, often shared by the authorities, that they were unethical in their business practices. On the other hand, by the late eighteenth century, leaders in the region had come into contact with Enlightenment ideas, and some were beginning to advocate removing the restrictions on Jewish economic activity, arguing that the only reason Jews were immoral in commerce was that the law gave them no other options. As one of the most famous Enlightenment advocates for broadening Jewish rights put it in 1781:

> As there are almost no honest means of earning a living left to [the Jew] it is natural that he falls into criminal practices and fraud. . . . Has one a right to be surprised if a Jew feels himself bound by laws which scarcely permit him to breathe, yet he cannot break them without being punished? . . . Can one be surprised at his hatred for a nation which gives him so many and so stinging proofs of its hatred for him? How can one expect virtue from him if one does not trust him?[9]

The seventy-three documents Szajkowski stole from the Strasbourg Municipal Archives bear witness to Jews living in a time of flux, in which trust was extended at one moment and retracted the next. Over the centuries Szajkowski had studied, lack of trust had forced Jews into the types of commerce considered most shady, and business relations gone wrong became a pretext for further restrictions. And for all the great differences between wealthy, respectable Jews like Cerf Berr de Medelsheim (the only Jew permitted to live within the city of Strasbourg on the eve of the Revolution, together with his large family and servants) and the many indigent Jews of rural Alsace, as rights expanded and contracted, they seemed headed for a common fate. As Szajkowski saw it, on the eve of the Revolution of 1789, it was unclear if that fate was to be expulsion or emancipation.[10]

With the benefit of hindsight, Szajkowski knew full well how that story would turn out. Emancipation, not expulsion, would be the fate of those Alsatian Jews. But he also knew that emancipation had not resolved the problems Jews faced in Europe, even in France. The vicious cycle of mistrust, legal restrictions, and economic insecurity had circumscribed his very own life, perhaps as much as any eighteenth-century Jewish moneylender in the Alsatian countryside. He never stopped asking what had gone wrong.

In Dollinger's mind, documents such as these could cast a powerful spell on certain people. The phenomenon is widespread, if pathological, and it is not without its theorists. "Every passion borders on the chaotic, but the collector's passion borders on the chaos of memories," wrote Szajkowski's contemporary Walter Benjamin, himself no stranger to that passion. In acquiring objects, Benjamin theorized, the collector sees through them to their past, and the act can feel something like redemption. Assembling them in the "magic circle" of his collection, the collector breathes life into the objects; in so doing, he renews his *own* existence, as well as theirs.[11]

For those who, like both Benjamin and Szajkowski, were forced by dangerous circumstances to relocate to strange countries, collecting held a particularly powerful promise for the restoration of a battered self. Benjamin described it, using decidedly militaristic terminology, as a campaign carried out especially well in foreign lands: "Collectors are people with a tactical instinct; their experience teaches them that when they capture a strange city, the smallest antique shop can be a fortress, the most remote stationery store a key position. How many cities have revealed themselves to me in the marches I undertook in the pursuit of books?"[12] For Benjamin, a Jewish refugee himself, collecting is a weapon of the weak, a scavenging project that ultimately aims to reassemble both a broken world and a broken self.

Benjamin's analysis seems especially apt for this particular collector of old and rare papers, a refugee who had fled France in 1941 but returned frequently after the war to scour the country for remains of the Jewish past. In the Strasbourg Municipal Archives that week, Szajkowski had found the very laws that circumscribed Jewish life in early modern Alsace, shaping their world by restricting their economic activity, keeping them out of cities, and limiting their interactions with gentiles. Each of the papers he had cut out provided a clue to the fate of these Jewish people in centuries past. The archives had ordered them according to the logic of the authority that had produced them (e.g., the Alsatian Sovereign Council or the magistrate of the Free City of Strasbourg), for in a fundamental sense, the archives were the extension of that authority, both its memorial and its reflection.

Back at the hotel, though, these papers from the archive of the city had become a Jewish archive. Selecting from the city's collection only what had to do with Jews, the collector-historian had rearranged these papers for his own purposes. And he had not stopped with merely gathering these Jewish documents together. He had organized them into an archive, dividing them into the folders he had marked according to an idiosyncratic filing system only he understood. Collectors like Szajkowski, Benjamin tells us, feel a "thrill" when they place individually gathered items within the system they have designed, their "magic circle." The act of "fixing" each object in place offers collectors "the most profound enchantment," even a sense of omniscience, allowing them to peer through the objects deep into the worlds through which they have traveled. "[F]or a true collector the whole background of an item adds up to a magic encyclopedia whose quintessence is the fate of his object."[13]

Writing history was of course another way to create that same magic circle, using facts rather than objects. Most of Szajkowski's scholarship on Jews in early modern France was noted less for the arguments it advanced than for detailed descriptions of new sources. Many of his articles even included appendices in which the sources themselves were reprinted in their original languages. One might even say that some of the articles were themselves, on some level, collections. And amazing collections they were, particularly for their time. Szajkowski had a remarkable nose for the archives, finding things where Jewish historians had rarely looked.

If Dollinger believed he was dealing with a historian who had yielded to temptation, others were casting the story in decidedly different terms. The local newspaper ran a story on the theft in late April, likely based on small bits of information obtained from an archives insider. Full of misinformation, the newspaper's version of the story is all the more interesting, for it provides a taste of the kinds of rumors that were circulating in the wake of the theft. False rumors such as these are of little use in a police investigation, but they are a rich source for historians, because they provide a window into collective cultural anxieties that can be otherwise difficult to see. The story in the *Dernières Nouvelles d'Alsace* was a fantasy constructed out of the deep sense of unease that its author and many of its Alsatian readers felt about Jews in 1961. It reported:

> If we are to believe what we hear in certain parts of Strasbourg, the "thief" was no stranger. In fact, the archive employees often received this visitor. It seems that this person might be a certain historian who answers to the name of Frydman. He'd be of Polish origin. His books, well respected in fact, could be found in bookshops. He would have two accomplices, Soza and Takowski. They believe—maybe with too much haste—that the three men, who were not arrested, were looking to fill out the dossiers for the Eichmann trial. It is quite hard to say if this is the case. Nevertheless, knowing that Interpol has been brought in, we can assume that the investigators will be looking for these three individuals abroad, where they would have gone.[14]

The theory here was that the Israeli state was sending agents all over the world to comb archives for proof of Nazi crimes and then steal the documents to support their case at the trial of Adolf Eichmann, which was then underway in Jerusalem. Szajkowski's thefts were framed as a daring rescue mission, outside the law but justifiable as a means to bring Nazis to justice, not unlike the Israeli Mossad's bold and illegal mission to capture Eichmann in Argentina the previous year. Indeed, an article in the same newspaper had recently reported on the role that Tuvia Friedmann, director of Haifa's Institute for the Documentation of Nazi Crimes, had played in the capture of 150 Nazis to date.[15] Perhaps the journalist had mistaken Frydman for Friedmann?

This theory about the Israelis was, of course, highly unlikely. The article itself had correctly reported that the documents in question were from the early modern period and thus had nothing to do with Nazi crimes. Surely no matter how deeply the Israeli prosecution planned to delve into the history of European antisemitism, the acts of the Strasbourg magistrate in the sixteenth century would not be relevant, at least not to the point that the documents would be needed. Besides, even if there was some point that required research, why would the *originals* be needed? A second error enhanced the mistaken interpretation. By turning Szajkowski into a gang of three (Frydman, Soza, and Takowski), a simple theft became a Zionist conspiracy, and archive-hunting became part of the Jewish struggle for justice and revenge for the Jews murdered in the Holocaust.

Incorrect as this reading may have been when it came to understanding what Szajkowski did, it nonetheless tells us something about the mood in Alsace in 1961, just sixteen years after its liberation from Nazi rule. Historian Henry Rousso has argued that during the 1950s and 1960s, France's collaborationist past was "repressed," and the myth that all Frenchmen had participated in the resistance reigned. The situation was particularly complicated in Alsace, which had been annexed directly to the Reich in 1940. Although the region had been an integral part of Germany for the remainder of World War II, its population had been treated in postwar France no differently than other Frenchmen. That is, they were assumed to have spent the war either as victims of Nazism or as *résistants*, rather than as collaborators or, most unthinkably, as former German perpetrators. In fact, the reality had been more complicated, but as elsewhere, pragmatic concerns made it difficult to deal fully with the wartime past.[16] For this journalist and his readers, a Jew poking around in the archives threatened to bring that difficult, repressed history back up again.

The fact that the chief archivist did not march Szajkowski down to the police station on the night of April 13th does not mean he did not treat the case seriously. In addition to filing a police report the next morning, Dollinger also sent letters of warning to the archives across the border in Basel, Switzerland, and Trier, Germany, believing Szajkowski might be headed their way. Just in case, he also reached out to Pierre Schmitt, the archivist at the municipal archives in Colmar in southern Alsace. "I am writing to inform you that the Archives of the City of Strasbourg have just become the victim of a theft of numerous documents carried out by a certain Szayako [sic] Frydman, of U.S. nationality, who specializes in research on the Jews before the Revolution," he wrote to his colleagues, each of whom quickly wrote back thanking Dollinger for the information once they had verified that although Frydman had been in their archives that spring, nothing appeared to be missing.[17] The thefts appeared to have been contained.

But then in May, an antiquarian bookseller's sale list arrived at the archives, and with it came new doubts. The catalogue came from one of the most important Judaica rare-book dealers of the day, A. Rosenthal, Ltd. of Oxford, England. Issued in two parts in May and June 1961, the mimeographed "Jews in France" lists were filled with rare items from across France, described with the kind of exquisite detail for which Albi Rosenthal's erudite catalogues were known. The lists were rich with information about each item, focusing not only on physical condition but also historical significance, often with reference to scholarly works produced in multiple languages. The more elaborate printed catalogues had beautiful illustrations on their covers as well, and they have become objects as revered by collectors as many of the rare books they described.

In the "Jews in France" lists of 1961, Dollinger's staff found several documents they knew must have come from their archives. Looking more closely, they also guessed that many of the others must have come from archives elsewhere in France: Bordeaux, Avignon, Carpentras, Colmar, Aix-en-Provence, Marseilles, Strasbourg, Metz, and Paris. These were, they knew, the cities Szajkowski wrote about and visited most frequently on his research trips in the 1950s. And to make matters worse, throughout the catalogue Rosenthal had cited Szajkowski's articles to explain the significance of the documents. No longer seeing April's thefts as a crime of passion contained by a quick response, Dollinger and his associate François Joseph Fuchs went back to the police with the catalogue, and after consulting with Strasbourg's Mayor Pierre Pflimlin, they moved forward to press charges.[18]

In the ensuing investigation, the police learned that Szajkowski had earned £1,160, then equivalent to about $3,400 (the equivalent of $27,000 today, adjusting for inflation), by selling items stolen in the 1950s from French archives to Maurice Ettinghausen, Rosenthal's Judaica specialist. The unsuspecting book dealers were shocked to hear the accusations against Szajkowski, whom they knew and trusted as a scholar, family man, and courageous World War II veteran, a paratrooper no less. That a scholar would also be a collector and occasionally a dealer was not uncommon in that era. Rosenthal's firm also frequently bought materials from the Jewish historian Cecil Roth, to cite just one prominent example.[19] But theft was a serious charge, and Rosenthal did not quite believe it when he was first informed of the charges in a detailed letter from Dollinger dated June 20, 1961, which was later followed by questions from André Chamson, head of the French archives system, as well as visits from the Oxford office of Interpol.[20]

Eager to get to the bottom of this and to protect his firm's reputation, Rosenthal spoke with Szajkowski in person that summer in New York. The historian vehemently denied having committed the crime, though he refused to return to France to defend his innocence because, he said, he was awaiting an operation to repair damage from the near-fatal chest wound he had suffered as a soldier in World War II. He also pointed the finger at another collector in France, Gershon (Georges) Epstein, from whom he claimed to have purchased the documents in Paris in the late 1930s. When questioned in late August by investigators at his home in Grasse, Epstein said that he didn't know anything about these documents, and that he hadn't spoken to Szajkowski since the two had fallen out in 1948, although he had crossed paths with him in the archives in Strasbourg in mid-May 1950. The sources don't tell us how Rosenthal reacted to Szajkowski's insistence on his innocence and wartime heroism, but the Strasbourg investigators saw it as irrelevant and Szajkowski as a criminal who had acted alone. Certain as they were of their case, city authorities decided it was not worth the expense to extradite Szajkowski from New York. So in January 1963, Szajkowski was convicted for theft in absentia and sentenced to three years in prison and a 5,000-franc fine. It is all but certain that Szajkowski never returned to France.[21]

For Dollinger, seeing materials from the city archives listed in Rosenthal's catalogue changed his mind entirely about what Szajkowski had been up to in the archives. The man whom he once viewed with some degree of empathy was no longer deserving of any special consideration. Clearly nothing more than a cold-blooded thief, Szajkowski had betrayed the archivists' trust to enrich himself by selling documents he stole from the archives. Engaging in this type of commerce was utterly despicable to the archives' staff, and Dollinger's associate François Joseph Fuchs reached across the ocean to spread the word in America that "[a] recent theft of documents [was] committed in our archives by an American citizen ... the Jewish historian [*historien juif*] Zosa Frydman alias Szajkowski."[22] As in English, there is some ambiguity in French about whether "*historien juif*" refers to a historian who specializes in the history of the Jews, or a historian who is himself Jewish.

It is noteworthy that Dollinger had not used this formulation in his April letters to colleagues in Basel, Colmar, and Trier, using instead the less ambiguous formulation "*Szayako* [sic] *Frydman, de nation-alité USA, qui faisait spécialement des recherches sur les juifs avant la Révolution*" (Szayako Frydman, of American nationality, who was doing research especially on the Jews before the Revolution). The phrasing in Fuchs's later letter may have reflected merely a different writer's way of speaking, or it may represent an evolution in how the archives staff was coming to think about the thefts and their author.

The Strasbourg judge who condemned Szajkowski did not mention his Jewishness, but did call him a "Russian refugee domiciled in the United States." The turn of phrase was inaccurate; the country Szajkowski had fled for the United States was France, not Russia.[23] The wording seems noteworthy. By the time charges were pressed, Szajkowski was seen not just as a historian with a weakness for old paper, but rather as a *Jewish* historian and a wandering one at that, a refugee from the East who fit a centuries-old stereotype of the Jewish criminal who broke the trust extended to him by public authorities by engaging in immoral and illegal forms of commerce.

Since Szajkowski worked outside of academia, the archivists' attempts to censure him produced little result. They did their best, beginning by contacting Franklin Ford, a Harvard professor recently appointed dean of the Faculty of Arts and Sciences to whom Fuchs had grown close when Ford had conducted research in the city's archives in 1952–53 and 1955–56.[24] Although Ford had met Szajkowski in 1955 in Strasbourg, he wrote to Fuchs that he was not in a position to do much to sanction the scholar, who was not, after all, affiliated with any university. He did put Fuchs in touch with the American Historical Association, whose executive secretary politely wrote Strasbourg that he had never heard of "Zosa Frydman," but he hoped that the incident would not change the warm reception American scholars had received in Strasbourg in the past. Responding to Fuchs's request, Ford had also provided the address of the Alexander Kohut Memorial Foundation, based at the Jewish Theological Seminary

(JTS) in New York; Fuchs had noticed that Szajkowski had thanked Kohut for research support in a 1959 publication, a copy of which he had sent to the archives. But Dollinger received no response to the letter he sent the foundation's officers detailing the crimes of this "professional thief."[25] In the end, despite their efforts, the news remained relatively contained.

Astoundingly, the conviction in Strasbourg was not the end of Szajkowski's career as a collector and dealer, nor was it the end of his career as a historian. Although his access to French sources was blocked, and Rosenthal would never again buy from him, Szajkowski was still able to earn money selling French Jewish documents to other buyers. Among these were many important research libraries in the United States, including the libraries connected to the very institutions they had contacted, Harvard and JTS. Many others also bought from Szajkowski. His sales to libraries began at least as early as 1950; they continued until his death in 1978.

The episode left a mark on Szajkowski nevertheless. Unable to return to France, he shifted the focus of his scholarship to new topics for which the sources could be found in the United States, particularly the history of American Jewish aid to Jews in Eastern Europe. His narrow escape must have shaken him personally as well. Those who remember him in his later years describe an eccentric man, prone to bitter and paranoid ruminations, who remarked to more than one confused listener that he could never go back to France because someone there had it in for him.

Szajkowski's criminal behavior did not stop. In 1978, it caught up with him, this time in the reading room of the Jewish Division at the New York Public Library, where he was caught once again. But this time, the outcome was different. A few days after the incident, the sixty-seven-year-old historian took his own life.[26]

Why did this respectable historian become an archive thief? Were his thefts intended to facilitate his research? Were they perpetrated on behalf of the Jewish people to avenge European antisemitism through scholarship? Were they the compulsive acts of a collector whose drive had turned pathological? Were they an illicit form of commerce to which a struggling refugee had turned when he could find no other means of supporting himself as a scholar?

Just as perplexing as those questions are the motivations of the librarians in the United States and archivists in Israel who bought these materials from him in the 1950s, '60s, and '70s. Why did they turn a blind eye to the signs of ownership that, one assumes, were surely present on at least some of the materials? The two issues cannot be addressed entirely separately. However pathological, however criminal, however ideologically motivated certain of Szajkowski's acts were, he would not have undertaken such risky activities had there not been willing buyers. These buyers provided a market that made his thefts profitable and, tacitly, an alibi that made them morally acceptable. Understanding their worldview as well allows us to deepen our understanding of Szajkowski's passion.

Both Szajkowski and those who bought Judaica from him can be understood only when we answer a larger set of questions. We must know what these sources of Jewish history, scattered in institutions across Europe, meant to Jews—Szajkowski, his buyers, and many of his victims—in the postwar era. During the Holocaust, six million European Jews had been killed and hundreds of thousands more had fled the continent as refugees, either before or after the genocide. Millions of cultural treasures had been looted during the war, and many cultural institutions, including libraries and archives, were left in disarray. What did the documentary remains of Jewish history found both inside and outside those institutions mean to the Jews who had survived the war? What did they mean to the French archivists whose institutions housed them? What did they mean to Jewish survivors in France, who sought to rebuild in a country scarred by occupation and collaboration? And what did they mean to the American Jewish and Israeli cultural elite as they assumed the mantle of leadership in the postwar Jewish world?

The story of how Zosa Szajkowski became an archive thief is the story of a preoccupation that was far from idiosyncratic. The passion that postwar Jews felt for the archival remnants of their European past—their desire to collect, arrange, preserve, and study them—was, indeed, a sentiment broadly shared.

2

A Usable Past

ZOSA SZAJKOWSKI LOVED JEWISH BOOKS all his life. Already in 1921, at the age of ten, Yehoshua "Shayke" Frydman was a cultural activist for whom books had special meaning. That winter, he and a few friends demanded that their school buy Yiddish books for its library. They raised the money themselves with a Chanukah concert and convinced their parents to keep the books in their homes until the school library finally took them. The children were tremendously proud of their accomplishment, and with good reason. Raising the money had been no small feat; their families were among the poorest in town. Theirs was a secular school for Jews, established as a private Yiddish-language *folkshul* in 1919 but absorbed into the Polish state system in 1920. Most Jews sent their children, at least the boys, elsewhere if they had the means. But the campaign for Yiddish books touched a nerve. Not just their parents but also the wider community joined in the campaign, which the precocious Yiddishists waged as a struggle against forced assimilation into Polish culture. The issue had been simmering for more than a year, because when the school had become part of the public system, officials had changed the language of instruction from Yiddish to Polish.[1]

Shayke and his friends were sensitive to the political and cultural currents reshaping Jewish life in their hometown of Zaręby-Kościelne

SZKOŁA ŻYDOWSKA. W ZARĘBACH·K. DN 29/92

An official photograph from the public primary school for Jewish children in Zareby. Szajko Frydman, age twelve, is in the fourth row, third from right; his brother Efraim is the boy with the flowers in the third row, second from left. Parents with means sent their boys elsewhere, which accounts for the high ratio of girls to boys in this public school. *From the Archives of the YIVO Institute for Jewish Research.*

(Zaromb in Yiddish), a small town in east-central Poland (Masovia) where Jews comprised 1,254 of 1,626 inhabitants.[2] The shtetl may have been small, but the political and cultural ferment of the interwar years had not passed it by. Following its destruction during World War I, some of its Jews had left for the nearby cities of Warsaw and Bialystok, and others had ventured even farther, to New York and Paris. Returning home to visit their rebuilt hometown, they saw that the Zarombers were growing increasingly impoverished. By 1938, 90 percent of Zaromb's Jews would be living off assistance from Jewish charities in Poland and abroad.[3]

Nevertheless, the Zarombers were energetically embracing the same ideas as Jews in Poland's larger cities. New movements were remaking the political, social, and cultural fabric of life in the little town and changing the way its Jews defined their very identities. Today, the idea that Jews constitute a unified "people" or "nation" is widespread, but the historical transformation of this concept over the past two hundred years is less well known. In post-Enlightenment Europe, Jewish peoplehood did not disappear as a concept, but what had once been a religious idea was reconceived in new, more secular terms. Nationalist movements based on language, culture, and history proved a particularly potent influence. Zionism, the movement to build a homeland for the Jewish people outside of Europe (in Palestine or later, Israel) is the best-known form of Jewish nationalism today, but in the first half of the twentieth century, other forms of Jewish nationalism also abounded. Among Jews in interwar Poland, Zionism competed against forms of diaspora nationalism, whose proponents agreed that Jews constituted a unique nation in the lands where they already lived, and should be recognized as such in Eastern Europe, both culturally and legally. The related movement of Yiddishism sought to cultivate Yiddish as Jews' national language and proved influential on many of these forms of diaspora nationalism. Even international socialism included Yiddish-speaking subsections or autonomous parties, the best known of which was the Bund, which fostered both Jewish national consciousness and working-class consciousness.

Energized by the political and intellectual ferment around them, the children of Zaromb's Jewish public school—especially the smart and ambitious ones like Shayke—became activists. When they demanded Yiddish books for the school library, it was in order to preserve and strengthen Jewish life in the face of the powerful changes that were threatening it.[4] The Poles too had embraced nationalism, and some of the bureaucrats setting up the public school system of the new state were not keen on educating students in any language other than Polish. For Shayke, not yet a member of any political party, Jewish books and a Jewish library were causes worth fighting for. He long remembered the excitement he had felt when the whole town had come together to support its children when their Jewish identities were at stake.

It was in Paris, though, as a young man, that this lover of Jewish books became a scholar who studied and produced them himself. Szajko Frydman came to Paris in 1927, when he was sixteen, to join two of his older brothers, Zilke and Zalmen, and his sister Dina. In France, he still used the Polish spelling (Szajko) to transliterate the Yiddish nickname (Shayke) he used as his official first name, even though it was as difficult for the French to decipher as it would later be for Americans. But in his world, it actually posed few problems, for he lived among Yiddish-speaking Jewish immigrants accustomed to Polish spelling conventions. Many, like himself, had been educated in Polish.

The highly politicized, culturally dynamic milieu that Szajkowski found in Paris was an important hub in the vast global diaspora of Yiddish-speaking Jews that formed in the turbulent 1920s and '30s. This meant that many of the same political and cultural ideas that Szajkowski had encountered as a boy in Zaromb—Communism, Jewish socialism, Zionism, and diaspora nationalism—also shaped life among the 90,000 immigrants who formed the majority of Paris's interwar Jewish population of about 150,000. In those years, antisemitism and economic hardship pushed many Eastern European Jews to migrate across the globe, as they sought new situations in which they could support themselves and live their lives in peace.

The scattering did not destroy the migrants' sense that the Jews constituted a nation. Instead, their shared experience of economic insecurity, social discrimination, frequent displacements, and bureaucratic struggles seemed only to have strengthened their sense that Jews constituted what Benedict Anderson calls an "imagined community."[5] Increasingly cut off from the religious practices, beliefs, and social norms of traditional Jewish life in Eastern Europe, the Yiddish-speaking Jewish migrants of the interwar years were on the move, exposed to new ideologies, and secular in outlook. They were also reading the world together through shared media: Yiddish newspapers, an emerging Yiddish literature, and mass-produced Yiddish scholarship, all mailed across long distances, within whose pages they affirmed a common identity and a collective fate, and debated how best to face the future. Dislocation heightened nationalism's appeal, and paradoxically, lent a distinctive transnational quality to the migrants' new sense of Jewish identity, as well as to the political and cultural movements they embraced.[6] In spite of their political disagreements, which could be quite bitter, fostering and preserving Jewish culture was deemed central to the agenda of all the Jewish political parties.

Szajkowski's particular passion—his love of history and the documentary remnants of the Jewish past—was ignited in the mid-1930s when he met Elias (Ilya) and Rebecca (Riva) Tcherikower, intellectuals originally from Ukraine who had moved to Berlin in the wake of the murderous pogroms of 1918–21, and then, with Hitler's rise to power, had come to Paris in 1933.[7] When Szajkowski met them, the Tcherikowers were associated with the Yidisher Visnshaftlekher Institut (the Jewish Scientific Institute, or YIVO), an academic institute founded in 1925, dedicated to the study of Jewish life, particularly in the Yiddish-speaking world. Founded in the same year as the Hebrew University of Jerusalem, YIVO too aspired to be recognized as the leading academic institution for the modern Jewish people, but its orientation was diaspora nationalist and Yiddishist rather than Zionist. As such, YIVO was an adamantly Eastern European institution, committed to fostering Jewish life in diaspora and supporting the development of a national Yiddish culture. Nevertheless, its leadership was geographically dispersed across the interwar Jewish diaspora.

Vilna, long a symbol of Jewish learning, was the organization's headquarters because of its founders' commitment to the Yiddish language and to Jewish life in Eastern Europe. But its leaders were dispersed, and its four "sections" were each headquartered in a different city. Max Weinreich chaired the Linguistics, Literature, and Folklore Section in Vilna, where an impressive modern building was constructed to house the institute. Together with two other scholars of Yiddish, Zelig Kalmanovich and Zalmen Reyzen, he also directed YIVO. Leibush Lehrer ran the Psychology and Education Section out of the "Amopteyl" (*amerikaner opteyl*, or American branch) in New York; Jacob Lestschinsky ran the Economics and Statistics Section in Berlin until 1933, then in Warsaw until 1938, and then in New York; and Tcherikower ran the Historical Section in Berlin from 1925 to 1933, and then in Paris from 1933 to 1940.[8]

Although academic, YIVO in the interwar years was anything but an ivory tower divorced from the struggles of the Jewish masses. Ideologically committed to the idea that the Jews were a national group and that developing national culture would fortify them to face the economic, political, and social challenges of the twentieth century, YIVO saw itself as a kind of Jewish university sitting at the pinnacle of Jewish intellectual life. To that end, it sponsored scholarship and trained teachers for the Yiddish school system that was established for Jews in interwar in Poland. YIVO also established a network of *zamlers* (collectors), recruited from across all the Jewish social classes, who collected all sorts of materials that documented Jewish life—folktales, oral histories, music, printed matter, copies of documents found in local archives—and preserved them in its archives for future study. Inspired by historian Simon Dubnow, a guiding force in YIVO's early years, YIVO's leaders saw collecting as a way to preserve Jewish culture, to make Jews care about it, and to make it possible for an emerging class of intellectuals to study, in an objective and scientific fashion, as many aspects of Jewish life as possible.[9]

As with so many others, YIVO changed Szajkowski's life. For this man of natural intelligence, YIVO offered a path to stretch himself intellectually in the service of the Jewish people. Perhaps just as importantly, it offered a point of entry to a new cultural elite within the transnational Yiddish-speaking diaspora, which appealed to his driving ambition.

Szajkowski met the Tcherikowers around 1935 when he was working as a journalist for Paris's Yiddish-language Communist daily, the *Naye Prese*. This was quite an achievement for a working-class Jewish immigrant, whose brothers, like most Jewish immigrants in Paris in that era, worked in the clothing trades, one as a tailor and the other as a watchmaker.[10] Shayke was a worker too. When he first arrived in Paris in 1927, he wrote on the registration form required of all immigrants by the local police that he was working as an "apprentice furrier"; a friend later recalled Szajkowski telling him he also worked as a milkman and a porter in a furniture factory at one point or another.[11]

By 1934, though, he was making his name as a writer, and in 1936, he successfully petitioned the police prefecture to reclassify him as such on his foreign worker's identity card.[12] The move was especially unusual for someone with such limited formal education. In Zaromb, Shayke had attended a *heder* and a public school for Jews. As an adolescent, he spent three years in Warsaw in a public Jewish secondary school, but his formal education ceased when he arrived in Paris at the age of sixteen.[13] Yet his curiosity about the world around him was boundless, and he found himself able to write even after having put in a full day in a factory.[14]

The results were impressive. Between May 1934 and February 1938, he published nearly two hundred articles in the paper. As was common practice in the interwar Yiddish press, Frydman published under a number of different names: variations of his legal name (S. Fridman, S.F.), as well as at least three different pen names, S. Feld, Tchaptchinski, and, transforming his first name into a last name, Z. Shaykovski, the pseudonym he also used later as a professional historian writing in English, adopting the Polish transliteration of his name, Szajkowski.[15] The "Z." was for "Zosa," the unusual diminutive for Yehoshua preferred by his parents, Minka Roza and Chaim Yankel Frydman, who had stayed behind in Poland, although they later moved to Warsaw.[16] Later in life, when Szajkowski read Jack London's novel *Martin Eden*, he experienced a shock of recognition. London's plucky protagonist, a self-taught journalist, relied on his sharp mind, steely determination, and thick skin to rise above his proletarian roots through writing. The self-taught Szajkowski had done just that, reinventing himself and cata-pulting himself into the cultural elite. Ironically, he had begun this journey to respectability within the nominally egalitarian milieu of Jewish Communists.[17]

Szajkowski had actually become a Communist in Warsaw. When he first arrived in Paris in 1927, the Party's Jewish section (*sous-section juive*) was a kind of home for him, as it was already for his brothers. Indeed, Communism was the most popular affiliation for new arrivals from Poland.[18] Most, like Szajkowski, had joined before leaving Poland, despite the fact that the Party was banned in interwar Poland. Once in France, they still found the affiliation meaningful. Poorer and less integrated than the smaller number of Jewish immigrants who had come before the war, the new migrants preferred the more politicized and working-class Party to the *Fédération des Sociétés Juives de France* (an umbrella group bringing together various immigrant associations, composed in large part of prewar immigrants). They were even more alienated from the long-established Jewish associations dominated by the French-born Jews, particularly the religious institutions of the Consistory system, which dated back to the Napoleonic period, or the *Alliance Israélite Universelle*, an international philanthropic organization founded in 1860.[19] The *sous-section juive* was also less dogmatic than the Party in interwar Poland and the Soviet Union, and many members were in fact ideologically more anarchist than was possible in Eastern Europe.[20]

For new arrivals like Szajkowski, part of the reason that the Jewish subsection of the Communist Party was a home away from home was that promoting Yiddish culture played an important role in its agenda. In 1925, the French Communist Party (PCF) formed its immigrant labor section, the MOE (*Main d'oeuvre étrangère*—which in 1932 was renamed MOI or *Main d'oeuvre immigrée* and included the *sous-section juive*, in which organizing was done in Yiddish). In creating the MOE, the PCF was actually building from an existing base. Jewish Communists had formed their own organization in France as early as 1921 when, following the larger split within French socialism, the Jewish Communists split from the Jewish socialists of the Bundist Medem Association, a group that Communists perceived as insufficiently critical of traditional Jewish elites (rabbis and bourgeois). The MOE was designed to integrate organizations such as the Jewish Communists into its larger structure as a way to reach more immigrant workers as their numbers were growing, and perhaps bring greater ideological uniformity to its membership.[21]

Szajkowski's early writing in the *Naye Prese* was intended to appeal to fellow Jewish immigrants in that highly politicized milieu, much of it investigating the situation of Jewish workers and their organizing in France. Many of his articles focused on the trades themselves, ranging widely in scope—the garment trades, the furniture-makers, and the grocers, to choose just a few examples. These depicted a Jewish lower class with a somewhat different profile from the proletariat imagined by strict Marxists, since so many in the clothing trades worked at home, often subcontracting work to their spouses and other family members. Furthermore, the class distinction between "workers" and petit bourgeois artisans and shopkeepers was less than clear. What they shared first and foremost were terrible living conditions, with whole families living in cheap hotel rooms or small one- or two-room apartments.[22] As Szajkowski's articles in the paper showed, the Jewish lower class in Paris had turned to organizing to face these challenges since the late nineteenth century.

Szajkowski's Communism was reflected in his interest in the struggles of lower classes; but just as strongly, he projected a Jewish nationalist sensibility that in this period was not yet at odds with his Communist beliefs. Many of his articles describe the activities of such groups as the Communist cultural organization, the *Kultur-lige*, as well as Jewish libraries, Yiddish theater, and Jewish summer camps for poor children.[23] As Szajkowski depicted them, the newly arrived French Jewish working class lived in a time of great motion and new experiences. In these times of change, Jewish culture remained relevant and dynamic, perhaps more so than ever before. For example, Szajkowski wrote articles showing working-class Paris's Jewish sites, as in his "On the Metro from the *Pletzl* to Belleville" (the city's main neighborhoods for Jewish immigrants); and, broadening the scope, in his 1935 series "To Nancy in the Fiat," for which Szajkowski took a road trip to eastern France, exploring the world of Jewish immigrants in Alsace-Lorraine. Some simply introduced the readers to Paris's attractions, such as the Musée Carnavalet, a history museum located in the *Pletzl*, or the little-known Catacombs of Belleville. He also reported on their experiences as long-distance migrants, as in his 1935 article "From Birobidzhan to Paris on Foot."[24]

Such reporting helped immigrants get to know their adoptive city. But the articles also tacitly affirmed the distinctiveness of the Jewish immigrants, circumscribing a Jewish city within the larger metropolis. Like the Yiddish-language newspaper *Forverts* in New York, the *Naye Prese* helped Jewish immigrants to acclimate to their new setting, but without abandoning their cultural, social, and linguistic identity as Jews. Although the "ethnic" identity that Szajkowski and his fellow writers at the newspaper were helping the immigrants to imagine seemed at odds with how previous generations of French Jews had defined their distinctiveness, even among the French-born Jews, an ethnic type of identity, more secular and cultural than religious, was emerging in this dynamic period.[25]

Like his contemporaries across the divisions on the Yiddish-speaking Jewish left—that is, Communists, Bundists, and members of the Marxist Zionist party, Poale Zion—in the mid-1930s, Szajkowski saw fostering a sense of peoplehood among Jews as a means by which the Jewish masses could organize and improve their lives materially and morally. And yet, even in his promotion of Jewish distinctiveness, Szajkowski did not reject acculturation altogether. Instead, he showed in one case after another that Jewish immigrants had always contributed to life in France and had participated in its tradition of democratic and social revolution, from 1789 to the uprising of the Paris Commune. In a seven-part series in August 1934, for example, he traced the history of Jewish workers' associations in France back to the nineteenth century, locating it within the general workers' movement. His five-part series in 1935 on Jewish immigration to France finds Jewish immigrants shaping France since the late eighteenth century, including a piece on Zalkind Hourwitz, a Polish immigrant who played a role in the French Revolution. For the readers of the *Naye Prese*, such studies provided what American critic Van Wyck Brooks called "a usable past," with a set of imagined ancestors who helped shape life in their new country without giving up their distinctive identity and connection to Jews (particularly Yiddish speakers) elsewhere.[26]

But Szajkowski was ambitious, and he wanted to be a scholar. Though journalism gave him a ready audience, it provided little opportunity to hone his craft as a historian. In 1936, he took a year-long break from the newspaper to try his hand at a different kind of writing. Late in the year, he published—at his own expense—a book called *Etyudn tsu der geshikhte fun ayngevandertn yidishn yishev in Frankraykh* (Studies on the history of the immigrant Jewish settlement in France) that contained versions of some of the historical essays he had initially written for the newspaper, as well as new pieces, and that represented his novel approach to the history of Jewish migrants from Eastern Europe, rooting them within both French history and the history of the Jewish diaspora.[27]

It was during this year-long break from journalism that Szajkowski became close to the Tcherikowers and the circle of scholars that congregated at their apartment at 34, rue Dombasle in Paris's fifteenth arrondissement. This was a kind of salon for the Yiddish-speaking Jewish elite, and many of the visitors were both community leaders and self-trained scholars. They spanned the political spectrum, from the revisionist Zionist activist and historian Julius Brutzkus, to the disapora nationalist president of the *Fédération des Sociétés Juives de France*, Israel Efroykin (known in French as Jefroykin), to the Bund leader and historian Franz Kursky, to the ex-Communist Yiddish poet and journalist Daniel Charney, who had left the Soviet Union after opposing the spelling reforms being imposed on Yiddish there.[28] The Tcherikowers were responsible for YIVO's history series, the *Historishe Shriftn*, in which scholars across the Yiddish-speaking diaspora published their original research and copies of their most exciting archival finds. Many in the Tcherikowers' circle in Paris were focusing on Jews in France, publishing articles in Yiddish in the *YIVO Bleter* on just the kinds of issues that impassioned Szajkowski (e.g., Motie Dobin's article on contemporary immigrant workers' lives, published in 1932, and Avrom Menes's more general study about the history of Jews in France, published in 1937).[29]

The apartment was not just a meeting place for scholar-activists; it was also an archive. By the 1930s, the Tcherikowers had amassed what would later become the massive Record Group 81 of the YIVO Archives in New York. The papers in the collection pertained to some of the most significant events in the recent Jewish past, most importantly, the Ukrainian pogroms of 1918–21. The Tcherikowers had smuggled much of this material out of the Soviet Union when they fled to Berlin in 1921 and had gone to great efforts to bring it along when they relocated to Paris in 1933. The collection must have filled the apartment. As they would learn in 1940, when leaving for the United States, the archival material alone weighed 2.25 metric tons. The collection made a great impression on the young Szajkowski, reaffirming his sense that here on the rue Dombasle he had found the true caretakers of the Jewish people, the scholars and activists who studied their condition in order to solve their most pressing problems.[30]

For the intellectually curious Szajkowski, the world around the Tcherikowers offered exciting possibilities for changing his life. Here he found potential mentors experienced in writing academic-style scholarship, a community of colleagues interested in history, and new forums for publishing. He was probably also interested in selling copies of his self-published book. The move was somewhat daring for the autodidact, but many in this world were trained outside the university system, and he approached the transition with courage. In May 1936, he made contact with Jacob Shatzky (a university-trained Polish Jewish historian who had moved to New York, where he served as secretary of YIVO's American branch, the Amopteyl), sending him some articles he had written about the history of Yiddish theater in Paris and modestly asking for feedback. "Please don't forget that I am not a historian by profession," he wrote,

Szajko Frydman on an outing with his mentors Ilya and Riva Tcherikower in France, in the late 1930s. *From the Archives of the YIVO Institute for Jewish Research.*

"but rather a simple worker. Therefore I won't be insulted if you tell me that I'm not, in fact, a historian, and certainly not a historian of Yiddish theater. Aside from that, I also wrote these articles very quickly. In any case, let me know if you can use them."[31]

A few months later, he sent Shatzky a copy of his *Etyudn*, hot off the presses. Still unsure about how his work would be received, but nonetheless promoting himself as best he could, he wrote to Shatzky, "I will appreciate any comments you make about the work. If you can, please write a review of the book somewhere, which was by the way, written evenings after working all day in a factory (I realize this is not relevant within a critical review)."[32] It was an emboldened Shayke Fridman who published a second scholarly study in 1937 about the history of Jewish labor organizing in France before 1914, entitled *Di Profesionele bavegung tsvishn di yidishe arbeter in Frankraykh biz 1914* (The Jewish workers' movement in France before 1914).[33] Encouragement from the YIVO historians was helping the "simple worker" turn himself into a professional Jewish historian.

But it was Tcherikower who mentored Szajkowski most directly. In early 1936, the young journalist reached out to the older scholar after reading in the press that YIVO had launched what it was calling an *aspirantur* (graduate study) program in Vilna. The graduate training program in Jewish scholarship offered its *aspirantn* financial support to pursue their own research, which would be overseen by the institute's impressive faculty. YIVO had created the program as both an expression of its cultural nationalist ambition to train a new elite class of Jewish scholars knowledgeable about its people, and a practical response to the increasing antisemitism that was keeping Jewish scholars out of the Polish university system.[34]

The program also appealed to Szajkowski in France, for parallel reasons. Hoping to become part of the emerging Yiddish elite, he faced practical problems that would have kept him out of the French university system, since he lacked a high school diploma.[35] At the time, there was no place in French universities to study the topics that interested him anyway; working with Tcherikower was a much better fit. Although it would take a few years to organize it, Szajkowski was eventually accepted to YIVO's program for the academic year 1938–39, with a unique arrangement set up to facilitate his work on the topic he eventually settled on: "The Relationship between French Jews and Russian-Polish Jews in the 19th Century." Unlike the rest of the *aspirantn*, who all worked in Vilna, Szajkowski's research as an *aspirant* was conducted in Paris under Tcherikower's direct supervision.[36]

The eager student had much to learn. His earlier books on Jewish immigrants had grown out of his journalism, and he had not yet tried out the social-scientific methods so valued by YIVO scholars. He had had little opportunity to learn such methods. His formal education had ended at age fifteen when he left Warsaw's State Seminary for Teachers of the Mosaic Faith, a school that trained teachers qualified to offer the course on Judaism in the Polish public school system. High as the quality of this modern, secular school appears to have been, Szajkowski was a mediocre student there, earning mostly the equivalent of Cs. He later remembered little about it beyond the free room and board it offered poor students like himself and his brother Berl.[37]

Nevertheless, Szajkowski was now in a different state of mind, and working with Tcherikower yielded impressive results. In 1938–39, the energetic Szajkowski published three article-length studies in Polish scholarly journals, two trying out sociological methods and one on the history of Yiddish in France.[38] Although one of these early sociological studies contains the kind of serious methodological flaws typical of a student paper, his output—and his ability to get published—was as remarkable as it had been when he was a journalist.[39] With the Tcherikowers' patronage and guidance, this Communist worker was turning into a scholar.

If YIVO saw itself as the national university for the Yiddish-speaking people, then Elias Tcherikower was the chair of its history department and its chief archivist. As the head of the Historical Section, he was responsible for publishing work by Jewish historians based all over Europe, in Palestine, and in New York.[40] Alongside philology, folklore, and social science, history was a central pillar in YIVO's overall mission as a Jewish academic institute. As a diaspora nationalist, Tcherikower saw in history a task of great national significance, as his friend Simon Dubnow had. In an 1891 essay, "On the Study of Jewish History," Dubnow had written that in order for Jews to have a firm sense of themselves as a people, they needed to chronicle their national past using modern scientific methods. The task, he had argued, was as incumbent upon the masses as it was upon the elite; the poorest classes of Jews needed to help "build the edifice of Jewish history" by collecting the material remnants that scholars would use. Dubnow's call to "search and research" had been heeded by the Jewish cultural elite in Russia even before the Revolution—for example, in the efforts of the Jewish Historic-Ethnographic Commission that, around the turn of the century, collected and published songs, stories, and articles about dance, theater, and dress. There too the objective was to preserve and study the traditions of their people using modern scientific methods.[41]

These efforts to collect and study the traces of Eastern European Jewish life continued with a renewed sense of urgency in the 1920s. War, revolution, and economic modernization accelerated the pace of change in all aspects of Jewish life, and the more traditional ways were receding rapidly. In the face of such loss, diaspora nationalist historians like Dubnow pressed their case that preserving the past was an absolutely necessary task. In fact, these nationalists were themselves modernizers, even as they expressed nostalgia for Jewish tradition. Like other European nationalists (German, French, or Eastern European), they were secular in outlook and sought to preserve the memory of the past because they felt fundamentally separated from it. In a sense, their work solidified the very break from the past that they bemoaned, since they thought about tradition in the entirely new terms of the modern sciences such as history, ethnology, and philology. They no longer lived traditions, nor did they inhabit the enchanted world in which religious belief connected them to one another through divine covenant. Studying the past using modern scientific methods and collecting its remnants were in fact crucial steps in creating a new and distinctly modern type of community: a nation.[42]

In this way, Jewish diaspora nationalist historians like Dubnow had much in common with the romantic historians of nineteenth-century Germany and France. In Germany, in the aftermath of the cataclysmic Napoleonic wars, cultural activists began to write the history of the German people and collect material for archives, even before the creation of a unified state. Feeling a sense of loss, unmoored from tradition, German cultural nationalists came to think of themselves as a nation and went searching for a common past. As historian Peter Fritzsche put it, "For archives to collect the past, the past has to come to mind as something imperiled and distinctive." Such collecting also presumes a "bounded national subject" (i.e., a present community that considers itself the custodian of that lost past, with an intelligentsia actively dedicated to seeking it out for study and preservation).[43] In France too, the changes of the Revolutionary era had shattered tradition. There too, in the nineteenth century, historians began to write national history rather than the history of kings, and the National Archives were created as a way to "restore order" after great disruption by connecting the French nation to a past from which it was perceived to be cut off.[44] In both contexts, a scientific worldview guided the collection, study, and preservation of the history that nationalists claimed as their own.

But the Dubnovian project to "search and research" was not just nostalgic; it was also the expression of deep concern about the material problems Jews faced in the present. The historians working in the orbit of YIVO showed a commitment to addressing social problems in the topics they chose for their scholarship. They were particularly drawn to the experiences of non-elites, and they used new methods borrowed from social science in their work in order to do so.[45] This distinguished their work from that of their nineteenth-century German predecessors of the *Wissenschaft des Judentums*, such as Leopold Zunz and Heinrich Graetz, the pioneers of modern Jewish history, whose works, in the eyes of the YIVO historians, had focused too much on rabbis and the wealthy.

YIVO's directors conceived of their work building archival collections in populist terms as well. Dubnow and his followers valued folkways—the beliefs and practices of the common people—and deemed them as equally worthy of collection as the manuscripts of venerated rabbis. Here too, the contrast with YIVO's predecessors elsewhere is telling. The first modern Jewish archive, the American Jewish Historical Society, founded in New York in 1892, sought to document the American Jewish past in a way that stressed Jews' American patriotism at a moment of heightened xenophobia. "The objects for which this society is organized are not sectarian but American," its founders declared at their inaugural meeting. As such, the achievements of the elite and dignified were stressed in the collection, and anything that might be construed as making Jews a separate nation with its own traditions was minimized.[46] A similar institution was founded in Berlin in 1905. The Gesamtarchiv der Juden in Deutschland preserved the official records of the Jewish communities (*gemeinde*) in Germany, and eventually also the papers of important communal leaders. It too defined Jews as a non-national group, in this case, in strictly confessional terms.[47]

The emphasis of the YIVO *zamler* (collector) program was different. *Zamlers* came from all walks of life and worked outside official institutional channels in order to reach non-elites. Indeed, an express goal of the project in forming the archive was to involve the Jewish masses in its creation. The program was relatively successful in Poland, if less so in the immigrant community of Paris.[48] YIVO also collected in other ways that creatively elicited Jewish voices that had previously gone unheard. For example, the institute sponsored autobiography contests for Jewish youth in the 1930s, offering a prize for the best one but with the express goal of archiving the resultant memoirs of young people.[49] In Paris, the YIVO committee sponsored a 1939 survey whose results documented the rich associational, cultural, and religious life of immigrant Jews. With efforts such as these, the experiences of ordinary people were documented in YIVO's growing collections and were deemed important subjects for Jewish scholars.[50]

Finally, in Elias Tcherikower's hands in particular, the historical endeavor was also linked to the politics of Jewish self-defense. In 1918–21, he was in Kiev when a wave of horrific pogroms spread across Ukraine in the context of the civil war. As the Ukrainian nationalists under Symon Petliura fought for independence from the Soviet Union, the Jews of the region fell victim to atrocities perpetrated by numerous groups involved in the fighting, particularly the Whites. More than a thousand incidents of anti-Jewish violence, characterized by an apparent sadism that would long haunt the survivors, claimed tens of thousands of lives. The best recent estimate places the number killed between 50,000 and 200,000 Jews, with almost a million more affected by the violence.[51]

The Ukrainian pogroms represented an important turning point in the Tcherikowers' lives and work. In their aftermath, they not only gave up on living in the Soviet Union; they also came to devote their lives to historical scholarship and documentation in the service of the Jewish people. Elias Tcherikower served as secretary of the Editorial Committee for the Collection and Research of Material Concerning the Pogroms in Ukraine that had been formed in 1919 in Kiev. Working alongside editor-in-chief Nokhem Shtif—a pioneer in Yiddish linguistics—as well as Dubnow, Lestschinsky, and other scholars and journalists, Tcherikower ran the day-to-day operations of this massive documentation project. The committee assembled an archive containing all possible evidence of the atrocities, particularly from the point of view of the Jewish victims, including eyewitness testimony, photographs, diaries and letters, records from Jewish communal organizations, government statements, perpetrators' statements, and press clippings. Riva Tcherikower served as archivist, cataloguing the materials and having copies made. The Tcherikowers called the archive the *Mizrekh-yidisher historisher arkhiv* (Eastern Jewish Historical Archive), and when they moved to Berlin following the fall of Kiev to Soviet forces in 1921, they managed to smuggle the archive out as well. When Szajkowski met them later in Paris, it formed the core of the collection they housed in their apartment.[52]

In Berlin, the Tcherikowers began to put together a study of the pogroms on the basis of these documents, entitled *Di Geshikhte fun der pogrom-bavegung in Ukraine, 1917–1921* (History of the pogrom movement in Ukraine, 1917–1921). The first of the anticipated seven volumes of the study was published in 1923 in Berlin, with an introduction by Dubnow. A second volume documenting the suffering of Jews in the Russian Revolution followed the next year, although financial difficulties prevented publication of the other completed manuscripts. In all these volumes, Tcherikower used the material he had assembled, including testimony from ordinary people, to show the pogrom's horrors. Relying on documentation to paint a picture of Jewish suffering, Tcherikower and his associates pioneered a new genre: objective writing, using scholarly methods, in the service of Jewish self-defense.[53]

The Tcherikowers' efforts in the wake of the Ukrainian pogroms were the forerunner of both the Oyneg Shabes documentation project that Emanuel Ringelblum directed in the Warsaw ghetto during the Holocaust and the post-Holocaust European Jewish historical commissions. The creators of these archives responded to catastrophe with objective scholarship and painstaking documentation. The historians involved evinced a faith in the power of careful scholarship to serve justice and memory; but at the same time, they demonstrated an equally deep suspicion that justice had not been served by the government authorities, and might never be.[54] The turn to documentation and scholarship was thus a way to put their hope for justice on hold, collecting and organizing proof of crimes until a context for their fair evaluation would emerge.

The archives these historians created differed in important ways from existing types of archives, particularly those of European nation-states, but also from European Jewish archives such as the Gesamtarchiv in Germany or even the YIVO collections housed in Vilna. The archives of catastrophe were designed to be portable, following their owners in their migrations, or, in the case of the Warsaw ghetto archive, hidden underground. And for all the faith these historians demonstrated in the power of documentation, their anxiety about when, where, and how the materials could be used in the service of justice was reflected in some of their scholarship, which relied much more heavily on documentation to support its interpretations than had been the norm in much of

Jewish historical scholarship. The new genre fell somewhere between a court case and a narrative history: Every point was carefully supported with evidence; the documents themselves were quoted directly at great length. Visual evidence was given particular pride of place, as documents and photographs were often reproduced in facsimile.

The connection between these archives of catastrophe and formal justice was not just in the minds of the creators. Indeed, the Tcherikowers first came to Paris in 1927 in order to use their archive in a court of law. Sholem Schwartzbard, a Jewish immigrant watchmaker and committed anarchist, had killed the Ukrainian nationalist leader Symon Petliura on a Paris street in 1926. In the ensuing trial, Schwartzbard's defense lawyer, Henry Torrès, made the case that the assassination had been an act of vengeance for the pogroms, which had claimed Schwartzbard's entire family. In a novel strategy, the defense made use of the eyewitness testimonies and photographs from the Tcherikowers' archive, in a sense putting Petliura on trial and casting Schwartzbard as defender of his people. The strategy worked, and Schwartzbard was acquitted in October 1927.

In the liberal context of Paris, the Tcherikowers' hope was thus fulfilled. Their archive, objectively assembled, properly catalogued, and transported before the eyes of a fair judge, was used to prove that Jews were victims of unjust authorities. The experience served to strengthen the Tcherikowers' commitment to scholarly history. Far from simply a retreat from politics, for the Tcherikowers, assembling archives and using scholarly methods to interpret that documentation were conceived as important weapons in the arsenal of Jewish self-defense, even if their use had to be deferred. For this nation without a state, an archive, used by those trained in scientific methods, was a portable tool that could be used in their struggle to achieve recognition and perhaps even justice from the world community, even as they themselves migrated from one country to another.

When Szajkowski started working with the Tcherikowers in Paris, the Yiddish-speaking Jews across Europe were facing new threats, and although he was taking a break from working at the *Naye Prese*, he was still committed to the political work involved in their defense. In Central and Eastern Europe, the antisemitic fascists who had come to power were stripping Jews of their rights and their economic well-being.

In France as well, the far right, xenophobic and often explicitly anti-semitic, was threatening the security of the 150,000 Jewish migrants who had settled there. In 1935, a new response to the fascist threat had emerged on the left, including among the Jews of France. Jewish Communists, Bundists, several Jewish workers' parties, some *landsman-shaftn* (mutual aid societies of Jewish immigrants from a same home-town), and LICA (the Ligue internationale contre L'Antisémitisme, a self-defense group founded in the wake of the Schwartzbard trial), put aside the differences that had divided them to form the *Mouvement Populaire Juif* (MPJ). The coalition was intended to parallel the broader Popular Front then forming among leftists of various stripes in France and elsewhere, for the express purpose of uniting to fight fascism.[55]

After the Spanish Civil War broke out in summer 1936, Szajkowski—then hard at work on his first efforts at academic writing—contributed to the efforts of the MPJ by recruiting Jews to fight in the conflict and by collecting funds to supply the Spanish republicans.[56] But a crisis within the *sous-section juive* soon shook his faith in the Party. In March 1937, the PCF dissolved the Jewish section, suspicious that nationally organized sections did not sufficiently foster solidarity among workers and were even perhaps inherently bourgeois. The move had also broken the MPJ, which lost the largest element in its coalition. Some Jewish Communists were bereft at this move, seeing it as a blow to Jewish agency at the very moment when a response was most needed, as fascism loomed across Europe.[57]

Szajkowski—always a diaspora nationalist and increasingly alienated from the Party's collectivism altogether—was forced to prioritize his commitments. The last straw, he later told friends, came when he heard that the Communists were killing their allies on the left in Spain rather than saving their fire for the fascists. The fact that by the late 1930s, Szajkowski had found a new home in the world of YIVO made the social and professional consequences of his break with the Party around this time easier to withstand, and he must have felt affirmed in his decision by the fact that the new friends he respected so much shared his critique of the Communists.[58]

When Szajkowski left the Communist Party, he did not join a new party. Rather, by 1938–39, he was moving toward a rejection of political ideology altogether. Scholarship itself became his new faith, different in content but not in passion from his earlier beliefs. He came to believe that embracing any of the modern, secular political ideologies—the nationalism of the organized Zionist movement, the socialism of the Bund, the Communism of the PCF, or the assimilationist liberalism of the Western European Jews—had divided the Jews and made them work against one another. He himself had done this, he recalled, when as a young man he "disrupt[ed] Socialist and Zionist meetings and even collect[ed] funds for the Arabs during the Palestine pogroms in 1929 ('for the victims of Zionist imperialism')."[59] Now, in leaving the Party, he saw such ideologically driven activism as ultimately suicidal for the Jewish people.

His move was not unique in this time of crisis, when many Jewish communal leaders were rethinking their strategies and allegiances. These included not only Jewish Communists he had known and worked with since the early 1930s, but also the intellectuals he met through the Tcherikowers. They too were radically rethinking their previous positions and exploring their ideas in conversations in their apartment, as well as in the pages of a new journal called *Oyfn Sheydveg* (At the Crossroads) edited by Tcherikower, Israel Efroykin, and, writing from Vilna, Zelig Kalmanovich. Although only two issues appeared in 1939 before war broke out, the short-lived journal was as rich in reflection as it was deep in despair. As they witnessed the failure of Western democracies and the Communists to address fascist antisemitism adequately, they were embracing the scholarly study of the Jewish past with a fervent desire to come up with new solutions.[60]

By the late 1930s, Szajkowski's role models had come to embrace a position that was tragic in the most classical sense. Their commitment to study as a way to solve Jews' present problems had led them to a deeply problematic stance. In the Jewish past, they were indeed finding a way of coping with difficulty, but it was foreclosed to them because their worldview had become too modern. Szajkowski wrote:

They had grown up in Russia, been active in the Jewish and Russian movements, witnessed the Revolutions of 1905 and 1917, and lost their faith in God. However, they never made a show of their secularism. Many of them still believed that religion was the basis for the endurance of the Jewish people, and some of them even thought of

themselves as religious Jews. They suffered because they were unable
to break away from the secular ideologies and habits. . . . Tcherikower
developed the idea that the Third Reich was not the first catastrophe
in the history of the Jewish people. However, the previous generation had been able to survive because their "religious faith created a
philosophy of suffering and prevented the fall of the Jewish spirit,"
but ours is "a weak generation."[61]

In debating these issues among themselves, these scholars were not
turning to Zionism or any other forward-looking ideology as they questioned their previous political stances. Turning their backs on Dubnow,
they called Jewish modernization itself into question in their discussions, newspaper articles, and scholarship, seeing it as having drained
the Jewish people of the ability to respond to persecution. And of
course, this radical self-questioning was taking place against the back-
drop of Nazism's growth, which contributed to the general sense of
hopelessness they expressed. As Szajkowski remembered the conversations, the scholars followed poet Jacob Glatstein's 1938 call for a "return
to the ghetto," a metaphor charged with anguish about the results of
the historical processes of emancipation and assimilation. They called
for a radical reappraisal of religion, arguing that the Orthodox had done
more to preserve Jewish life than modern Yiddish cultural activists ever
had. All this questioning was motivated by a deep sense of despair. It
made a particularly strong impression on Szajkowski when one day at
the Tcherikowers' apartment he saw Charles Rappoport, a philosopher
and former Communist leader now estranged from the Party, "perusing
a volume of Graetz; [when] all of sudden he said, 'What an idiot I was,
my entire life I have toiled for strangers.'"[62] Jewish history was making
it possible for these intellectuals to think outside their most deeply held
political beliefs and to see, in Jewish tradition, an alternative.

And yet, although these scholars were revaluing Jewish tradition, they
did not actually see themselves as capable of genuinely returning to a
traditional way of life. The very conversations in which they had called
Jewish modernization into question were predicated on the participants' fundamentally modern worldview. As Szajkowski put it, "They
were people to whom the individual was more important than state,
collectivist ideological or political forces."[63] Or, one might add, religion.

The very vehicle of their shifting worldview—scholarship itself—was a modern, secular enterprise. Theirs was the nostalgia of the truly modern, the hopelessness of nationalists cut off from the traditions of the national past they were studying.[64] Even in their rejection of politics and appreciation for Jewish tradition, they could not access for themselves the enchanted worldview they had come to hold in such high regard. In spite of themselves, they remained committed to reasoned debate, to scholarly inquiry, to the power of the individual. And therein lay the tragedy, as Szajkowski was well aware.

Even so—or was it for that very reason?—in Szajkowski's recollection, these discussions were some of the most stimulating he had ever heard, and left him a lifetime believer in Jewish scholarship.[65] He became a major contributor to the large, multi-authored project that Tcherikower was editing in Paris, a collection of historical studies called *Yidn in Frankraykh* (Jews in France), finally published in early 1942 in New York.[66] This was pioneering work, for the first time locating French Jewish history within a larger story of Jewish history and bringing it to the attention of the growing international body of Jewish historians writing in Yiddish.[67] Tcherikower's contributions in particular were also radical in their reappraisal of the history of Jewish emancipation, reflecting the conversations Szajkowski was hearing. Although by the late 1930s, many Jewish intellectuals across Europe had come to rethink their previous celebration of the history of Jewish emancipation and assimilation, Tcherikower's work stood out.[68] In his two articles on the French Revolution and the Jews, Tcherikower created what Joshua Karlip has called a "counter-genealogy of Jewish modernity," interpreting the French Revolutionaries' decision to grant Jews citizenship as a move that denied Jewish autonomy and thus set the stage for the destruction of the rich Jewish culture he treasured.[69] He reread the sources, looking back at the speeches made by the supporters of Jewish emancipation in the French National Assembly in 1789, pointing out that Jews had been forced by their supposed friends to give up their communal autonomy, and that they had tried to resist. For Tcherikower, Clermont-Tonnerre—admired by generations of Jews for speaking out in favor of citizenship for Jews—was in some ways as bad as the antisemites he had fought when he argued in the Constituent Assembly in December 1789, "We must deny everything to the Jews as a nation; we must give them everything as individuals." Looking back at the source, Tcherikower noted that this was in fact an affirmation of rights, but one predicated on the destruction of the Jewish nation.

Although some Jewish leaders from Alsace and Lorraine had petitioned to maintain their communal rights—their right to live separately, according to Jewish law, and under their own Jewish leaders—the terms of emancipation had made that impossible. Clermont-Tonnerre himself said explicitly that if the Jews refused to give up their communal rights in favor of citizenship as individuals, "they must inform us, and we shall be compelled to expel them."[70] It was thus emancipation itself—the specific terms by which Jews had acquired equal rights—that had brought Jews so far from their traditions, unable to cope with the antisemitism that persisted and made true equality impossible. The new heroes in this account were the Jewish leaders of Alsace and Lorraine, Cerf Berr, Berr Isaac Berr, and Isaiah Berr Bing, who had fought for equality *and* communal rights. Although they had failed to achieve it, it was they who were the best models for Eastern European Jewry in the contemporary crisis, although there also it was probably too late.[71]

Tcherikower's arguments may have been bleak, but they were unquestionably new and the debates passionate and deeply meaningful. His history of emancipation in France was what Foucault has called a "history of the present." Rigorously source-based to be sure, it was designed to get to the roots of the current crisis that Jews were facing across Europe, and to bring to light the paths not taken. The work put France on the mental map of Yiddish diaspora, incorporating this new home into the history of their imagined community.

3

A Salvage Operation

WORLD WAR II BROKE UP the circle of YIVO historians in Paris. Most had already migrated at least once in their lives; now many uprooted themselves once again. Some left for military service, not knowing whether they would be able to return home at the end of the conflict. Others sought shelter in places that seemed safer based on judgment calls that were ever subject to revision as the situation shifted. A lucky few secured the needed paperwork and left Europe altogether. These were arduous undertakings that required tremendous time, effort, and expense. Even so, rather than abandoning their scholarship to focus on the difficulties of the moment, the YIVO scholars remained as dedicated as ever to documenting their world for posterity. Indeed, for many of them, collecting the documentary traces of the current crisis and writing its history was as important as saving themselves and their loved ones from harm. In this, Szajkowski was no exception.

Szajkowski sensed that he was in danger from the moment the Germans invaded Poland on September 1, 1939, prompting the French to declare war against Germany on September 3. In Paris, antisemitism—palpable since 1938—became even more acute. The police began to stop Jews on the street and "not only asked for their regular papers but also for evidence that they had enlisted in the 'French Army,' that is, the Foreign Legion."[1] For Jewish immigrants who, like Szajkowski, did not have French nationality, the situation seemed risky. Wisely, then, he heeded the calls of Jewish leaders and volunteered for military service on September 2, 1939.[2]

It was months before he was actually called for duty; in the meantime, he continued his research in Paris for his contributions to Tcherikower's *Yidn in Frankraykh* collection. In mid-November, he was finally called to Vancia, just outside Lyon, to be evaluated for service in the Foreign Legion. By then, the Tcherikowers had become as dear to Szajkowski as his own family, perhaps more so. In his break from the Communist Party, he had grown increasingly alienated from his working-class Communist brothers and particularly from his sister, and he spent more and more time at the rue Dombasle.[3] It was Ilya Tcherikower, not his family, who gave Szajkowski the parting gift he found most meaningful. This was a Hebrew Bible that Tcherikower's own grandfather had given him, and he told Szajkowski he had kept it "during his wanderings in Palestine, the United States, back to Russia after the Revolution of March 1917, Germany, then France." "[I]t will also keep you safe," he had told Szajkowski. Riva, for her part, gave him an amulet inscribed in Yiddish with a single word, "YIVO," which he kept with him until losing both in battle on June 15, 1940.[4] Szajkowski also gave the military officials the Tcherikowers' name and address as the people to notify should anything happen to him.[5] From his training camp, Szajkowski wrote the Tcherikowers several times a week, sending regards to mutual friends and asking for updates on their collective project, *Yidn in Frankraykh*.[6]

To buoy his spirits, Szajkowski spent much of the long wait from November to June, when his unit was finally mobilized, thinking about his scholarly work and particularly *Yidn in Frankraykh*. His mind was filled with ideas for finding new sources that would be useful for studies for the volume. He suggested that Tcherikower get copies of all the questionnaires—he estimated that there were likely 10,000 of them—that had been filled out by young Jewish immigrants signing up for the Foreign Legion. "This is not material for a work about Jewish volunteers because at present we don't have a complete picture," he wrote, "but on the other hand, it's quite good material for a statistical-economic survey of the Jews that have come into Paris."[7]

Later, he sent Tcherikower a collection of "folklore" from the Jewish legionnaires—mostly bawdy songs, sayings, and slang.[8]

He also sought to expand the circle of historians to be included in the volume. Better integrated than his mentor into the circles of French-born Jews, he instructed Tcherikower about how to contact various native-born French Jewish historians whose work might be included in the book, such as Professor Moïse Ginsburger of Strasbourg and Paul Bettelin of Boulogne-sur-Seine.[9] In a number of ways, then, Szajkowski was an important partner in *Yidn in Frankraykh*. Beyond conceiving of studies and finding authors, he also wrote many of the chapters himself, more, in fact, than any other author. In addition to his six single-authored articles, he co-authored another with Tcherikower (they signed it "Tcher-ski") and transcribed a set of primary documents that appeared as an appendix to volume 2.[10]

In this period, though, Szajkowski was also a soldier. In fall 1939, after getting glasses, some dental work, a uniform, and a gun, Szajkowski was moved to La Valbronne, where he joined the 12th Regiment, which was about 30 percent Jewish and otherwise relatively diverse in terms of nationality. It eventually saw heavy fighting. He later estimated that of the 5,000 or so men in this regiment, only 350 to 500 survived the war.[11] Early in his training, Szajkowski wrote to Tcherikower, "I don't forget even for a minute that this is a holy war for us Jews and we need to put extra effort into being soldiers."[12]

After months of waiting, expecting to be deployed any day, the 12th Regiment finally saw action in June 1940. Szajkowski faced danger with remarkable courage and a cool head. In his first report to the Tcherikowers from the front, he wrote: "We fight and we will win! I assure you that the Jewish soldiers are fighting bravely! As you see, I'm still alive. I've seen death before my eyes many times, but I keep my course and do my duty. In spite of everything we will conquer and destroy the Hitler beast."[13] Yet when the next letter arrived at the Tcherikowers' address, it was in unfamiliar handwriting, and in French rather than Yiddish: "My dears: I think of you, I am wounded, but it's nothing, it's not serious. In spite of everything, France will vanquish. Your Friedmann [sic]." Only a shaky additional signature from "Frydman," just below the first, proved the letter really was from Szajkowski.[14] His courage at the front did not go unnoticed. On

Szajko Frydman as a soldier in the French Foreign Legion, 1940. *From the Archives of the YIVO Institute for Jewish Research.*

October 3, 1940, he was awarded the Croix de Guerre with a bronze star; the regiment had honored him in the citation as a "Légionnaire courageux et de sang-froid [courageous and composed legionnaire]."[15]

In fact, his injury was quite serious. On June 15, 1940, he was hit by a bullet in the left part of his chest, wounding his lung; it passed through his body and came out his right arm.[16] The battle had taken place near Pont-sur-l'Ain in Franche-Comté. He had been fighting alongside several other Jewish legionnaires whom he knew from Communist circles, and none stopped to help him. He wrote the Tcherikowers with great bitterness about how they had abandoned him there because they knew he had quit the Party. Luckily, though, his Sergeant Henry—an old-time legionnaire—came back for him and saved his life.[17] He was then sent by ambulance to a Bordeaux military hospital, where he stayed for a few weeks, until the Germans arrived in that city at the end of June. On July 3, the hospital was evacuated and Szajkowski was sent to another hospital in Carpentras, where he would remain until August 13.[18]

As Szajkowski quickly surmised from his hospital bed, serving in the Foreign Legion would not protect him from potential persecution as a foreign Jew anywhere in France. Since the armistice of June 25, 1940, the north had fallen under direct Nazi occupation, and the unoccupied south, where Szajkowski found himself, was governed by Marshall Philippe Pétain's collaborationist Vichy regime. Exchanging news with friends who had fled Paris in the June exodus, he learned that many Jewish legionnaires were being sent to detention camps in the south. His dear friend Henoch Gelernt wrote from Toulouse to advise him to stay away from his unit once he was released from the hospital: "Do not go back to the base. Absolutely, do not remain. In these times it is healthier not to write about such things.... [I]n any case I want to protect you from the Hell in which our friends that I've mentioned find themselves." This confirmed Szajkowski's sense that Jewish immigrants were in greater danger than ever before, now "simply acting as a shield for the country."[19]

Much later, working as a historian with access to documentation, Szajkowski had the opportunity to learn that Gelernt's intuitions were quite correct. Indeed, many former soldiers were soon interned in the French labor camps called Groupes de Travailleurs Etrangers (GTEs, literally Groups of Foreign Workers). These were established by the law of September 27, 1940, in the Southern Zone for all male immigrants aged eighteen to fifty-five who could not return to their countries of origin, could not work, who had crossed illegally into the unoccupied zone, or had been volunteers in the army. Jews comprised a third of the 60,000 men sent to these GTEs. By staying away from the base, Szajkowski managed to avoid the eventual fate of many of his fellow Jewish legionnaires. Although at the time their fate was not yet known, Szajkowski later learned that, eventually, immigrant Jews, including many former legionnaires, were sent from the GTEs to the French concentration camps of Pithiviers and Beaune-la-Rolande. From there, in August 1942, they were deported to Auschwitz.[20]

What his fate might be was much on Szajkowski's mind from the time he arrived in the Carpentras hospital on July 4, 1940. Rendered stateless by the war, an injured Jew with no means of support, he remained at risk; as time went on, these risks became much more acute.[21] In his hospital bed, he thought frequently of the Tcherikowers, whom he had come to see as surrogate parents. In the chaos of June, he had lost touch with them. Late in July, after sending many frantic letters, he finally made contact with them; they had fled Paris in the June exodus and had landed in Bagnères-de-Bigorre, a village in the Pyrenees. They wrote him that YIVO's New York office had pulled strings for them, and they were relatively certain they could obtain a visa from the American consulate in Marseilles and would leave as soon as possible for New York. Szajkowski urged them not to wait and especially not to try to return to Paris to collect their books and papers, which he promised to retrieve and send on to them in America.[22]

In the meantime, he needed to figure out how to support himself in Carpentras. He had been released from the hospital in mid-August, well before his wound had healed completely, and chest pain compounded his worries. The essential thing was to find work. As he wrote the Tcherikowers, without a certificate from an employer in the unoccupied Southern Zone of France, he might be interned in a labor camp (a worry he expressed even before the law of September 27, 1940, made it official policy).[23] Although he had met some local people—a few had visited him in the Carpentras hospital soon after he had arrived there, and one kind person, Monsieur Gold, even invited him to stay with him once he was released—his needs clearly exceeded the charity they offered.[24]

Such material support was, of course, hard to come by. In mid-August, shortly after leaving the hospital, he tentatively sounded out the Tcherikowers to see if YIVO would be able to help if he were to "create a commission to try to save everything possible for YIVO in America.... Hopefully, America will agree to a small subsidy to cover the expenses for sending these things."[25] But YIVO's resources were stretched thin at this time and, even in this letter, he stopped short of proposing they pay him a salary. After seeing a doctor in Marseilles in September, he realized that jobs requiring physical labor would be out of the question. He was told that with a lung injury, chest pain can take years to ease. With no means of support, Szajkowski was in danger and he knew it.

He was officially demobilized on September 15, which kept him temporarily out of the labor camps, where other Jewish legionnaires had been moved. By October, he appears to have been out of money, hungry, and quite ill. Those of his friends who had managed to get to New York worked tirelessly through the fall to secure a visa for him. In late October, Franz Kursky wrote to Max Weinreich, who was now heading YIVO from New York: "the main thing is, the urgency to get him a visa because right now they take Polish citizens in France into concentration camps. And the first ones are former soldiers of the Polish or French army. So without looking at his illness, he is the first candidate of all for the concentration camp. From Toulouse I had written already for a visa for him. But nothing came out of it. So you look to all the possibilities to get him a visa but in the meantime, material support."[26]

An American visa was Szajkowski's greatest hope, but realistically, he knew that his chances were slim. "Before issuing a visa, the American Consul now demands evidence that you are someone of worth. Without that, there's no getting a visa. I have nothing at hand—not even a book of mine," he wrote the Tcherikowers after he had traveled to Marseilles to gauge his chances.[27] He imagined that once the Tcherikowers were in New York, they could help, and before they left in September, they reassured him that they would do everything possible for him. Together with other YIVO leaders in New York (Naftali Feinerman, Jacob Shatzky, and Max Weinreich), the Tcherikowers were able to pull off the impossible, getting Szajkowski the necessary documentation by early 1941. But at that late date, papers were not enough; connections were needed too. He was one of the lucky few. YIVO leaders managed to get him on the lists of the Emergency Rescue Committee, which helped about two thousand of the most prominent writers, artists, and anti-Nazi activists, including Hannah Arendt and Marc Chagall, to escape France. In this way, Szajkowski managed to obtain a quota immigrant visa (QIV) from the American Consulate in Marseilles on April 18, 1941.[28]

As uncertain as his future was during the months he spent in Carpentras, Szajkowski never abandoned his work as a scholar. In his first months in the Foreign Legion, he had kept anxiety at bay by training his mind on his research. In Carpentras too, he felt danger approaching, and again he buried himself in his work. A first project was about Jewish soldiers' experiences in the war, particularly in the Foreign Legion. His journalistic instincts told him there was an important story there, and he wanted to memorialize his fallen comrades. "Collecting the material should take a year, maybe more," he wrote. "*I have to do it.* I can't do otherwise. You certainly understand me. It is my duty to the fallen Jewish volunteers and to those who still suffer." In spite of his own traumatic experience, having felt abandoned by his Jewish comrades when he was shot, he swore he would be capable of proving their heroism. "It should be objective but glorious for the Jewish soldiers, which may be difficult for me," he confided to the Tcherikowers, alluding to the many (mostly politically motivated) criticisms he had leveled at his comrades in letters written during the long months of waiting. "Whatever faults, however, that I took note of prior to the front, are small details in comparison with the pain and heroism they showed at the front."[29]

But thoughts about leaving France transformed the project and forced him to defer it, minimizing its impact and shrinking his audience considerably. As initially conceived, the study was intended for a French audience; the book would prove immigrant Jews' devotion to their adopted land. But he was coming to realize that the time for such apologetics was running out.[30] He did the envisioned research and used it for several pieces over the course of his life. These were published in Yiddish, English, and Hebrew for audiences both scholarly and popular, the most in-depth being his 1975 book *Jews in the French Foreign Legion*.[31] But he never published anything on this topic in France or even in the French language. Instead, his audiences would be American and Israeli, and his work would be contextualized as part of the history of European antisemitism rather than as a defense of Jewish immigrants' loyalties.

Like the project on Jewish soldiers, *Yidn in Frankraykh*'s status also seemed uncertain. The collection was complete in June 1940 on the eve of the German invasion. From his hospital bed in Carpentras,

Szajkowski worried about what had happened to the manuscript, and wrote to Tcherikower that once he was well, he would travel to Paris to have the essays typeset and galleys printed up.[32] But just as they began to envision their own futures elsewhere, they abandoned the idea that *Yidn in Frankraykh* had much of a future in France. First of all, the practical problems were immense; it was dangerous even to travel from the unoccupied south to occupied Paris. But more fundamentally, Szajkowski thought that printing the collection in Paris no longer made sense because "[t]here aren't any more friends of YIVO left here. Everything's on its way to America."[33] As he himself came to terms with the fact that most of his YIVO friends were emigrating, he came to believe that the future of the project lay in New York, and it should be printed there instead of Paris. His instincts matched the Tcherikowers' exactly. The aging scholars had carried the manuscripts with them on their arduous journey, which took them from Paris to the Pyrenees, from the Pyrenees to Marseilles to get their visas, back to the Pyrenees again, this time crossing into Spain, then through Spain and Portugal to get to Lisbon, where they caught the *Nea Hellas* to New York on September 2, 1940. The collection was finally printed in New York in early 1942.

Szajkowski was coming to see *Yidn in Frankraykh* in terms that went far beyond a scholarly study. In his most self-aggrandizing moments, he thought of its fate as emblematic of a historic change in Jewish civilization. As he wrote to Weinreich shortly after the Tcherikowers' departure, "Our dear friends left France by foot, with a small package in their arms—a few draft pages of our planned Paris YIVO writings. This is how our forefathers left for *Galut* [exile]."[34] The analogy helped Szajkowski make sense of the confusing circumstances. This modern scholarship was, for him, like the ancient knowledge taken by the rabbis into *Galut*. If the Yiddish scholars were modern rabbis, New York was their Yavneh. After all, weren't the ancient rabbis precisely the keepers of Jews' early national history, writing down the ancient ways in order to keep Jewish life alive in new contexts? Today's Yiddish scholars were bringing the no-less-sacred manuscripts that would allow future generations to know what had happened to their people in the days when they had dwelled in Europe. As he wrote to the Tcherikowers, even before learning that they had indeed taken the manuscripts with them on their flight from

Paris, "I've met so many refugees, but in my mind I can see you carrying manuscripts and galleys of the planned YIVO collection book. Can we imagine a dedicated keeper of Jewish culture escaping the Germans in any other way?"[35]

Szajkowski's sacralizing terminology was not a sign of any religious conversion; he remained as secular in outlook as he had been as a Communist. Rather, he used this terminology to place the current crisis in a broad historical context, and to assert a central role for Jewish scholars in that history. In Szajkowski's mind, the center of gravity in the Yiddish-speaking scholarly diaspora was shifting to New York, a change that he, earlier than some, already perceived as permanent. A true Dubnovian, Szajkowski saw one center of Jewish history fading away just as another was rising. The exile of Yiddish scholars from Europe was of historic proportions, inaugurating a new chapter in Jewish history. Seeing the moment in these terms, Szajkowski imbued *Yidn in Frankraykh* with a sacred character. The questions it asked about emancipation and the social and economic changes it had wrought were, to his thinking, the essential questions Jews needed to grapple with as they rebuilt Jewish culture in a new setting.

After a few months, a third scholarly preoccupation emerged as well: the history of Jews in the Comtat Venaissin, the region around Carpentras, where by sheer luck Szajkowski found himself when he emerged from the hospital. Although Carpentras was small, it boasted a longer continuous Jewish presence than anywhere else in France. Whereas Jews had been expelled from France proper in 1394 and readmitted only centuries later, Jews had lived in the four towns of Avignon, Carpentras, Cavaillon, and L'Isle-sur-Sorgue continuously since medieval times, because this area, under Papal sovereignty, was annexed by France only during the Revolution. Their long presence in the Papal States was not, however, without difficulty. They were confined to cramped ghettos called *carrières* (streets), forbidden from holding public office, and forced into money lending and petty trade. Nevertheless, by the eighteenth century, their economic situation was comparable to that of the Sephardic Jews of Bordeaux and Bayonne and much better than that of their brethren in Alsace-Lorraine. After their emancipation, many of the so-called Papal Jews were relatively well off and, when the opportunity presented itself, they moved out of the region. The Jewish population of the towns thus declined precipitously in the nineteenth century, falling from 544 people in 1809 to 289 in 1900.[36] By the time Szajkowski arrived in Carpentras, few descendants of the old communities remained and little research had been done on them.

Researching an abandoned Jewish ghetto intrigued the young scholar, and he approached the task with characteristic energy, despite his troubles. Little by little, Szajkowski found sources in Carpentras's Bibliothèque Inguimbertine, the libraries and archives in nearby towns, and the private collections of individual Jews he met. With the nose for sources that would become his trademark, Szajkowski assembled materials voraciously in the six months between his release from the hospital and his departure for America via Marseilles. Between 1942 and 1948, he used the research he had done in an impressive series of studies on the Papal Jews: an important Yiddish monograph, two long and three short articles in Yiddish, a published version of a set of primary documents, and a substantial article in a prestigious English-language journal, a language he began to study only upon his arrival in America in the fall of 1941.[37]

It was not simply the pace of his work that was remarkable; it was the creativity involved. If the Carpentras he was getting to know was home to very few Jews—interesting enough, but far from the cosmopolitan cultural scene he was used to—the Carpentras he was discovering in his research was a thriving, fascinating place filled with Jewish life. He explored the Carpentras cemetery, which dated back to the fourteenth century, overgrown with weeds but still in use, and the synagogue rebuilt in the eighteenth century to enlarge a medieval one. He used the archival records he found in nearby Marseilles to compile demographic statistics that documented the exodus of Jews from the region after emancipation freed them from their ghetto. And most exciting of all, in the library, he read and deciphered "Lou pés enleva," a fascinating satirical poem from 1803 written in the language the local Jews spoke. Far from the Yiddish scholars who had trained him, Szajkowski now engaged more fully with French historiography to understand the contours of Jewish life in the carrières and to make sense of why Jews had abandoned the region in such large numbers once they were permitted to.

The questions he explored surely made Tcherikower proud. Like his mentor, Szajkowski was in certain ways nostalgic for the lost world of the ghetto. This is clearest in his intriguing monograph on the defunct language of the Papal Jews before emancipation, entitled *Dos Loshn fun di Yidn in di arbe Kehiles fun Komta-Venesen* (The Language of the Jews in the Four Communities of Comtat-Venaissin), published in Yiddish in New York in 1948 with YIVO's support.[38] The language was previously unknown to Yiddish scholars, and although it was better known in France, previous accounts had been cursory. For the most part, the language had been described as the Jewish dialect of Provençal, or a Jewish slang.[39] Szajkowski, however, saw Judeo-Provençal as a language in its own right and called it "Chuadit," a word for "Jewish" that he found in "Lou pés enleva." The name has stuck, as has Szajkowski's claim that Judeo-Provençal constituted a distinctive Jewish language spoken only by the Papal Jews, comprised of a mixture of Provençal, French, and Hebrew and written in Hebrew characters. Sitting in the Carpentras library, having had no formal training in linguistics, Szajkowski spent much of the winter of 1940–41 reconstructing the language's vocabulary and structure based on just a few manuscripts. With his natural capacity for languages, Szajkowski pushed into uncharted territory, his confidence in his interpretations later buoyed by the positive feedback he got from Weinreich, who advised Szajkowski on his work in New York after the war.[40]

Szajkowski brought to his studies of Jewish life in the *carrières* all the urgency that Tcherikower had brought to his study of Jews in the French Revolution. Under Tcherikower's influence, Szajkowski had come to question whether emancipation and assimilation really made for a better life for Jews. In the language study, Szajkowski reconstructed a world in which Jews lived largely in peace with their neighbors, in spite of the restrictions on their movements and economic activities, and the texts he used testify to a rich and distinctive cultural life. Had the abandonment of the ghetto really made Jews happier? As he mused, "Our forefathers here with their beliefs were definitely more fortunate than we are, and better prepared to withstand all their troubles."[41] The study evoked a lost world in which Jews had a language of their own and their separation from their neighbors was generally unaccompanied by violence. Although prejudice did thrive, they had the strength to flourish anyway. In his presentation of Judeo-Provençal folklore, sayings, songs, and expressions, Szajkowski painted a picture of a dynamic, if now forgotten, Jewish world in which Jews clung to Jewishness even as they borrowed from and interacted with the surrounding culture.

Szajkowski's language study has been read in two contrasting ways, depending on whether the reader identifies the history of Papal Jews as part of Jewish history or as part of French history. The study's Yiddish readers were predisposed to appreciate the idea of a distinctive ghetto world flourishing in its separateness from gentiles. Weinreich saw in Szajkowski's application of Yiddish linguistics methodology to Chuadit the beginnings of what he called "Jewish inter-linguistics," the comparative study of Jewish languages that had been called for by the eminent Yiddish linguist Solomon Birnbaum in an earlier study of Yiddish.[42] French linguists, in contrast, have pointed to the study's methodological shortcomings in their critiques, which aim to re-situate Papal Jews in the context of French history. As a result of certain errors in transcription and pronunciation, they have argued, Szajkowski overestimated the degree to which Chuadit was distinct from Provençal. Indeed, as Szajkowski himself noted, no examples could be found of non-Jewish Provençal speakers unable to understand Chuadit. Although he conceded this point, Szajkowski failed to follow it to the logical conclusion that this may not, in fact, have been as distinct a "Jewish language" as, say, Yiddish. Rather, for these critics, Chuadit was comprised of a set of terms used by Jewish Provençal speakers to refer to certain specific Jewish things or practices. The difference is important. As Michel Alessio, an expert on minority languages in France, has put it:

> Is [Chuadit] really a Jewish language? If by that we mean that the sentence, "We are going to look for the *chametz* and participate in the Passover *seder* that requires three *matzot*," clearly represents a special code with its own expressive or demarcating character. But can we truly say that we have left the realm of [English]? You be the judge.[43]

Indeed, as Alessio further notes, linguists now see true Jewish languages less as a product of ghetto life of the type lived by the Papal Jews, who were relatively settled, than a result of expulsion and mass migration. For example, Judeo-Spanish developed after the Spanish expulsion. That language was based in the Spanish these Jews had spoken before their expulsion, but it developed independently from peninsular Spanish and, in time, took on a distinctive character. Yiddish was similarly a language of exile, developing among Jews driven from Germany who had relocated to Eastern Europe and mixed the language of the country of origin (Germany) with words from Hebrew and others from Eastern European languages. Like the German-speaking Jews of pre-expulsion Germany and the Spanish-speaking Jews of pre-expulsion Spain, for the Papal Jews, bilingualism would have had no use. The community was relatively isolated and its residents' only external interactions, beyond the Jewish street, were with Provençal speakers. Accordingly, they spoke Provençal except when they needed words to express certain specifically Jewish concepts.[44]

For Szajkowski and the other Jewish historians who made up his intended audience, though, the Papal Jews were Jews first and foremost. The history of the Papal Jews was a story in which Jewish life was nurtured because it remained closed off from gentiles. Their decline began with the end of the ghetto. As soon as they were able to leave the confines of the *carrières*, the Jews of Carpentras had begun their own exodus. Writing in English in *Jewish Social Studies* in 1944, Szajkowski acknowledged, "The papal province was not in fact the 'Jewish paradise' which so many writers [here he cites French ones] would represent it to have been."[45] Seeking economic opportunity and fleeing the intolerance of their neighbors, Jews had moved from the four towns in droves. They went first to the larger cities nearby and then eventually to the capital. The richer ones went before the poorer ones, leaving the community without the means to support its educational and charitable institutions, impoverishing Jewish life in the region tremendously. Szajkowski saw the effects all around him. Early in his stay in Carpentras, he estimated that there were only about ten Jews left in the town.[46]

Szajkowski never contextualized his findings in terms of French or Provençal patterns of urbanization; nor would his readers in *Jewish Social Studies* and *YIVO Bleter* have done so. Rather, he and they would have seen in the story a pattern familiar in modern European Jewish history. The Papal Jews' abandonment of their towns following emancipation is, in this account, strikingly similar to the more recent exodus from the shtetls of Eastern Europe in which many of these scholars, Szajkowski included, had themselves participated. Readers of these publications were not used to entertaining the idea that, even before emancipation, Jews like those in the Papal States might have been as comparable to their gentile neighbors who were also migrating to urban centers as they were to Polish Jews, which would have forced them to consider the migration patterns in a different light. Rather, they saw in this tale a story with a familiar arc, in which Jews abandoned their closed world to become assimilated because modern opportunities proved too attractive to resist. The end of his 1944 article, "The Decline and Fall of Provençal Jewry," thus strikes an elegiac note, mournfully describing the emptiness of the towns he visited in 1940. He wrote, "Of the Jewish community in Lisle-sur-Sorgue, nothing remains. Even its location is uncertain" and described how, in the Carpentras synagogue, services were no longer offered even though a few Jews still lived in the town.[47] Readers of Szajkowski's wartime Jewish studies publications would have immediately seen the comparisons to Jewish communities elsewhere. When opportunity had come calling for the Jews of Europe, only cemeteries were left.

Szajkowski's research on the Papal Jews was facilitated by his monumental collecting efforts. Judging from what he wrote to the Tcherikowers, collecting provided some comfort in a time of imminent danger by connecting him to community: new friends in Carpentras and old friends in the YIVO world. YIVO was and always had been as much a community of *zamlers* as a community of scholars. Sending things to YIVO in New York brought them close to mind in those dark days, and helped him make new friends too. He began to collect even before he was released permanently from the hospital, when he first met local Jews like Gold, who offered him a place to stay and took him to see the town's Jewish sites, notably the synagogue and the cemetery. At the synagogue, he met Mademoiselle Mossé, the daughter of the deceased synagogue caretaker, who gave him things from her family's collection, including a photo of her father Ulyssé, who was reputed to have died with the synagogue's keys in hand. On one of those August outings, Szajkowski went to the post office and sent some of those things to the Tcherikowers to bring to YIVO in New York: "a

Megilas-Ester [Book of Esther], a synagogue chandelier, three *tefillin* bags, a little box for *havdalah* spices, a Torah crown, a circumcision chair, a tin vessel used to snuff out the candles in the synagogue, and two stamps."[48] Later, after they left in September, he sent them a Torah scroll via their mutual friend Henoch Gelernt, then on his way with his wife and son to New York.[49] In this way, Szajkowski kept loneliness at bay in his time of isolation and anxiety.

But collecting Judaica, and boasting about it in his frequent letters, also allowed Szajkowski to paint himself as a hero in his friends' eyes when he needed their affections the most. Showing Tcherikower and Weinreich what he could collect was a form of special pleading, proof that he was in fact, a person of worth. More often than not, Szajkowski reminded the Tcherikowers of the gifts he had sent just when he was asking for help gathering the proper papers for his visa. Collecting materials for YIVO made Szajkowski feel less like a burden and more like a faraway representative achieving heroic feats. We can see this heroic self-construction in the exuberant description of the "wondrous" things he was sending by ship just after he finally obtained his visa in April 1941. He proudly listed the following:

> a collection of Hebrew grammar books from the 16th and 17th centuries, prints from the end of the 15th century, a dossier about Yiddish music, wondrous things from a giant dictionary for which I don't even have funds to use for shipping the crate. I asked Efroykin to lend me some but I haven't gotten a reply. I'll figure something out. I'm borrowing it with the promise of returning it from New York. The crate of things is very valuable. This time I out-did myself. I ask that if I'm successful in giving Henoch the suitcase from Paris, I'd like my archive to be tied together with all the things I'm sending you. My old dream: a collection in YIVO in the name of my mother. I am really praying for that. But I am on my own. I would be able to collect so many things, but there's no strength. There would perhaps be energy, but there's no money, and no one wants to help. Wherever I turn, I get the same answer. "Look what a crazy guy is thinking about these days? Archives! Like they might accomplish something." All people do is wait for visas,

and in the meantime, they prepare banquets (Yes!) for those who are leaving, and they buy everything they can. They can go to hell.[50]

Compensating for the long months of fear and anxiety, Szajkowski celebrated his deliverance by bragging about his feats and expressing contempt for those around him who thought merely of saving their own skins. Salvaging archives had proved that he was someone of worth, and thus someone worth saving.

All this would have made sense to the Tcherikowers because at YIVO, collecting separated the insiders from the outsiders. Both the activity and the objects collected were valued tremendously, so much so that Szajkowski wrote of honoring his mother by naming his Carpentras archive for her. The Tcherikowers were particularly devoted *zamlers*. They had always treated their own collections as the most precious of their cargo in each of their migrations. Each time they had fled danger—from Kiev to Moscow, from Moscow to Berlin, from Berlin to Paris, and now from Paris to New York—they had gone to great lengths to bring along the archives they had amassed. In this most recent move, Szajkowski was their main partner, and it was thanks to his tireless work that their enormous collection was sent from Paris to Marseilles, and then after the war, through the Thomas Cook travel agency, on to America. Indeed much of the Szajkowski-Tcherikower correspondence in this period is devoted to frantic discussions of the details of sending the library and archives. Szajkowski imagined *Yidn in Frankraykh* as a secular, modern Talmud; the Tcherikowers thought of their archive in similar terms. As their protégé, Szajkowski worked hard to emulate them. By salvaging the archives, he asserted a place for himself within the Yiddish cultural elite when, it had become clear, only the elite had a real chance at securing American visas.

Szajkowski would wear his work collecting documents of historical value in Carpentras as a badge of honor for the rest of his life. In "The Decline and Fall of Provençal Jewry," the study he would publish in 1944 using the materials he found in Carpentras, he wrote:

In the tragic days of 1940, on the eve of the German occupation, the writer was able, by a peculiar combination of circumstances, to salvage much of this material and to bring it for safe keeping to this

country, where it has been deposited in the library of the Yiddish
Scientific Institute in New York. The present study is based largely
on these new sources.[51]

Among the Jewish historians Szajkowski knew, salvaging archives was
understood as tantamount to rescuing national treasures. Writing for
them in this article, he depicted himself as a plucky kind of hero: He
had seen the storm approaching firsthand, but rather than buckling
under the weight of fear, he had kept a cool head, and capitalizing on
some good luck, he had seized the moment to act selflessly. Salvaging
those archives remained burned in his memory as the noble and brave
act of a hero, a sign of his devotion to scholarship and the Jewish people.
Much later, with thirty-five years' hindsight, he recalled, "In spite of
the difficulties and uncertainties of the era, this was a truly beautiful
period of time and probably the most exciting period of my life."[52]

Heroes are literary figures shaped for an audience. The reality is
usually more mundane and often more complicated. While Szajkowski's
heroic self-representations tell us what was valued in his world, it
is more difficult to get at the messy and often more ambiguous reality
that lies hidden beneath their surface. Curiously, even as he boasts
in "The Decline and Fall of Provençal Jewry" that he found this rare
material himself, he makes no mention of the people from whom he
acquired such rare and precious things. Using the term "salvaged" to
describe the materials erases the intermediaries completely. Yet the
documents were not found abandoned in a cave, or in a garbage dump,
or at the bottom of the sea after a shipwreck. Rather, they were acquired
from real people under a "peculiar combination of circumstances," as
Szajkowski put it in the article, giving the entire undertaking an air of
mystery and romance. This leaves open an important question: What
events, calculations, relationships, values, and emotions actually shaped
this first salvage operation?

Although the traces are few, it is possible to reconstruct, at least to
some extent, how Szajkowski went about his collecting in Carpentras.
In early September 1940, when the Tcherikowers were leaving for
America, Szajkowski reported in separate letters to them and to
Weinreich about several major finds. First, there was "a big pack of
documents from the Commission to liquidate the debts of the old

Carpentras community from the first two decades of the last century" that had been kept in "a basement" by someone whose name he did not mention.[53] Then there were several eighteenth-century Hebrew manuscripts about "events (partly unknown) in the Jewish communities in southern France," but he did not describe them in any further detail, nor did he mention where or how he got them. Did he find these items by canvassing the Jews of the region? If there really were only ten Jews left in Carpentras, this would have meant that 30 percent of them had items of real historical interest stored in their houses. Was it possible? To read Szajkowski's letters, it appears so. These local Jews appear to have been quite welcoming of the wounded foreigner, who was still in quite a bit of pain, and they willingly helped in his collecting efforts. Szajkowski even told Weinreich, "If I need to leave here and can't manage to send things to you before I leave, I will leave a package at a Jewish farmer's in this region, Monsieur Estzin, Venasque (Vaucluse), which he'll send to you at his first opportunity."[54]

The most exciting of Szajkowski's finds were the *pinkassim* of Elie Crémieux of Carpentras, two eighteenth-century communal record books called the *Sefer ha-Yakhas* [Book of genealogy], and the *Hazkarat ha-Nefashot* [Memorial of the souls], kept from the 1730s to the 1780s. The *pinkassim* have been quite valuable for historians. Like parish record books, they contain the vital records of the Carpentras Jewish community on the eve of emancipation, and they also document such things as religious events, maintenance of the synagogue, and even the arrival of emissaries collecting charity for the Jews of Jerusalem. Szajkowski published an excerpt of these rare texts in *Yidn in Frankraykh* in 1942 and followed up the next year with an article about them in the *YIVO Bleter*.[55]

Some mystery surrounds the acquisition of the Carpentras manuscripts. In a 2005 article, historian Simone Mrejen-O'Hana accused Szajkowski of having stolen them from the Archives Départementales du Vaucluse (ADV), based largely on his reputation today as an archive thief. Is she right? It is hard to know; in this case, the backstage of the archives is too poorly documented to be certain. The ADV has no record of any such documents going missing, because in 1940, no inventory had been created for these types of records. Many archives, particularly smaller ones, lack a complete record of their holdings.

This was the case at the ADV, where even today, the inventory for the Carpentras parish records is incomplete, lacking any mention of the Jewish documents.[56]

Another strategy for evaluating Mrejen-O'Hana's charge would be to make a reasonable guess about where such a document *should* have been in 1940. As she notes, in the period from 1763–92, information on births, deaths, and marriages was required of the Jews by the local authorities, who had grown eager to track Jewish inhabitants as their wealth had grown. It is therefore reasonable to think that, like the town's Catholic parish records, they would have been in the ADV, which was the heir to the pre-1791 archives of the former Papal States.[57] On the other hand, the ADV today is still in possession of a Jewish communal record book from Carpentras listing circumcisions, marriages, and deaths in the community, covering the actual period required by law, unlike the Crémieux manuscripts, which cover the period of 1736–69.[58] This calls the accusations of theft into doubt. It is entirely possible that, like many pre-emancipation Jewish records in France and elsewhere in Europe, these *pinkassim* were created for purposes internal to the semi-autonomous community before its emancipation, and after its dissolution, the records remained in private hands until Szajkowski acquired them.

Szajkowski's own correspondence about acquiring the manuscripts does not fully solve the mystery either. He first reported finding the manuscripts at his moment of greatest panic, shortly after his release from the hospital, upon returning from his final visit with the Tcherikowers before they left France, reporting boastfully:

> You can imagine how wonderful it was for me to spend several hours with you before you left France. I was very sad after you left. I found one consolation in a basement in Carpentras, where I found a big pack of documents from the commission to liquidate the debts of the old Carpentras community of the first two decades of the past century. After that I got a suitcase of your presents from the driver. Real great things so one can't be at all mad at you. . . .
>
> At the home of a local Jew, we have the register of the community [*pinkas*] of the 18th century. There are circumcisions listed, births, and deaths from 1736 to 1780. He won't however release them

without being paid. I'll try to buy it from him. What do you think? It is a very interesting document, several hundred pages, densely written in Hebrew. Let me know if it's worth buying.[59]

The next day he wrote to Weinreich in similar terms:

A local Jew owns the register of the Carpentras community from around 1730–1780; several hundred pages written in Hebrew—all the births, deaths, circumcisions, and weddings. He won't give it away for free. Is it worth buying from him and how much to offer him? Write me.[60]

Was there really such a "local Jew," or was this a dishonest way of asking YIVO for money when he most desperately needed it? After all, just a few weeks before, he had proposed to Tcherikower that YIVO offer him support for his collecting, and we know that his sense of desperation was growing. Had Szajkowski already begun his criminal career as a dealer in archives, stealing from one archive to sell to another? He never mentioned the "local Jew" or his documents again in these letters, so we cannot be sure.

Whether Szajkowski acquired the *pinkassim* and the other treasures through purchase, donation, or theft, his ability to construe his collecting as heroic built on a long-established rhetoric of scientific salvation, in which scholars are depicted as the heroic rescuers of forgotten treasures decaying in obscurity in faraway places where no one is left to appreciate them. The emphasis is on the scholar-collector in such accounts, not the intermediaries who sold, donated, or were robbed of the materials. Putting himself in the foreground, Szajkowski tells us little about the people who gave him these rare artifacts from the synagogue and sold him old manuscripts. Only the smallest of details are given: the day at the synagogue with Mossé, the daughter of the last synagogue caretaker; the encounter with the man who kept the communal debt records "in his basement"; the man who would not part with the *pinkassim* without being paid; the Jewish farmer Estzin who offered to store the materials and send them on later. These are hazy figures at best, particularly when compared to the detail Szajkowski provides when describing the objects and the manuscripts, their rarity and their potential utility for scholars. He sees through these intermediaries as if they were mere ghosts, connecting him to the long-ago ghetto.

In this way, Szajkowski's collecting in Carpentras is reminiscent of that of European orientalists, who since the nineteenth century had gathered antiquities in the course of their journeys. Many a British, French, and German scholar traveled to Greece, Egypt, and even Palestine, claiming artifacts and manuscripts they found there as part of the European cultural heritage and bringing them to new homes in museums and libraries in Europe.[61] As early as the mid-nineteenth century, Jewish scholars had participated in these efforts as well and saw their efforts in the same terms as non-Jewish scholars: heroically and altruistically collecting materials for study, in spite of the difficulties involved in traveling to distant lands.[62]

Best known are the Jewish scholars who, at the turn of the twentieth century, participated in the "salvaging" of an immense trove of documents from the Cairo Geniza, a repository of discarded texts found in an Egyptian synagogue. On the basis of the texts they collected, these Jewish scholars reconstructed the contours of Jewish life across the Mediterranean over the course of centuries.[63] The story of that salvage operation is well known, but most versions of the tale focus on the scholars rather than on the Egyptian intermediaries. Similarly, the story of the salvaging of the Dead Sea Scrolls in a cave in Qumran in 1946 focuses more on the scholars who studied them (and later fought bitterly for the right to own them) than on the Bedouins who found them.[64] The pattern is strikingly similar, and has less to do with orientalist racism than we generally imagine. When scholars find precious manuscripts or objects in the field and use them for scholarship, it is they who are remembered. The people who helped them along the way are forgotten, and their motivations become impossible to reconstruct.

In the same way, since Szajkowski wrote so little about them, it is hard to know much about why the Jewish intermediaries who gave or sold him Judaica in Carpentras might have done so. Even if Szajkowski stole some of his treasures from the local archives, we know that at least some of what he collected was given to him by the last synagogue caretaker's daughter, who was friendly enough with the historian to have remained in touch with him for a long time. Why did she give away the synagogue's treasures? Given that the salvaging occurred in Vichy France in 1940, one might wonder if she and the other mysterious donors were trying to protect the materials in their possession from the perceived threat of the Germans or the Vichy authorities. France had, after all, just fallen to the Germans and though Carpentras was in the unoccupied south, the new regime was already showing itself to be antisemitic. Might they have seen YIVO as a safe haven for their Jewish treasures? It is unlikely. Nowhere else in France, not even in the occupied north, did leaders of Jewish institutions seek to protect their documents from the approaching Germans by sending them abroad, even though many took pains to protect their documents in other ways. In Paris, for example, leaders in two institutions—the native-born Jews' Consistory and the immigrant-dominated Jewish Communist organization—went to great lengths to hide their documents from the Nazis at the moment of the invasion. Consistory leaders are said to have transported their papers to the Rothschild chateau in southwestern France, where they were hidden until the end of the war. Jewish Communist records are said to have been buried in the ground of a garden in Paris.[65] When French Jews felt that papers in their possession were valuable, they did not protect them by sending them abroad; they hid them in France.

The fate of the Bund archives is a bit different, but equally instructive. Like the Tcherikowers' archives, the Bund archives had been moved westward as their caretaker had fled persecution. They had been moved from Russia to Berlin and then from Berlin to Paris, all under the supervision of Szajkowski's dear friend Franz Kursky. In 1934, Kursky had contracted to send the Bund archives to Amsterdam, where they were to become part of the collections of the International Institute of Social History. Yet by 1940, he had sent only part of the materials, and upon fleeing Paris in June 1940, he hid the remaining documents in Paris, returning in 1945 to retrieve them and bring them to New York, where he himself had emigrated. Even this transfer of materials out of Europe took place after the war, not at the beginning. This archive was saved by hiding it rather than sending it away. As Gelernt wrote to Szajkowski in July 1940, Kursky's intention had been to keep the materials in Europe. Indeed, Gelernt wrote, he himself had packed the archive and was ready to send it to Amsterdam in June, but in the confusion of the German invasion, there had been no time, so he hid the materials instead.[66] Only later, after the war, did Kursky reevaluate his decision to leave the materials in Europe and bring them to America. We know of no other French Jewish institutional collection that was sent out of France for safekeeping in 1940 or 1941. For those French Jewish leaders who cared about their archives, hiding them within France seemed a better way to protect their materials than sending them to America.

The more plausible scenario for the sales or donations, then, is that the individuals who had the materials believed they had met someone who treasured the old papers and objects they possessed, remnants of an abandoned community, and they were happy to learn that they would become part of an archive for historians to use. After all, Szajkowski never mentioned in his letters that he might one day return the materials to Carpentras once this threat had passed, and in his publications, he proudly announced their addition to the YIVO collections. He was not hiding his salvaging work from the previous owners; he was wearing it as a badge of honor. They must not have seen the materials as a part of the regional patrimony, needing protection in a brief moment of danger. Rather, they were giving things to a collector who prized them and promised to give them value by making them part of something greater, part of an archive.

In this first salvage operation, Szajkowski depicted himself as part of the scholarly elite. A lone hero in a dangerous place, he had gathered treasures for his friends to admire and use. By studying what he had collected, they might also be able to answer the difficult questions they were raising about the price Jews had paid for their emancipation. Szajkowski in 1940–41 had no concept of a particularly *French* Jewish patrimony. Rather, these materials were remnants of a larger story in *Jewish* history, and could be gathered up and taken anywhere that Jews lived. Indeed, he saw the world they evoked as archetypical of the abandoned ghetto, not so different from other ghettos and shtetls Jews abandoned as they embraced the opportunities modernity offered them. The universal nature of the story they contained made salvaging them seem all the more important. As with the Geniza fragments at Cambridge University or the Dead Sea Scrolls at the

Hebrew University, the best place for these remnants of the European Jewish ghetto was understood to be a place where there were Jewish scholars who understood their meaning and value and had the means to preserve them. Carpentras at that moment was certainly not such a place, but YIVO was. As Szajkowski witnessed the end of an era in Jewish history, he hoped that these salvaged materials could be used as part of the material foundation for a new Jewish culture. After all, had he not written from his Carpentras hospital bed to the Tcherikowers, "Can we imagine a dedicated keeper of Jewish culture escaping the Germans in any other way?"

On May 15, 1941, Szajkowski finally left Marseilles aboard the French Line steamer *Wyoming*, bound for Martinique. Like most of the other refugees lucky enough to be on the ship with him, his plan was to go on from Martinique to New York. But the *Wyoming* did not get beyond the Moroccan coast in its journey west. Fearing that the British would seize the ship, French authorities stopped it off the coast of Casablanca and made the passengers disembark. They were sent to a camp in a town called Oued Zem, about 150 kilometers inland, in central Morocco. Szajkowski's letters to his friends in New York from the camp, which he called "Had-Gadio" (here a Yiddish slang term for prison, likely used to get by the French censors), were frantic and full of despair. "Will I ever see you again?" he wrote in French to the Tcherikowers. "In any case, my very dear friends, I wanted to tell you that I love you like my own parents and I think of you often. Do everything necessary via Washington to let the American consul in Casablanca know in case my visa needs to be extended. Love, your Frydman."[67]

The situation must have been terrifying. Having just escaped potential imprisonment in a labor camp in the Southern Zone of France, now he found himself interned by the French police in Morocco for an indeterminate period, with the clock ticking on his visa. What's more, the French police officials at Oued Zem seemed just as antisemitic as in metropolitan France. As Szajkowski later remembered, "When I demanded that they free me because I was wounded in the war and decorated with the Croix de Guerre, I received this answer from a high French police official: 'If you volunteered in the army, it is a sign that you wanted the war. In that case, a concentration camp is the place for you.'"[68] And in the middle of all this, he was also anxious about the fate of the Tcherikowers' possessions, some of which were en route and others of which were still in Marseilles. Now, the fate of those boxes, full of priceless archival treasures, was completely out of his hands. In fact, his letters from his stay in Morocco reflect greater worry about those boxes and bags than about his own fate, reflecting how profoundly his sense of himself was bound up in the materials.

We can probably credit Szajkowski's personal resourcefulness for getting him out of Oued Zem. He received little in the way of reply to his frequent letters and telegrams to Ilya Dijour, a friend and the head of the French office of HICEM, the immigrant aid organization that was arranging his travel plans ("HICEM does much for many people, except for its own friends," he wrote the Tcherikowers angrily, in French, from Morocco).[69] What news Dijour did send was bad. There was no room for him on any of the few ships that would depart from Casablanca. Instead, he would have to make his way to Seville to board the *Navemar*, due to depart on July 10. This was his only option, in spite of the fact that it was all but impossible to obtain a Spanish transit visa.[70] No records remain of how Szajkowski actually got out of Morocco, how he gained entry into Spain, or why HICEM paid for his passage on a ship for which tickets were rumored to cost $1,000 each.[71] Yet the *Navemar*'s ship manifest tells us that, indeed, Szajkowski was on board when it finally left Seville on August 4, after weeks of being stuck in port.[72]

As if Szajkowski's journey had not been arduous enough, he now found himself on one of the most notorious of all refugee ships. The ship was in fact a banana freighter, a merchant vessel in no way equipped to transport passengers. Accommodations were available for fifteen crew members only, and yet the ship was transporting nearly 1,200 refugees. The *Navemar* stopped in Cadiz, Lisbon, Bermuda, and Havana on its journey to New York, which took a grueling six weeks. It was hot, food was scarce and repulsive, the facilities grossly inadequate, and there were no medical supplies. There was little water for washing, and soon, many on board the ship contracted dysentery. By the time they arrived in Bermuda, Szajkowski had heard that four passengers had died (in fact, only one had, and he had been buried at sea for fear of contaminating other passengers). The few toilets, showers, and sinks were covered with diarrhea and were never cleaned. There were thirty-two accidents onboard, eight cases of typhoid, numerous heart attacks, and fevers. There was nowhere to sleep. Passengers who had the strength climbed into the lifeboats on deck for a little comfort.[73] After it landed in New York and the conditions onboard were publicized, the ship was dubbed "Hell on Water" by the local press, and with good reason. Representatives of the American Jewish Joint Distribution Committee called the ship's conditions "criminally inadequate" and, indeed, hundreds of passengers filed a class-action lawsuit shortly after landing in the United States.[74]

For Szajkowski, as for several others who wrote about their experiences on this ship, the worst part of the trip was dealing with the other passengers. The refugees were desperate Jews from all over Europe. Victor Brombert, who called the ship "the Floating Camp" in his memoir, remembers the "uncivil behavior and outbursts of minor violence" that plagued the ship, remembering a particular "contingent of former inmates of German concentration camps who had been liberated recently" that he and his family called "the wild ones."[75] He remembered that in the absence of any official security staff, passengers organized themselves into groups in order to protect themselves, taking turns keeping watch over each other and their bags. René Bravmann, a child at the time of the journey, remembers his mother later reminiscing about the unruly passengers; her strategy for survival on board was to keep her mouth shut and not talk to anyone.[76]

Szajkowski too was wary of the Germans, though he seemed not to know that they had been recently released from a concentration camp. "On top of everything else, we're all suffering the majority of passengers who are German Jews, coming directly from Germany. They are horrible people, with a horrible German spirit with which we are really having a hard time." Yet, as he seems to have done in so many terrible situations, Szajkowski kept his head. He found friends on board, people he had known prior to the trip, among them Mark Zborowski, the ethnographer who had traveled in Trotskyist circles in Paris and would later work for YIVO in New York; and Marc Slonim, a Russian literature specialist.[77]

After thirty-nine horrific days at sea, the *Navemar* landed in New York on September 12, 1941, reuniting Szajkowski with his dear friends, the Tcherikowers. By then, they had received part of their treasured collection that Szajkowski had arranged to be sent from Marseilles before he left in May. For the bulk of the materials, though, they would have to wait for Szajkowski's return to France as a soldier with the American forces.

4

The Parachutist

WHEN SZAJKOWSKI FINALLY ARRIVED IN New York in September 1941, a postcard from his father in the Warsaw ghetto, dated April 23, was waiting for him. Conditions in the ghetto were awful, his father reported, and he asked Szajko to send a parcel of food right away because the family was starving.[1] It must have been pure anguish for Szajko to realize that his arrival in America, delayed by several months, might have caused his father and his brothers Efraim and Mendel further suffering. He also worried about his sister Dina and his brothers Zalmen and Zilke, who had stayed in Paris with their families despite the German occupation. Lack of news compounded Szajkowski's anxiety, and he found it hard to settle in during his first year in New York.[2]

Szajkowski always found work a consolation. Luckily, he was able to join YIVO's *aspirantur* program for a second year, this time in New York, working with the rare materials he had brought from Carpentras. YIVO's small stipend of thirty dollars a month covered his meager needs, especially when supplemented by payments for articles in New York Yiddish papers such as *Der Tog*. The *aspirantur* program also gave him a sense of purpose. He worked closely with some of YIVO's finest established scholars, such as the institution's head Max Weinreich, who had arrived from Vilna in March 1940; the linguist

75

Yudl Mark; historians Raphael Mahler, Koppel Pinson, and Jacob Shatzky; as well as several scholars he already knew from Paris who were teaching courses in the program: Julius Brutzkus, Franz Kursky, and Avrom Menes. Of course, he continued to work closely with his mentor Elias Tcherikower on the Jews in France.[3] Szajkowski also made a few new friends at YIVO, including the American-born historian Lucy (Libe in Yiddish) Schildkret, who later would become a pioneering historian of the Holocaust, publishing under her married name, Lucy Dawidowicz. When Szajkowski met her, the still single Schildkret had recently returned from a memorable year as an *aspirant* at YIVO in Vilna in 1938–39 and had begun working as Weinreich's secretary in New York while pursuing her own research.

Despite his professional opportunities at YIVO, in late 1942, Szajkowski signed up for the U.S. Army. As an immigrant, he was not subject to the draft, and he was still experiencing pain from the chest wound he suffered in France in June 1940. Yet if other Jewish refugees' memoirs are any clue, his ardent desire to serve—apparent in the letters he sent the Tcherikowers from basic training in Fort Dix, New Jersey—was fanned by the numerous advantages service offered. These included a quick path to citizenship, a steady income, a way to avoid the social discomfort of staying on the home front, and most importantly, a way to contribute to Hitler's defeat.[4]

For a few months, it seemed unlikely that he would be allowed to fight. Although welcome in the armed forces, recent refugees were routinely viewed with some suspicion and assigned to the medical corps. This is what happened to Szajkowski in Camp Pickett in Virginia in early 1943.[5] Then, after a new policy enabled greater use of the linguistic and cultural skills of these refugees, he was sent to Fort Ritchie in western Maryland for training in military intelligence and interpreting. Most of the so-called "Ritchie Boys" were from Germany, Austria, or Czechoslovakia; Szajkowski himself was among a smaller group of Jews from France. "In the new barracks they are all French-speaking," he wrote. "Real Frenchmen: none. And it makes for a good atmosphere that reminds me a little of France."[6] Together they kept their distance from the German Jews ("We call them *boches*, after all, we are not friends," he wrote of them), explored nearby Hagerstown, and took classes to prepare for their exams.[7] The training pleased him. With a

Szajko Frydman in his U.S.
Army uniform, with Ilya
and Riva Tcherikower in
New York, 1943. *From the
Archives of the YIVO Institute
for Jewish Research.*

gun in his hand, he would return to battle the enemy that had forced
him out of Europe.

In late August 1943, Szajkowski received devastating news. Ilya
Tcherikower had died suddenly from a heart attack. He rushed from
Fort Ritchie to New York for the funeral, and since the Tcherikowers
had no children, Szajkowski said *kaddish* at the graveside. Back in
Maryland, his thoughts turned to scholarship for the first time in
months. "I would like to compile a bibliography of Ilusha's works," he
wrote to Riva. "I am writing to Libe [Schildkret] to ask her to do this
with me and to start collecting a bibliography.... I can't see another
person who could do it."[8]

At the end of November 1943, he left for an army base in England. Szajkowski—Technician Third Grade Frydman—had volunteered to serve as a paratrooper and interpreter in the 82nd Airborne Division, a division that had already seen action in Italy, but was then regrouping at its base in England. Its headquarters were in Oadby, a village on the outskirts of Leicester, where the paratroopers awaited the anticipated invasion of France. The training was demanding but also thrilling. The additional pay, $50 on top of his regular wages of $110 per month, was attractive to Szajkowski, who never forgot how uncertain his job prospects would be at the end of the war. But beyond the financial considerations, he had volunteered for the 82nd Airborne out of a keen sense that on invasion day, the paratroopers would be at the center of the action. Besides, he was a natural when it came to parachuting. As he wrote to Riva, "The main thing is to keep your senses, keep your feet together. . . . You always said I was a very nervous person, a hunk of turmoil. Now, as I've been jumping, I'm convinced that I'm not that nervous after all. As with everything else in my military life, my fatalist philosophy helps me out. I don't know where and how I got infected with it, but I feel fine about it."[9]

Keeping in touch with Riva was a lifeline for him in those days, as it was for her. Just a few years earlier, when he was about to leave France for the United States, Szajkowski had politely refused Riva's offer to come live with her and Ilya in their Washington Heights apartment because "as you know, I'm a bit screwed up and have the habits of an old bachelor."[10] But now that Ilya was gone, he understood that she needed him as much as he needed her, and he began to address her with the intimacy of the son she never had. In the rare instances when more than a few days passed without receiving a letter from her, he grew frantic with worry, knowing she was finding it hard to eat and sleep without her lifelong companion. At a time when it was impossible to get news of his family in Warsaw and Paris, Riva truly became a surrogate mother. Despite the fact that he had regular contact with his brother Harry in Chicago and was even able to visit his sister Sarah in nearby Hull, England, on several occasions, it was Riva, not either of his siblings, whom he listed as next of kin on his army papers. He gave her power of attorney in case something should happen to him and frequently sent her money and gifts.

126463

Technician Third Grade Szajko Frydman in his U.S. Army paratrooper uniform, England, 1944. *From the Archives of the YIVO Institute for Jewish Research.*

Szajko also wrote to Riva about his increasingly intimate friendship with a young English woman named Elaine whom he met in the spring quite by chance, when he was out walking by the water near his army base. The romantic situation was complicated. Not only was Elaine not Jewish; she was also engaged to another man. But Riva did not disapprove. On the contrary, it reassured her to hear that Szajko was not too lonely. He had dated a lot in his Paris days; Riva teased him endlessly about all the women on his *"carnet de bal"* (dance card). But he had always had trouble finding someone to settle down with, and since he had arrived from New York, he had barely dated. It made her worry that at thirty-three, he might be alone forever; and Szajkowski himself was more or less resigned to the possibility.[11] He seemed to know there was something a little strange about the way he closed himself off, but he backed away from simple diagnoses. "I personally could be good material for Freudian study, but I've never been able to make peace with that theory. It's too simple," he once explained to Riva.[12] Perhaps a more complex theory would have taken into account the personal toll of multiple migrations and self-reinventions.

In the liminal space of the war, the soldier finally opened his heart a little, even if it did not commit him to anything. Like many soldiers—especially the refugees—he thought it a bad idea to make plans for the future given the current circumstances.[13] And so he permitted himself the pleasure of the unlikely affair without necessarily giving in to fantasies about a shared life, following Elaine's own advice, "You have to love a lot, but never lose your head."[14] Szajko was good at that. When pressed about the extent of the relationship, he always responded that he and Elaine were "just friends," in part because he harbored relatively strict ideas about women's virtue, and he disapproved of intermarriage. Perhaps that is what freed him to let her in. He even let her call him Zosa, the childhood diminutive his parents had used. No one had called him that in years. There must have been something truly special about her. As his brother-in-law in Hull told him, "The big secret of how a Jewish historian can fall in love with a gentile becomes understandable when you meet Elaine."[15]

From time to time, Szajkowski was able to get away from camp for a break. During these times, his thoughts returned to Jewish culture and history. In March 1944, he headed to London. In just a few days, he managed to connect with a few important players in the Yiddish world and learn how they were planning for the future. He reported to Riva about his amazing chance encounter on the London subway with the Yiddish poet Itzik Manger, whom they knew from Paris in the late 1930s. "His first words to me were 'I will not be writing in Yiddish anymore.' And he immediately began cursing everything and everyone. Nasty as he ever was! No respect for anyone!"[16] In a time when it seemed that the entire Yiddish-speaking elite was on the move, old acquaintances might turn up anywhere. Despite his contempt for

Manger, running into him felt like seeing a distant relative, reconnecting him to a world far away.

He also had a longer and more serious conversation with Aaron Steinberg, a friend of the Tcherikowers who, like them, had followed a path from the Soviet Union to Berlin in the early 1920s, and then from Berlin to Western Europe in the early 1930s. Steinberg's destination, however, was London. There he became deeply involved with the World Jewish Congress (WJC), an organization founded in 1936 in Geneva to defend Jewish rights, and he served as head of its cultural department in London from 1948 until 1971.[17] After receiving a reliable report in 1942, the WJC was the first organization to publicize the news that the Nazis planned to exterminate the Jewish people. Its leaders were deeply concerned with the ever-widening scope of the tragedy unfolding across Nazi-occupied Europe. Spending the day with Steinberg, Szajkowski heard quite a bit about the WJC's work on behalf of European Jews, and the news of their plight depressed him. To Riva, he dwelled not so much on the news of the mass murders, but rather on Steinberg's stories about the endless "intrigue and pettiness" among the WJC leaders, who came from a diverse set of backgrounds and had different ideological commitments.[18] Why, he complained to Riva, did Jews do nothing but quarrel in the most difficult of times?

Steinberg talked to Szajkowski about Nazi looting in Jewish libraries and archives across Europe. The discussion brought the younger historian's attention back, for the first time in months, to the artifacts of the Jewish past—books, papers, and other cultural treasures—that had so occupied his thinking a few years earlier in Carpentras. Though the extent of the looting was not yet known, it was already clear that it had happened across Europe, in every country under German occupation. Steinberg said that the WJC was proactively forming a committee to deal with the problem, but that in this realm too, they were bogged down in political disagreements. As Szajkowski wrote to Riva, "The highly assimilated circles (a French Jew) argued that this was a subject for world governments and not specifically for the Jewish committee. The Zionists demanded that we get everything back from the Germans and send it to Hebrew University in Jerusalem."[19] Szajkowski immediately thought of Weinreich and asked Riva to talk to him. As the head of one of the largest libraries and archives that had fallen into German hands, surely he would want to participate in this conversation.

Szajkowski did not have to worry; Weinreich was already involved in similar conversations in New York, where the discussions were no less contentious. By 1943, thirty-two different Jewish research groups across the diaspora were studying the question of how Jews could rebuild after the war. Several of them demonstrated particular interest in the restitution of cultural property, most importantly, the Commission on European Jewish Cultural Reconstruction, led by the Jewish historian Salo Baron of Columbia University in New York; the World Jewish Congress's branch in New York (where jurist Jacob Robinson ran its research arm, the Institute on Jewish Affairs); Hebrew University in Jerusalem; and the Jewish Historical Society of England, headed by the historian Cecil Roth.[20] Viewing the rescue of Jewish people and Jewish books as part of the same task, even the most secular leaders among them saw it as a sacred duty. As Roth put it in April 1943, "to our fathers, the rescue of Jewish books from piratical hands was regarded as an integral part of the fundamental *mizwah* of *Pidyon Shebuyim*, the Ransoming of Captives."[21] Although the Talmudic commandment to ransom Jewish *people* who had been taken captive was well known, Roth's application of it to books was far more obscure. Yet at that moment, it made sense. As many Jews came to think of themselves as a nation in the early part of the twentieth century, they began to speak of Jewish books in the terms usually reserved for Jewish people.

The debates about libraries and archives on both sides of the Atlantic turned on the question of whether reconstruction in Europe would be possible, even if the Allies won the war. The questions were existential; the debates were passionate and divisive. Szajkowski still hated the way Jews always seemed to fall into entrenched camps, endlessly tearing at each other. But even so, his conversation with Steinberg piqued his interest and led to action after he reached the continent.

As Szajkowski himself learned in London, Allied leaders already knew the broad outlines of Nazi plunder. Yet the troops on the ground were unprepared for the full extent of Nazi looting. Just as troops making their way to Berlin in 1945 stumbled unprepared upon emaciated Jewish prisoners in German concentration camps, as part of the same advance into German territory, they also stumbled unprepared upon cache after cache of booty in secret depots in castles and caves. The loot they found was extensive. In every country under Nazi occupation, beginning in Austria in 1938, German authorities had systematically confiscated art, furniture, musical instruments, books, and archives.[22]

By World War II, great libraries and archives were considered national treasures, and so Nazi looting of these institutions was first and foremost a symbolic act to proclaim German superiority, even when it also served strategic ends, as, for example, in France, where the archives of the train agency, the postal service, and the diplomatic service were looted.[23] Archives in the part of Poland that was directly incorporated into the Reich were also plundered with the intention of undermining Polish national identity. Some of the most extensive library looting took place after the German invasion of the Soviet Union, when more than four million books were stolen from Kiev alone, and many other valuable volumes were taken from other cities.[24]

There were precedents for this kind of looting. Napoleonic armies had once plundered works of great artistic and cultural value in their conquest of Europe, including from the German lands, and had brought them to the Louvre. The emperor deemed this a work of "protection" of these treasures, as the Nazis would later claim about their own plundering. In addition, Napoleon also envisioned a vast "archival palace" to be built in Paris, and had seized archival collections to be housed in it. Though the project was never realized, it too foreshadowed Nazi policies. At the Congress of Vienna in 1815, the powers that vanquished Napoleon demanded that the archives and other cultural treasures be returned, much as the victorious Allies would do after World War II. Actual restitutions after the Napoleonic wars were limited by the fact that victorious armies had already taken many valuable items from the Louvre as war trophies. This too prefigured the situation that Allied leaders would face in the aftermath of World War II.[25]

Napoleon had looted archives and libraries because, since the Revolution, French authorities deemed such collections to be of great symbolic importance. In France, the Revolutionaries saw "nationalizing" the archives as part of their project of claiming sovereignty. By seizing their contents from the nobles and kings who had created or inherited them, deeming them the property of the nation, they supported their claim to rule legitimately. For them, as for the succeeding regimes of nineteenth-century France, archives came to represent national sovereignty, for they were the physical repositories of the laws of the realm.[26] And while the French were the first to treat these collections as national property, simultaneous developments in international law also speak to a direct association between archives and sovereignty. This association is clear from the fate of the Polish archives in the partitions of the late eighteenth century, when Polish archival documents were moved first to St. Petersburg and later divided among the beneficiaries of the partition, the Habsburgs, the Prussians, and the Russians.[27] Here too, the archives were understood as the repositories of law, and thus had to be moved when sovereignty changed hands.

In the century that followed, the logic connecting archives and libraries to sovereignty was developed more fully in international law, and for that reason, archival transfers became more common when territorial sovereignty changed hands. For example, in 1831, when Belgium became independent, the new state was given all the archives relevant to governing it by the kingdom of the Netherlands, from which it had seceded.[28] At the end of the Franco-Prussian war, the archives of Alsace-Lorraine were transferred to German control.[29] As nationalism grew, so too did the concern for archives and libraries. The 1907 Hague Convention forbade the looting of cultural treasures in wartime, while it permitted the seizure of "depots of arms, means of transport, stores and supplies, and generally, all moveable property belonging to the State which may be used for military operations."[30] The breakup of the Habsburg Empire at the end of World War I led to massive transfers of archives, as several international treaties gave the new nations of Eastern Europe the right to possess archives relating to their respective pasts.[31]

Other sorts of cultural treasures—such as rare books, manuscripts, and art—were also increasingly treated as national property and as such, subject to international treaties. The Treaty of Versailles held Germany responsible for the destruction and looting of cultural treasures, and was required to return items still in existence (such as the original Koran of the Caliph Uthman and the skull of the Sultan Mkwawa). There was also a specific provision regarding cultural treasures destroyed in the war: Germany was required to compensate the Louvain University library in Belgium by furnishing it with books and manuscripts from its own collections.[32] This last provision represented the introduction of a notable principle in international law that reparations, as well as restitution, could be made to nations that had lost cultural treasures as a result of military aggression.

Much of the German looting in World War II was both illegal (since the Germans were signatories of the Hague Treaty of 1907) and extremely meaningful. Although the plunder of supplies to arm the German troops was acceptable under the provisions of the Hague Treaty, the systematic appropriation of occupied nations' cultural treasures, including the archives taken for their historic and cultural value rather than their strategic use, was not. Such action had been declared illegal precisely because of the meaning that such cultural property had acquired since the time of the French Revolution. Like Napoleon, Hitler plundered cultural treasures to assert his imperial sovereignty and his regime's status as the arbiter and protector of civilization, as he and his supporters defined it.

Nazi looting of cultural treasures was an important part of genocide. The looting of Jewish books and libraries began in France in the summer of 1940 under Nazi ideologue Alfred Rosenberg, whose organization, the *Einsatzstab Reichsleiter Rosenberg* (Reichsleiter Rosenberg Task Force, known as the ERR), systematically looted books, manuscripts, and archival documents, as well as other items of cultural value, such as art, furniture, and tapestries, from Jewish individuals and institutions. It was also the agency that took charge of the plunder of art from France's public collections.[33]

The ERR focused its efforts on plundering Jewish institutions and individuals. The goal was multifold: to impoverish Jews, to destroy their culture, and to provide Nazi scholars with material for study. Even though prominent French Jewish institutions, such as the Consistory and the Jewish Communist organizations, took pains to safeguard their collections, hiding them as part of their preparation for Nazi occupation in June 1940, many others fell victim to the ERR soon after the occupation began.

The most important Jewish library in Paris was the Alliance Israélite Universelle (AIU), an international aid organization whose prewar library of around 100,000 volumes contained many rare treasures, including Geniza fragments and illuminated medieval manuscripts. It also housed an archive of the organization's work around the world dating back to its foundation in 1860. Its stacks had been renovated just before the war began. When Rosenberg and his men visited the AIU library in the summer, they not only packed up 700 cartons of books, manuscripts, and archival documents and sent them to Germany; they also confiscated its building at 45, rue la Bruyère to use as their base of operations. Its stacks then became a stopping point on the eastward journey of hundreds of thousands of books that were confiscated from individuals and institutions across Paris.[34] These included the large collection of the Ecole Rabbinique, which contained manuscripts dating back to the fourteenth century, and some smaller collections as well. The Jewish-owned publishing house Librairie Lipschutz lost 20,000 books, and prominent Jewish book collectors were looted as well, including the Rothschild family, who lost 20,000 volumes.[35] Though Slavic libraries and libraries of Freemasons were also plundered, the pillaging of Jewish collections was the most thorough and systematic effort the ERR undertook in French libraries.

The ERR sent French Jewish books mostly to Frankfurt, for the Institut zur Erforschung der Judenfrage (Institute for the Study of the Jewish Question), part of Rosenberg's Hohe Schule, established in 1938. The Hohe Schule was the centerpiece of a new Nazi university system that would educate the new elite, advance Nazi racial science, and study the regime's enemies. Even in their propaganda efforts, the Nazis were committed to scholarly study, and for this reason, a library of Jewish books and archives was required. The collection already contained many books from German Jewish libraries that had been seized in the 1930s. At its height in 1943, the library comprised at least 550,000 volumes, more than five times the size of the largest French Judaica library before the war.[36]

After the German invasion of the Soviet Union, Rosenberg was appointed Minister of the Occupied Eastern Territories, and he set up a looting operation in that region similar to the one he had established in France. Large operations were established in the region of Minsk and around Kiev where German staff, with local help, went through local libraries and archives for material deemed worthy of Nazi study. Particularly important operations were carried out in Vilna. There, the ERR removed an estimated 100,000 books from the city's famous

Jewish libraries, including YIVO's library, as well as the Strashun library, the first public Jewish library collection, reputed to have held some 40,000 volumes, including many rare books and manuscripts.

The ERR used YIVO's library as its base of operations in Vilna, as it had done with the AIU library in Paris. Johannes Pohl, a Nazi Talmud specialist, oversaw a team of Jewish slave laborers required to select which books would be sent to Frankfurt. The team included a number of prominent intellectuals: Zelig Kalmanovich, one of the directors of YIVO; Herman Kruk, a refugee from Warsaw who ran the Vilna ghetto library; and the writers Abraham Sutzkever and Shmerke Kaczerginski. They found the task excruciatingly painful.[37] The books they selected would be "saved," but only by putting them into the hands of the enemy, while the rest were destined for destruction at a nearby paper mill. Unlike in France, the ERR destroyed the majority of the Jewish books it plundered in the East; of the 100,000 books estimated to have been looted from Vilna's Jewish libraries, only about 20,000 were sent to Germany.[38]

These Vilna library workers were among those most committed to resistance. They soon established a ghetto underground operation to protect Jewish books from being transferred to Germany, or worse, destroyed. From March 1942 to September 1943, the "Paper Brigade" (as it was called in the ghetto) smuggled thousands of books and tens of thousands of documents out of YIVO and back into the ghetto, where they were hidden for safekeeping. Although many of the members of the Paper Brigade were eventually murdered by the Nazis, some, including Sutzkever and Kaczerginski, survived by joining the partisans. They returned to Vilna in July 1944 and established a Museum of Jewish Art and Culture, the very first Jewish institution to be reestablished in the city. Despite the extensive losses, the survival of some of the treasured books and documents in the face of Nazi persecution was, for them, a symbol of the survival of the Jewish people. After Sutzkever and Kaczerginski realized that the museum would not survive in Soviet Lithuania, they again rescued the books, bringing them along in their baggage on their own emigration to Paris via Poland in 1946. They then sent the books on to YIVO in New York.[39]

While Jewish resistance fighters were attempting to safeguard Jewish libraries and archives under Nazi occupation, Allied leaders were attempting to coordinate their plan for dealing with Nazi loot. On January 5, 1943, representatives of sixteen Allied countries in London (including some whose countries were under German occupation but whose governments in exile were working with the Allies) signed an Inter-Allied Declaration against Acts of Dispossession Committed in Territories under Enemy Occupation or Control. The agreement signaled their clear intention to "defeat any methods of dispossession, whether or not they had the appearance of legality."[40]

The Declaration was based on international law. For the Americans, British, and French, it also responded to popular sentiment. The feeling was most widespread in Britain and France, where the toll of German destruction was already felt. But it was also palpable in the United States, where throughout the conflict, journalists frequently expressed concern about the fate of Europe's cultural treasures. The dangers were multifold, from new military technologies, such as aerial bombard-ment, to Nazi cultural policy. Popular pressure did much to push the Americans to prepare to protect Europe's cultural treasures before their troops landed on the continent. Yielding to the demands of concerned librarians, museum administrators, and academics, American military authorities created the Monuments, Fine Arts & Archives (MFA&A) program at the time of the Italian campaign of 1943. These "Monuments Men"—specialists in art, archives, and books—were assigned to work with the military units in the course of action.[41] As they advanced across Italy and Northern Europe, these officers identified and protected price-less treasures from looting and destruction.[42]

Restitution was another matter. Although the Declaration of January 5, 1943, did represent a commitment to the principle of returning looted property, it identified no specific means for restitution, nor did it establish an agency or agencies to take charge of the effort. Among the Allied forces, only France was invested in developing a full plan in advance for the restitution of looted materials. As early as April 1944, its representatives sought to create an international organization to handle restitutions after the war.[43] The British and Americans were less certain that restitution was a good use of Allied resources, and so they hesitated. The Soviets showed no interest whatsoever in establishing formal processes for restitution, fearing that any agreements they might conclude with the Allies might interfere with their plans for assuring security in Eastern Europe after the war.[44] As the Allies converged in Germany, they continued to disagree on restitution policies.[45]

Szajkowski knew that Jewish organizations were pushing aggressively for inclusion in whatever Allied restitution processes might eventually take place. But he had a prior commitment. On the night before D-Day, he jumped from an airplane over German-occupied Normandy, in advance of the Allied troops that would arrive on boats the next morning. He plunged into the Merderet River, near Ste.-Mère-Église, eight kilometers inland from Utah Beach. At dawn, holding his gun up over his head, he made his way across to the other shore, up to his neck in the water as the bullets flew by. It was a bad landing, and he

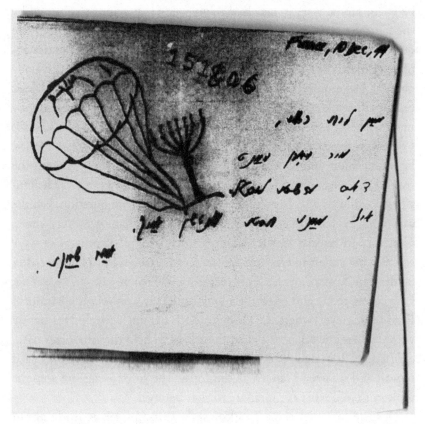

A drawing that Szajkowski made and sent to Riva Tcherikower in a letter from France, where he was serving as a paratrooper with the U.S. Army, wishing her a Happy Chanukah, December 1944. *From the Archives of the YIVO Institute for Jewish Research.*

made an easy target for snipers when he crossed the river. But somehow, Szajkowski got lucky again and survived, this time uninjured. The paratroopers told each other that the Germans were terrified of soldiers who dropped from the sky. The idea gave them courage. Still, he slept with "one ear open" and "eyes ready to pop open" too.[46]

For the next five weeks, he served at the front, acting as a translator in his unit's dealings with local Frenchmen and also in their interrogation of captured POWs. The enemy was not quite what he expected. These Germans were cowardly, which gave him some satisfaction. Actually, many of the *Wehrmacht* soldiers were not German at all, and soon he found himself speaking not only French and German but also Russian and Polish. More than a few of the enemy soldiers he encountered were in fact Red Army soldiers previously captured by the Germans, and some of them were as young as sixteen. They bore devastating news. One Russian had seen firsthand the brutal massacres of Jewish children in Minsk. Another, a Pole, had been in the Lodz ghetto a few months earlier and estimated that only a few hundred Jews remained. Szajkowski suspected the Pole might have been more than a mere witness to the slaughter of Jews. He preferred the Russians.[47]

Unwavering in his disgust for the Nazis and suspicious of the Poles, he was far more ambivalent toward the French. In five long weeks at the front, he looked again and again for evidence of where the French actually stood in this war, particularly regarding the Jewish question. On the one hand, evidence of collaboration with the Germans was everywhere. Contrary to reports in the American press, signs of resistance were scarce.[48] Yet suffering was apparent everywhere he went. Not long after landing in Normandy, he reported, "an old Frenchman, a brave man, hugged me today and cried for a long time." And although portraits of Pétain hung everywhere, he also wrote Riva about a whole Normandy village where the villagers risked their lives to help the American parachutists.[49] Ultimately he adopted a cautious attitude, writing "we need to wait and see what France will put forth. The very courageous step she took in 1940 doesn't compensate for her betrayal."[50]

Despite his even tone, Szajkowski's wait-and-see attitude about France was not that of a disinterested journalist. That summer, he worried constantly about his family in Paris, his two brothers and his sister, their spouses, and their small children. The civilian mail was not operating that summer while the war raged on, so getting even the smallest piece of news of them would have to wait until after liberation.[51] In the meantime, he found himself suspended between identities, uncertain where to imagine his future. At times he felt like a Frenchman, as when he jumped for the first time into Normandy, writing, "it's not for nothing that the French are the best fighters (See, I've got too much pride)."[52] Sometimes he even imagined staying in France after the war, at least for long enough to finish Tcherikower's research on Napoleon and the Jews.[53] More frequently, however, at least in his letters to the grieving, insomniac Riva, he promised to return to New York. Like many refugees who fought on the front, Szajkowski was poised between his old identity as a Jewish immigrant in France and a new one as an American. Uprooted and alone, Szajkowski knew that until he learned what happened to his family, he would have trouble planning for the future. "Somewhere in France, perhaps not far from here, are a lot of my relatives," the melancholy soldier wrote from the front in July 1944. "I don't know if I'm longing for them or for New York, but I'm longing for everything."[54]

After liberation, Szajkowski was finally able to get furloughed from duty on a regular basis and moved about more freely. In early November 1944, he took a few days off and made his way to Paris. There he finally learned how badly his family had suffered under the occupation. No one had escaped the persecution. His brother Zilke had been arrested in the first major roundup of immigrant Jewish men in Paris's 11th arrondissement on August 20, 1941, and had been sent to the prison camp of Compiègne. From there, he was deported to Auschwitz on March 27, 1942 as part of the very first French convoy of 1,112 men sent to the death camp, from which only nineteen would return. Szajko's brother Zalmen and his wife Deborah were arrested in July 1942 in Paris and sent to the Drancy concentration camp. They too were deported to Auschwitz, in August 1942. Szajko's sister Dina and her husband Jonia were also sent to Auschwitz.[55]

But not every family member had been deported. Zilke's wife Marjasza and their daughter Monique, born in August 1939, were luckier. Marjasza spent the occupation shuttling back and forth from a room she had rented in Paris under an assumed name ("Maria Marseille") and a cabin in an anarchist nudist colony in Chevreuse, in

the Paris suburbs, where she and Zilke had spent many happy week-
ends before the war. At some point after her husband's arrest, Marjasza
began to fear for her daughter's safety. Non-Jewish friends in Chevreuse
connected her to a woman in the countryside who agreed to take
Monique and also Cecile, Marjasza's sister Frejda's daughter, born in
1933. Frejda and her husband Jeszua Mitagsztejn were involved in the
resistance. They were arrested separately and both sent to Auschwitz,
where Frejda died in 1943. Marjasza had also taken charge of Szajko's
other brother Zalmen's daughter Michelle, born in 1935, whose parents
were deported in the summer of 1942. Through the same contacts, she
placed Michelle with a different family in the countryside.

Szajko found his sister-in-law in her old apartment in November
1944. By then, the courageous Marjasza had reclaimed Monique and
Cecile, and was about to bring Michelle home as well. Despite her
traumatic experiences—the fear, the starvation, and the grief at losing
those she loved most—Szajko's sister-in-law was already on her way to
recovery. She planned to raise the three surviving children together as
sisters, promising Szajko she would stop working if he could find the
money to support her. She was destitute.[56]

Szajko felt terrible. As a soldier, he could not stay, but he promised
to come when he could, and now that he had a regular salary from the
army, he would send money. He expected his older and more established
siblings—Sarah in Hull and Harry in Chicago—to contribute as well.
He even dared to hope that one of them might adopt the bright and
sensitive Michelle, who suffered serious health problems and was in and
out of the hospital for two years after her return to Paris in late 1944.
Harry promised to send money, but since he and his wife were on the
verge of divorce, he declined to bring Michelle to Chicago. Szajkowski
was disappointed, but he understood.[57] He was furious, though, with
Sarah and her family in Hull. Szajkowski's English friend Elaine went
there on his behalf to plead for Michelle, but reported back that they
would not be able to adopt her. It was not a question of money but
of emotional strain. She would be a constant reminder of the beloved
family they had lost. Szajkowski was absolutely heartbroken.[58]

How could Szajko help Marjasza and the girls without compromising
his own future? He sent money to friends in New York asking them to
send packages of food. Money was no good in Paris, he said, since it

lost its value too fast; it was better to send goods.[59] The girls' health, both physical and emotional, was precarious. Marjasza was a loving mother to all three of the girls, but she was also deeply traumatized, and supporting the family was quite difficult in those early months. Frejda's daughter Cecile, the oldest of the girls, assumed extra responsibilities. Monique and Michelle were quite ill for a time. Monique could not go to school that first year because of malnutrition and a bout of meningitis. The tiny Michelle—at age eleven she weighed only about forty pounds—was in even worse shape. Deeply marked by the loss of her parents and a difficult time in the countryside, she refused to eat, getting so thin that the doctors eventually put her in the hospital for electroshock therapy, which, along with the healing power of time and the love of her surviving family, seems to have helped.[60]

In late April 1945, Jeszua Mitagsztejn, Marjasza's brother-in-law and Cecile's father, had turned up. He was one of the lucky few to survive Auschwitz and, after the SS closed the camp in January 1945, the brutal death march to the Buchenwald concentration camp, where he was liberated. (Another astonishing return would soon follow, when Jonia, Szajkowski's sister Dina's husband, returned from Auschwitz in July. The two were among the mere 3 percent of French Jewish deportees who returned.) Jeszua was still quite ill. It would be months before he was well enough to leave the apartment, and he would never quite recover his zest for life. But he was there. By the end of the year, the five were joined by Jeszua's father Gabriel, who had survived the war in Paris, and all six lived in the Mitagsztejns' old apartment in Belleville. They kept Marjasza's smaller place nearby as a workshop for making sweaters, the same work they had done together with Frejda before the war. Jeszua and Marjasza married in 1948 (changing the spelling of their name to Mitastein and formalizing their adoptions of the girls at the same time), in part to facilitate the family's planned emigration to Mexico, where one of Marjasza's sisters had moved before the war. But the decision to form a family had been made as soon as Jeszua returned from Germany, in the context of their deep sadness and mutual need.[61]

Szajkowski worried for the girls' Jewish identities. Having spent so much time in non-Jewish settings, they had emerged from the war knowing no Yiddish, and this pained him greatly. Stationed in Belgium and hearing stories of Jewish children there being forcibly converted

Szajkowski's surviving family in Paris in the late 1940s. From left: his niece *Michelle Frydman, Cecile Mitagsztejn, Szajkowski's widowed sister-in-law* Marjasza Frydman, and her daughter (and Szajkowski's niece) Monique Frydman. Together with Cecile's father Jeszua Mitagsztein, the family moved to Mexico in 1949. *From the Archives of the YIVO Institute for Jewish Research.*

by their Catholic rescuers both during the war and after liberation, he came up with a plan to preserve the girls' Jewishness. He would put $500 of his own money aside for each child, to be given to them when they could speak, read, and write Yiddish well.[62] If this interference annoyed Marjasza and Jeszua, they kept it to themselves, and had the girls make an effort to write him in Yiddish. But they never really did learn to write it, as their letters to him from Mexico in the 1950s show; they preferred French or English.[63]

Szajkowski's concerns about his nieces reflected his general concerns about French Jewry. His initial impression on his first trip back to Paris in November 1944 was one of total devastation. Visiting his old haunts, he reported to Riva that "[v]ery, very few are alive and they all look so old."[64] And a week later: "The pain is unbearable. When you come into a club, you hardly find anyone you know. Everyone's been sent off to death."[65] French Jews, particularly the Eastern European immigrants, had been devastated by deportations and property seizures during the occupation, and their agony had not ended with the liberation of Paris in August 1944. As historians with access to a wider scope of information have since confirmed, about 76,000 French Jews had been murdered after being deported to death camps in Poland, although it would take some time for those at home to realize that very few of the Jews deported would return. Although far fewer than the 150,000 to 180,000 Szajkowski had estimated initially, the number was significant nonetheless, and disproportionately so within the immigrant community.[66] Perhaps he overestimated because so many Jews were still missing from the capital when he first traveled there in November 1944. Of the approximately 250,000 French Jews who did survive the war, dislocation was the norm. Two hundred thousand of them had had to move during the occupation—to hide and resist deportation— and this applied especially to those who lived in Paris. And the poverty was indeed immense. By the end of the war, 30,000 to 35,000 were directly dependent on aid from Jewish welfare organizations for their very survival.[67]

From the survivors, Szajkowski heard stories of terrible suffering. He visited the Drancy concentration camp, where his sister and brother had been incarcerated by the French before they were deported to Auschwitz in 1942 and 1943. Pondering the question of French responsibility, he wrote, "Am I anti-France? No. But there's no reason to pray for France either."[68]

Events in post-liberation Paris did not improve his judgment of the French. Many Frenchmen refused to give Jews back the apartments and belongings they had had to abandon when they sought refuge in the provinces. Szajko thought the core of the problem was simple greed. From what he saw, most of the French neighbors who had appropriated Jews' apartments and belongings as they fled simply did not want to give back what they had acquired unless forced to do so. He reported:

> The poverty is huge. People live on a little bit of cooked something in one of the kitchens. There's nowhere to sleep. The French don't want to return the apartments that were taken from the Jews nor the bundles that had been hidden in their care. "You're alive??" the French say in astonishment when you come to get your things back. Forget about taking your business back. All of our friends have the same question: Does the world know what happened to the Jews in France? Does anyone have the courage to tell what happened, especially in America?[69]

The scope of wartime looting had been vast. Throughout the Occupation period, all Jews were subject to the legal confiscation of their property by the authorities. Expropriation was conducted in a variety of ways, depending on the kind of property in question. The Aryanization laws had named *administrateurs provisoires* to manage the businesses formerly owned by Jews and to arrange their sale to new, Aryan owners. Household items were seized directly by the German authorities for redistribution in Germany. Jews across all social divides had been robbed: rich and poor, French-born and immigrant.[70]

Reclaiming lost property was a difficult problem that would not soon be resolved, even after the Nazis were gone and the republic reestablished. Although the Provisional Government explicitly renounced all legislation that discriminated on the basis of race in its ordinance of August 9, 1944, the ordinance did not address the question of property restitution. Returning Jews found themselves bereft of property of all sorts, from high-value items like works of art, book collections, and furniture to smaller items like clothing, linens, tools, and pots and pans.

The new authorities were unwilling to annul the forced wartime sales of Jewish businesses. It was impossible to recover the household items that had been sent to Germany. It was no easier to reclaim what had been found after liberation in Parisian warehouses and at train stations where the Germans had abandoned them upon their retreat from France. No lists linked these items to their previous owners.[71]

The only items that were really possible to reclaim were those that had been appropriated by French neighbors when Jews had fled their apartments and homes for safety. But this too could be dicey. Szajkowski's sister-in-law Marjasza, for example, had returned to the apartment she had left behind to find it completely emptied of its contents and had no way of knowing if her French neighbors were being truthful when they told her everything had been taken by the Germans. This was a typical scenario. In fact, Marjasza considered herself lucky that no one had moved into the apartment itself. Given the terrible housing shortage, Jews in that situation had little chance of getting their apartments back. As late as 1951, fully half of the estimated 65,000 Jews who had lost their apartments during the war had not yet gotten them back.[72]

The Provisional Government's failure to adequately address the issue of looted property was related to how it envisioned Jews' reintegration into French society. In the year following liberation, the government had a hard time meeting the needs of Jews in the capital, despite, or perhaps in some ways even because of, its anti-racist commitments, which made it difficult to recognize Jews' suffering and needs as different from those of other Frenchmen. Committed first and foremost to restoring order, they had to balance the demands of returning Jews against those who had legally acquired their property. Other tricky issues were at play in dealing with housing. Jews were not the only Frenchmen made homeless by the war; of paramount concern were the many whose houses had been destroyed by the fighting in 1944.[73] Now that they were once again legally considered Frenchmen like any others, Jews were unable to show how their special situation called for a special response.

Szajkowski believed that French Jews made their own problems worse by refusing to discuss or even envision their plight in "Jewish" terms. True to form, he complained that Jews across the political spectrum—from Communists to Bundists to Zionists to the assimilationist native-born Jews, whom the immigrants derisively called "*israélites*"—were too worried about the future of the nation and of humanity and lacked a real Jewish consciousness concerned specifically with Jewish matters. As he wrote in late November 1944:

> I visited the [Bundist] Medem Club at 110, rue Vieille-du-Temple. . . . It's sheer heartbreak looking at the pathos and emptiness of it all. A few people will miss it but for other people nothing's changed. They're still talking a lot of politics and in actuality doing nothing to put damaged Jewish life in Paris back together—politics and more politics! A group of Jewish children still sit at the rue Vieille-du-Temple and talk about world problems, about everything in the world except Jewish problems.[74]

Szajkowski was predisposed to see things this way. He had undergone a major transformation in his outlook in 1938 when he quit the Communist Party and, under the Tcherikowers' influence, had eschewed *all* political commitments, placing his loyalties instead in a belief that scholarship could unite Jews and return them to their authentic identities.[75] Now, more than ever, Szajkowski expressed bitter contempt for anyone who still believed that political parties could provide solutions for Jewish problems. It put him at odds with his old friends in Paris and distorted his perspective on their efforts at communal reconstruction.

This stance made Szajkowski feel tremendously isolated in liberation France, even though it enabled him to make new friends across the deep fracture lines dividing the community. As he wrote, "You see, I've come far enough along that I think of others, not as Bundists or Zionists but as Jews. The ultimate question is whether they think of themselves that way."[76] The longer he stayed in Europe, the less faith he had that any of them would come around to his point of view. By February 1945, he would write derisively of his Bundist friends, "Why hide the fact that my friends at the Medem Club are barely Jews? They're interested in politics and nothing else. Nothing's changed for them."[77] Of course, the political debates at the Medem Club were taking place in Yiddish, and concerned communal reconstruction among other things. A different observer might have said that they were still, in essence, Jewish debates. But at this moment, Szajkowski did not see them as such. For him, any engagement with larger political questions ultimately led away from Jewishness.

Szajkowski was not surprised to see this problem among the French-born Jews, long used to minimizing their Jewish identities in public. Enraged, he vented to Riva about how the Socialist Party's general secretary Daniel Mayer, a French-born Jew who had been a key figure in the Resistance, was urging the Jewish Bundists to "assimilate" and to "stop grouping themselves in segregated Jewish groups."[78] From the republican center as well as the left, postwar French leaders did not want to treat Jewish issues around reconstruction separately from those of other Frenchmen, and Jews like Mayer tended to agree.

But the worst offenders, Szajkowski believed, were the Communists. In the fall of 1945, they tried to sabotage an event planned by the major French Jewish groups called the Week of the Martyred Jewish Child. The Communists objected; they did not want to honor Jewish children separately from other Frenchmen. Szajkowski found their position galling. As he put it, "They want this commemoration to be carried out in conjunction with one for all French children, as if there were a lot of French children killed by the Germans."[79] Even worse, Joseph Millner was going along with them. Millner was the head of the Oeuvre de Secours aux Enfants (OSE), the Jewish organization dedicated to children's welfare, which had taken charge of hiding thousands of children in France and abroad during the war. Szajkowski found it outrageous that the head of such an organization would go along with the Communists in refusing to commemorate the murder of Jewish children. But Millner wanted to keep the peace.[80]

Szajkowski was even more exasperated when the Communists thwarted his efforts to memorialize the death of his friend Charles Rappoport, the one-time Communist militant who had broken with the Party in 1938 and had come to associate with the Tcherikowers. Born in Russia, Rappoport had been expelled for revolutionary activity in 1887, and once established in France, he had helped build the socialist movement there. An anti-reformist, he had helped to establish the PCF after the split within French socialism in 1920 and was faithful to Stalin in denouncing Trotsky in 1928; but he broke with Stalin at the time of the Bukharin trial of 1938, when he left the Party altogether. In 1940, Rappoport fled the Germans for a small town in southern

France, where he died of natural causes. The way Szajkowski saw it, this old-time Communist died "as a Jew" in exile because of antisemitic persecution, rather than in the workers' struggle. The distinction was a little forced, but it meant a lot to Szajkowski. He was proud to have undergone his political conversion with Rappoport in the late 1930s, and now he wanted to honor his friend properly. His hope was to have a memorial stone erected in Rappaport's memory specifying that he died "as a Jew."[81]

Thinking the Zionists might be inclined to help, he wrote to his friend Marc Jarblum, editor of the Zionist newspaper *Undzer Vort* and head of the largest Jewish immigrant association in France, the Fédération des Sociétés Juives de France (FSJF), who was now emerging as an important figure in French Jewish reconstruction. Initially, Jarblum was excited to publish a letter from Szajkowski in the paper with the idea, and even promised Szajkowski that he would build the memorial. But later, Jarblum thought better of the plan and did not even publish the piece. It would make the Communists too angry, he told Szajkowski, and now was no time to sow the seeds of division in a community in such need of unity.[82] Today, the headstone on Charles Rappoport's grave in Montparnasse Cemetery in Paris reads simply, "Socialism without freedom is not socialism, freedom without socialism is not freedom." For Szajkowski, the whole affair exemplified what was wrong with French Jewry. Even for a Zionist like Jarblum, political considerations overshadowed Jewish ones. Ultimately, Szajkowski believed, the cost was tremendous, stripping Jews of their very identities, as well as their ability to recognize the signs of danger before their eyes.

Jarblum may have agreed privately with Szajkowski's position, given his Zionism. But politically, going along with the Bundists and the Communists allowed him to build the bridges necessary for communal reconstruction. In Belgium in spring 1945, fights between Zionists and Bundists over whether surviving Jewish orphans should be sent to Palestine threatened to rip the community apart, with the Bundists going so far as to ask authorities to intervene to keep the children in Belgium. In contrast, French Jews managed to work together in greater harmony, thanks in no small part to Jarblum's skills as a leader within the immigrant community.[83] But such accommodation looked to

Szajkowski like even the Zionists were abandoning the Jewish cause by giving in to the spirit of the day.

In the leftist world of Szajkowski's surviving friends, a variety of forces were converging to keep Jews' Jewishness almost as hidden as it had been during the war. Szajkowski probably did understand that the pressure for suppressing Jewishness was coming in large part from the broader French political parties and their strategy for building unity and suppressing antisemitism. Indeed, he had been told as much by his old friends.[84] Nonetheless, he placed that blame on the French Jews themselves, and complained constantly to Riva that they were more interested in "politics" than Jewishness. The complaints represented a continual statement of loyalty to his beloved Riva and to YIVO, where he hoped to return after his army service, but they came from a place of deep conviction that Jewishness could not survive what "politics" demanded of the Jews.

To Szajkowski's way of thinking, what was at stake here was the very survival of the Jewish people. Jewish continuity had been threatened when Jewish children were hidden for safety during the war in gentile families, often under assumed identities. Now that those children had returned, who would teach them Yiddish? Who would serve as a Jewish role model, if the adults they returned to continued to hide their Jewishness? And who would produce the great works of Jewish scholarship needed to sustain a people?[85] In spite of the fact that the majority of French Jews survived the war, and communal institutions were starting to rebuild the material foundations of their Jewish lives, the fact that Yiddish and Yiddish culture had suffered such a blow under German occupation made Szajkowski worry that France's future as a home for Jews remained imperiled, even after war's end.

This same worry for the future of French Jewry shaped Szajkowski's collecting in France in the months following liberation. Just as he worried that, without Yiddish, his nieces would not really grow up to be Jews, so too did he fear that, without Jewish books, the Jewish survivors in France would never fully recover from the war. For Szajkowski, ever a cultural nationalist, reconstruction could not simply be material; it had to have a foundation in scholarship, for which libraries and archives were the cornerstone. He was deeply skeptical that this would be possible in France. Certainly there were surviving Jews. But were they really committed to rebuilding Jewish culture? As he saw it, the Communists in particular would use any Jewish document to serve their own short-term political ends. He hated to imagine what they would do if they beat him to Marseilles, where in 1941, he had been forced to leave the better part of the Tcherikower archives, including the papers of the diaspora nationalist Jewish historian Simon Dubnow. "Dubnow's diary in [Communist journalist Ilya] Ehrenburg's hands!" he wrote to Riva, in English, "My God! He will use the diary only for his propaganda."[86] The thought propelled him to make his way, as soon as he could, to Marseilles and have the thirty boxes he had left at the Thomas Cook office sent on to New York at YIVO's expense.[87]

But the problem went beyond the Communists. Across the political spectrum, French Jews were disinclined to see their problems in specifically Jewish terms.[88] Would they really do what YIVO had done in the interwar period, that is, dedicate some of their meager resources to supporting scholarship on Jewish life? At the moment of liberation, Szajkowski still imagined that this role was best filled by YIVO itself, and so he helped to reestablish YIVO committees in Paris and Brussels. In Brussels, he learned that YIVO's prewar committee had preserved its archives during the occupation, and it was ready to begin collecting again. He himself collected Jewish periodicals systematically, particularly ones that had been produced underground during the war, and sent them on to YIVO's library in New York.[89] He also prepared bibliographies of these wartime periodicals, first for France, which he sent to Riva in late March 1945, and then a second one for Belgium, which he sent in May 1945, for publication in the YIVO newsletter.[90] In Brussels, Szajkowski also established a contest for the best essay on Jewish experiences under the occupation, asking YIVO to pay for the $100 cash prize. The contest was fully in the spirit of YIVO's interwar essay competitions. It would encourage Jews to write their life stories, and YIVO's archive would be the beneficiary of many narratives documenting recent Jewish experiences, which Szajkowski already understood as an unprecedented time in Jewish history.[91]

In Paris, he found two passionate and erudite collectors—Gershon Epstein and Lion Herman, both immigrants to France from Eastern Europe, as he himself had been—who were happy to start collecting material for YIVO. At least some funding was promised by his friend

Yehuda (Jules) Jacoubovitch, the general secretary of FSJF's youth organization, the Colonie Scolaire, which had functioned semi-clandestinely during the war as a welfare organization with the name the Rue Amelot committee. Epstein himself planned to appeal to the American Jewish Joint Distribution Committee (known as "the Joint") for additional support. Epstein and Herman would continue the task of collecting items of historical value, focusing on the war years. They too planned an essay contest like the one Szajkowski had established in Brussels, and Jarblum promised that the FSJF would provide the prize money. But Szajkowski's excitement at the reestablishment of YIVO in Paris was tempered by his fear that the French Jews would not really support the endeavor in the long run. As he wrote to Riva, "Jacoubovitch promised to be sure that they would, in no way, devolve into politics. But we have to be prepared in the event they want to do something silly. Parisian Jewish life is overrun by politics."[92]

While Szajkowski was still in Europe, Epstein, Herman, and Jacoubovitch sent important materials, such as records from the Joint's work in wartime France and lists and photographs of inmates from the Drancy concentration camp near Paris.[93] Szajkowski engaged in this work too, setting up contacts with Jewish newspaper publishers in France and Belgium on behalf of YIVO in New York, asking them to send copies of their publications even after he had left Europe.[94] And yet, these Western European YIVO committees were destined to fail. As Szajkowski would learn with some frustration, Weinreich was not willing to fund the Belgian essay contest, even though he offered to house the resultant essays; Szajkowski wound up paying the winner from his own pocket.[95] Similar problems hampered Epstein's efforts in Paris. The obstacles to the success of the new YIVO committees in France and Belgium were thus greater than Szajkowski had imagined. In the end, with its meager postwar resources, YIVO was no longer able to support branch offices. What Szajkowski had initially helped to create became, in time, a relatively minor effort to collect and send materials of historical interest on an ad hoc basis to YIVO in New York.[96]

Szajkowski was in a bitter frame of mind in Paris in 1945, but wearing his U.S. Army uniform made him feel powerful. Alienated, he passed judgment on the Jews of France. To his way of thinking, no Jewish institution left in Western Europe could rise above politics and material

troubles sufficiently to collect. Any interest they had in the documentation of the recent past was for short-term political aims, not scholarship.
Fearing that the rare material documenting Jewish experiences in the
war would disappear, he sent everything he could to YIVO, the one
place he trusted to keep them safe. This included a complete run of
the periodicals produced by the Union Générale des Israélites de France
(UGIF), the wartime umbrella organization that brought together the
prewar Jewish welfare organizations in a single framework representing
French Jewry, answerable to the Nazis. Szajkowski wrote Riva excitedly
that he believed it was the only complete run of the *Bulletin* and the
Informations still in existence.[97]

He also sent a 300-page document he called "the Protocols of
the UGIF," the meeting minutes of the administrative council of the
UGIF in the Southern Zone over the course of its existence.[98] With
the Germans' departure, the UGIF had been declared defunct, and no
Jewish institution was interested in declaring itself heir to an organization
they viewed as collaborationist. As such, its papers were ownerless; this
particular document was found abandoned in a building in Marseilles.
As in Carpentras, Szajkowski proved to be an extraordinarily able *zamler*,
fueled by the adrenaline of a high-stakes scavenger hunt. Sending this
stuff was legal, if controversial. Writing to Riva, Szajkowski was unusu-
ally coy about the donor, saying merely that "he trusts me completely."[99]

The controversy about the UGIF's wartime record was entirely
political. The donor had given Szajkowski the UGIF papers for YIVO
believing they would testify to the "unscrupulous doings" of its leaders,
many of whom were eager to erase the traces of their work, fearing they
might be perceived as collaborators. For his own reasons, Szajkowski
agreed that France was not "a secure spot for Jewish archives" because
everyone wanted to use wartime papers for political finger-pointing rather
than for objective scholarship.[100] But he knew that sending these papers
on to YIVO would go against the explicit wishes of his friend Jarblum
at the FSJF, who begged him not to send anything, especially this document, to New York, at least until Jewish leaders had a chance to conduct
a proper investigation and use the document in an intra-communal *jury
d'honneur* (honor court).[101] Although he promised to send Jarblum a
copy of the papers for future use within the community, Szajkowski
went ahead and sent the originals to New York.[102] In a sense, the origin

of YIVO's UGIF collection lay in a desire to preserve these materials by moving them beyond the reach of the Jews who were most interested in them at the time, for the purposes of self-exculpation and communal reconstruction.

In the years to come, many more records of the UGIF would join this first document in YIVO's collection. Although detailed acquisition records do not exist, the "Finding Aid" that Szajkowski completed in 1957 notes that the materials came in between 1944 and 1957, with most arriving in 1946.[103] The resultant record group is quite large. According to the inventory, it contains 169,057 pages and fills 63 linear feet. They have been photographed for consultation on 104 microfilm reels. Though the collection is fragmentary, having arrived piece by piece from different sources, it provides a relatively comprehensive view of the work of the UGIF in wartime France. In addition to the minutes of the administrative council in the Southern Zone, it has come to include records of the UGIF's establishment in both zones, materials related to the 1941 census, memos and correspondence with the Germans, financial reports, and the records of social services, youth activity groups, children's homes, health centers, and soup kitchens. It also includes quite a few records of French concentration camps.[104] The papers of the Rue Amelot committee are also at YIVO, testifying to Jacoubovitch's lasting connection with that institution as well.[105] The FSJF papers, in contrast, remain in Paris, at the Centre de Documentation Juive Contemporaine, which eventually acquired a smaller but still very significant collection of some 28,000 pages of UGIF papers of its own (most of which would come from Szajkowski, but under quite different circumstances, in 1949–50).

In fact, although Szajkowski does not seem to have become aware of it until later, his intuition that some of the UGIF materials might not have been safe in France was correct. The biggest threat came not from the Jews themselves, though, but from the republican government. Beginning in 1944 and continuing through at least 1947, the republicans issued numerous instructions to state agencies ordering the destruction of wartime records relevant for documenting the experiences of Jews in France from 1940 to 1944. The destructions were completely legal. They were ordered by the Provisional Government in two circulars implementing paragraph 3 of the law of August 9, 1944, that repealed all existing racial legislation and reestablished equality before the law. To that end, these particular circulars required government agencies to destroy any and all records that identified citizens by race, as the many lists of Jews (treated in hospitals or served in soup kitchens, for example) contained in the UGIF papers did.[106]

Here too, the motives of the Provisional Government and Fourth Republic are questionable. Reestablishing republicanism was getting in the way of Jewish reconstruction, in this case, making it difficult for Jews to document their suffering under the previous regime. Szajkowski, learning of this later, must have been all the more glad that he had decided in 1945 to bring items that documented Jewish wartime experience to YIVO, where the circulars did not apply (although not all French agencies actually complied with these circulars, and many documents that should have been destroyed are still, in fact, in existence, such as the controversial *fichier des juifs*, lists of Jews compiled in 1940 and discovered by famed Nazi hunter Serge Klarsfeld in the Ministry of War Veterans in 1991).[107]

But at the moment of the liberation, Szajkowski believed the problem lay not with the republican government but with the Jews. He condemned the leaders of the established institutions for not seeing the value of documenting their wartime suffering as extending beyond the material and political needs of the moment. Too many of them agreed with Samy Lattès, the Consistory representative in Grenoble, who wrote in 1943, "As interesting as the writing of our martyrdom might be, I contend that at the present moment, too many urgent and tragic problems absorb our energy for it to be possible to find the leisure for the work of writing about it, which necessitates spending hours with our heads down before a desk."[108] When Szajkowski first encountered this perspective at the end of the war, he was outraged and consequently considered it justifiable to take materials out of France. His decision to start collecting these papers in 1945 had an important long-term effect, creating at YIVO one of the largest collections in the world on the experience of French Jews in World War II and the largest on the UGIF in particular.

Yet some French Jews were more interested in documenting their wartime suffering than Szajkowski acknowledged in his letters to Riva. Granted, at the beginning, their goals were short term. The Centre de

Documentation Juive Contemporaine (CDJC) was founded in 1943, when a diverse set of French Jewish leaders met clandestinely in the Grenoble home of the Russian-born rabbi-turned-industrialist Isaac Schneersohn, who would become one of Szajkowski's dearest friends by the late 1940s, although it is unclear whether the two knew each other before the war. Under Schneersohn's leadership in Grenoble, the group had worked tirelessly to document the actions taken against Jews, particularly expropriations. The work was illegal and conceived as part of the resistance to the Nazis and their French collaborators.

In many ways, the CDJC's work was similar to that of the members of Emanuel Ringelblum's Oyneg Shabes group in the Warsaw ghetto, who had also gathered documentation illegally to chronicle Jewish life in the ghetto. But the expectations of how the documentation would be used were somewhat different. As the leaders of Oyneg Shabes came to understand that the Jewish people were targeted for total extermination, they gathered material so that after the war, a proper, objective history could be written even if all the Jewish eyewitnesses had perished.[109] The CDJC's wartime goals were different. This documentation center was to supply evidence for use in the short term, particularly in getting back wrongfully seized property. As such, it speaks to its leaders' wartime expectation that survival and reconstruction, not extermination or exodus, were in French Jewry's future.[110]

To this same end, the CDJC gathered a tremendous amount of documentation in the chaotic moment of the liberation. Finding himself in the right place at the right time, the industrious CDJC documentarian Léon Poliakov collected many records abandoned by the Germans shortly after they fled Paris—including the ERR, the Gestapo, and the German Embassy—as well as records of some of the disbanded Vichy agencies, such as the Commissariat Général aux Questions Juives. At a moment when the Germans were in retreat, the French were more interested in distancing themselves from these institutions than in claiming the papers that lay in their offices. This proved fortuitous for the CDJC, whose researchers appropriated the papers as swiftly as Szajkowski appropriated the UGIF papers he was handed.[111] The political climate in liberated France made it difficult for the CDJC to effectively achieve its early goal of helping Jews reclaim lost property. But the institution was surprisingly successful in helping to achieve a different sort of justice.

In 1945, Poliakov and another researcher, Joseph Billig, were asked to accompany the French delegation to Nuremberg and used their archive to help the prosecutors document their case against the Nazis for crimes against humanity before the International Military Tribunal. While in Nuremberg, Billig and Poliakov were permitted to copy many of the documents that American prosecutors had gathered in Germany in 1945, and they brought them back to the CDJC in Paris.[112]

The expanded archive changed CDJC researchers' understanding of what they could do with their material. Whereas in 1945, they still conceived the CDJC as a temporary institution for immediate use as a "documentation center," by 1947, Poliakov, Billig, and other staff researchers had trained themselves to use the documents they had collected for rigorous, source-based historical studies, and the institution was reconceived as a permanent research center and archive (for which funding would soon become a constant concern).

Even better than Szajkowski, the CDJC historians understood the dangers their endeavor faced, given the political demands of the day. They worried constantly in their early years that their records were in danger of being destroyed, perhaps by one of the antisemites who had posted flyers on their door or by people eager to hide the traces of their wartime collaboration. But the CDJC leaders' solution was not to send materials to New York, but rather to place their microfilms in a bank vault and keep their card catalogue in a location other than the archive itself.[113] By the late 1940s, the CDJC became the center of Holocaust history writing in France. In fact, in 1947, when the CDJC hosted the first international conference of historians working on the recent catastrophe, Schneersohn wrote to Max Weinreich at YIVO, "We told the world that our goal is clear and beyond politics; it is purely scientific, which proves that our friend Szajkowski's fears did not turn out to be justified."[114] Perhaps they could have taken care of the UGIF archives after all.

Szajkowski's assessment of French Jewry was thus at odds with what others were thinking. Although he no longer considered France a safe place for Jewish archives and libraries, for others—Jarblum and the CDJC historians—collecting and using these materials in France constituted an important part of the work of reconstruction in both the short term and the long term. Szajkowski rejected short-term uses and instead sought to preserve these documents in a library where only scholars untainted by political commitments would be able to use them. Indeed, he was hoping his own future lay in that institute, and his wartime donations must also be seen as an effort to make himself essential in its directors' eyes.

But his collecting of the UGIF materials was motivated by sincere belief as much as by professional ambition. He was deeply committed to the goal of objectivity that lay at the core of the historical profession at the time. Separating scholarship from politics was, for Szajkowski, the only way forward for the Jewish people, who had sold their souls to the European political parties in the early twentieth century and been destroyed in the process. Most of the remaining Jews in Europe were, to his thinking, a lost cause, incapable of reconstructing authentic Jewish culture. Only Jewish scholarship could provide the foundation for a new and more robust way of being Jewish.

In his dedication to scholarship, Szajkowski remained naïvely unaware that his very decision to send this material to New York did, in fact, represent a kind of political position. Even as he rejected all the political parties, his collecting for YIVO showed that he had become a partisan of what he himself called, in a letter to Riva, "*Yitzias Eyrope* (the Exodus from Europe)."[115] The biblical allusion was a way to emphasize the world-historical proportions of the mass migration he had come to advocate.

If Szajkowski found himself in the minority in France, his views did find echoes elsewhere. They reverberated especially strongly among Jewish refugees in New York. This was particularly the case at YIVO, where the packages he began to send from Europe in the spring of 1945 soon became legendary, earning him a hero's welcome when he returned home in early 1946. Such a reception in New York, where he had decided to rebuild his life, must have helped to ease any misgivings he may have felt after his conflict with Jarblum about his decision to send the UGIF papers to New York.

Surely Szajkowski was also thinking about Ilya and Riva Tcherikower as he collected materials on the experience of Jews under the occupation in France. Like his mentors, who had assembled and moved the Ukrainian pogrom archives westward in the early 1920s, Szajkowski had made his own archive of atrocity, a vast repository of documentation that scholars could use to make sense of this hideous crime against the Jewish people. It was as difficult a mission to accomplish as Tcherikower's had been, and the stakes were just as high. Saving these papers required a cool head under pressure and an inner confidence that his mission was right, knowing full well that others saw it differently.

5

Partisans of the Exodus

IN MAY 1945, SHORTLY AFTER the German surrender, Szajkowski received new orders and left the 82nd Airborne for Germany. At first, he was assigned to work as a translator for the First Allied Army. Then in early July, he moved to Berlin, where he was assigned to the Allied Command, the joint Allied military government for the city. The Command desperately needed interpreters who knew French, English, and Russian. Most of the officers there spoke only one or two languages, and coordination among the Allies was of the utmost importance. Szajkowski was also expected to speak German with the conquered Berliners on behalf of the Allied Command. It was ridiculous, he wrote Riva. He had told his superiors many times that he did not really know German, only Yiddish. Plus, as a Jew, the assignment made him nervous. "The thought of knowing German and coming into contact with Germans has never filled me with joy; definitely not," he wrote. "You see, dear Riva, when you're in the occupying army, you've got to put all feelings as a Jew aside."[1]

Even in uniform, Szajkowski was unable to put his feelings as a Jew aside. The news in the Yiddish newspapers that Riva sent him in early June was just too awful. As the Allies made plans to bring the Nazis to justice, it appeared that war crimes would be the focus of the prosecution, not the attempted annihilation of the Jews. "The day I read

Technician Third Grade Szajko Frydman with the U.S. occupation forces in Berlin in 1945, standing under a sign that quotes Stalin's message to the Germans: "History tells us that Hitlers come and go, but the German people and the German state live on." *From the Archives of the YIVO Institute for Jewish Research.*

the declaration that the Germans' murder of millions of Jews was not considered a war crime was the day I completely stopped believing in the word 'democracy,'" he wrote in early June 1945, disgusted with the Allies for their indifference.[2] In fact, the prosecutors would not settle on specific indictments until months later, and as it turned out, many of the war crimes charges did concern the mass murder of Jews. But in early June, Szajkowski was in no mood to wait to see what the actual charges would be. The war in Europe may have been won, but given the political realities of the day, real justice for the murdered Jews seemed beyond reach.[3]

Szajkowski's thirst for justice was not satisfied by seeing the suffering of ordinary Berliners around him. The city lay in ruins from the 450,000 tons of bombs dropped in March and April 1945, killing 20,000 Berliners. The Americans who entered the city in July came on the heels of the Soviet army, which had been there since late April. Years of anti-Soviet propaganda under the Nazis had terrified the Germans, and to some extent, the terror proved justified when the Soviets arrived. As many as 110,000 women in Berlin, one in three, were raped in the first weeks after their arrival, some more than once.[4]

Szajkowski struggled not to feel any pity when he heard the stories of what the Germans, particularly German women, had gone through. In his daily letters to Riva he shored up his strength by writing about how much he hated them. Only by reminding himself that they were still the enemy responsible for the murder of his people could he fortify himself to exercise the power of the conqueror over the people he saw suffering before him:

> Today I had the occasion of being in the home of a German woman (in the line of duty). She told me how she had to kill her small child herself when the Red Army entered. Sometimes I have to requisition things from the Germans. When they start to cry, argue, or become pathetic saying that their neighbors have better things, I always say the same thing: "I'm still more of a gentleman than your Germans in the occupied countries were." But when the Germans try to get to me by telling me that the Russians have already taken everything from them, I have to start screaming at them. They all have suddenly become anti-Nazi and prepared long speeches in English about what they did to fight Hitler. They can all go to Hell. Fortunately, I don't let anyone of them get to me. I'm a little tired today. I spent all day running around German houses, requisitioning items.[5]

If Szajkowski himself was able to resist feeling sorry for the Germans as he carried out his orders to requisition supplies from them, he knew that most of his fellow Americans were weaker. The suffering of the

German women served to endear them to the American occupiers. Always a traditionalist when it came to women, he refused to understand how the dynamics of the occupation had changed the rules. "Women are very immoral here," he reported to Riva, disapprovingly. "Mothers and daughters get together with the soldiers. Naturally, they're all begging for food. You understand that the [fraternization] rule is only on paper."[6]

Indeed, Szajkowski saw fraternization everywhere, especially on Unter den Linden, central Berlin's wide main street, where "whores and more whores" stationed themselves, calling out to the American GIs.[7] They called out to him too, but never for a moment did he forget that he was a Jew, and he taunted them. "Women sometimes say I have 'beautiful eyes.' Even German women have told me that. I like to respond with 'If the Führer ever knew... I'm a Jew and you're complimenting me like that....'"[8] Szajkowski had enough hate in his heart not to break the fraternization order, but many of his fellow soldiers did not. Even officers were taking German mistresses. Seeing how they warmed to the German civilians only strengthened Szajkowski's certainty that Nazism would never really be purged from Europe. Ordinary Americans, like their leaders, had little will to see the Germans punished, particularly when it came to the crimes against the Jewish people. "We won the war, but we're losing the occupation," he wrote Riva.[9]

Szajkowski could not stop thinking about what had happened to the Jews in Europe. Soon after arriving in Berlin, he began to meet survivors from Poland and spent many evenings listening to their stories. German cruelty no longer had the power to surprise him; he had been hearing about it since he landed in France a year earlier. Now, it was the treachery of the Poles that astounded him. "It was the same story from all over: Lodz, Kielce, Siedlce, Warsaw. The martyred Polish people sold out Jews everywhere, for ten pounds of sugar."[10] In the partisan units too, he learned, Jews had been murdered by their supposed comrades as they fought the Nazis together.[11]

Since the German surrender, the situation in Poland had not improved much. The Jews arriving daily from the East reported that when they had attempted to return to their homes after the Germans had left, they had been driven out in a new wave of pogroms. Szajkowski understood the violence as "elemental expressions by the Polish masses" who ultimately proved to be "no better than their German neighbors." The postwar violence in his native country convinced Szajkowski to renounce one of his few remaining political commitments, his belief in "the principle of the freedom of small nations." Although it unnerved him to do so, he nonetheless abandoned his conviction that Poland had a right to exist as an independent entity. Whether or not the new wave of atrocities had been ordered by the Lublin government was beside the point. "In the final analysis, I have to be honest with myself. My opinion about most people and things is formed by how they respond to me as a Jew. . . . No, it's not worth shedding tears over the fate of Poland."[12]

Szajkowski was more concerned about the Jewish survivors. Shortly after beginning work at the Allied Command in July, he went with a few Jewish friends to visit the Berlin Jewish Hospital. Miraculously, the institution had survived the war intact. A gap in the German bureaucracy had left the 800 Jews among the patients and staff untouched, to the amazement of the Soviet soldiers who liberated them in April 1945.[13] Some of the Jewish refugees arriving from Poland were now joining the German survivors in the hospital, which had become a sort of displaced persons (DP) camp, although unlike most such camps, it was administered by the Berlin municipal government rather than by the United Nations Relief and Rehabilitation Administration (UNRRA), the agency established in 1943 to tend to the needs of those displaced in the war. When Szajkowski first visited the hospital, conditions were deplorable. The city had given its patients category 5 ration cards, the lowest level, sometimes referred to as the "*himmelsfahrkarte*" (ticket-to-heaven card).[14] The consequences were quite serious; the food rations were insufficient to sustain life. The cruel irony of it made Szajkowski furious; these fragile survivors were now classified as being of lower priority than many non-Jewish Germans. Moreover, municipal authorities had denied the hospital the right to access the money in its frozen bank accounts to supplement the rations or get needed medicine. "The food is horrible," Szajko wrote to Riva. "Now that I've gotten a taste of the place myself, I believe the Jew with whom I spoke a week ago on Unter den Linden. He said that he ate better in the German camp where he awaited death than he's eating now in the camp post-liberation."[15]

As in France, the refusal to classify Jews as a separate category in the immediate aftermath of the war prolonged Jewish suffering in Berlin. Whether democratic race-blindness or antisemitism caused Jews to be lumped in with the others, the results were the same: The Jews in the hospital were in worse condition than ever. Some Russian Jewish officers who happened to be visiting the same night were as shocked as Szajkowski and his American friends, and drew the same conclusions. "One of them simply said to me, 'Stalin will not live forever.' He's a good Communist and believes that as long as Stalin is alive he won't be in danger," Szajko wrote.[16] Confronted with the evidence of how Jews were treated in the war, and how little the Allies were doing to address the needs of the survivors, Jews in the Soviet Army offered the same prognosis as Jews in the U.S. Army: The Jews of Europe, subject to the most violent hatred from their neighbors, would not last much longer.

Szajkowski was already convinced that Europe was no longer a safe place for Jews. "I've become a supporter of the Exodus from Europe, even though it's not a political position of mine. I didn't start thinking this way by reading newspapers and going to meetings. I've recently met Jewish refugees and try to give them advice."[17] Firm in his convictions, he asked Riva to have Jacob Lestschinsky, one of the few Zionists at YIVO, publish his observations in the *Yidishe Kemfer*, whose Zionist readers were predisposed to favor the departure of all Jews from Europe.[18]

In the meantime, at the Berlin Jewish Hospital, Szajkowski took matters into his own hands. In late July, he sent a report to the Paris office of the Joint, reporting on the conditions there; they quickly promised to send a representative, but help was very slow in coming.[19] After two months passed, Szajkowski took a leave from his duties to call on the Joint office in Paris in person.[20] In early October, packages with food and medicine were finally delivered to the Jewish Hospital, courtesy of the Joint. Since the international aid organization had not yet sent a representative, the DPs quarreled over the distribution, and Szajkowski told Riva he had to step in himself to assure that the Eastern European and German Jews got their fair share. Szajkowski's proactive efforts to secure, eventually, aid from the Joint brought some relief to these Jewish DPs. Still, only a change of policy could preserve them during the coming winter.[21]

Szajkowski's adoption of a can-do attitude in Germany in the summer of 1945 represented an important step in his becoming American. Indeed, he was but one of many American Jewish GIs who decided spontaneously to take matters into their own hands when they saw the condition of Jewish DPs in newly liberated Germany. Jewish soldiers commonly wrote letters home imploring their families to publicize the plight of the surviving Jews and to get help for them from the Joint. Some went even further, stealing army supplies and bringing them to needy survivors in vehicles borrowed without permission. Others participated in the illegal Zionist *Bricha* (Flight), the operation that brought Jewish survivors from Eastern Europe into the U.S. Zone of Germany, and from there, led them to Palestine, brazenly violating British restrictions on Jewish immigration.[22]

Perhaps the best known of these American Jewish advocates for the Jewish DPs was Chaplain Abraham Klausner, who had been sent with a team of doctors and nurses to care for the desperately sick in the newly liberated Dachau concentration camp in May 1945. Klausner, like Szajkowski, acted on his own by organizing *She'erit Hapletah*, a campaign to help survivors find news of their lost loved ones by publishing lists of names. Together with Max Braude, another Jewish chaplain, Klausner helped to establish Feldafing, the first DP camp in Bavaria exclusively for Jews. The charismatic chaplain went much farther than Szajkowski in his efforts on behalf of DPs, leaving the army unit to which he had been assigned without permission in order to help survivors organize and articulate their increasingly Zionist demands to the occupation authorities.[23] Such actions eventually put Klausner at odds with military leaders; Allied indifference to the needs of Jewish DPs so dismayed the chaplain that he eventually left the army. Klausner was an unusual personality, unafraid of conflict, as his later career as an outspoken Reform rabbi would prove. But in newly conquered Germany, he was no outlier. Across Germany in 1945, many Jews in the U.S. Army saw themselves as seeking justice even when they had to break the law. Like Szajkowski, they felt they were filling a vacuum left by absent institutions, writing angry letters to the Joint and to Allied authorities that something more needed to be done to help Jewish DPs.[24]

The White House eventually heard their complaints. In June 1945, President Truman sent the law professor Earl Harrison to Europe, where

he toured DP camps and spoke with many Jewish DPs and their advocates. Harrison was qualified to report on the condition of refugees; he
had previously served as commissioner of immigration and naturalization, and then representative on the Intergovernmental Committee on
Refugees. In his report submitted in late August, Harrison lambasted
U.S. military authorities for their mistreatment of the Jewish DPs.
Harrison believed the root of the problem lay in the race-blind policies naïvely instituted by the democracies, which differentiated among
the DPs solely by nationality. The special needs of the Jewish DPs
were not met, and their frequent conflicts with other DPs, some of
whom had assisted the Nazis, were misunderstood and systematically
ignored. Harrison was convinced that Jewish DPs were different from
the many other Europeans who had been displaced in the war, such as
slave laborers and POWs. The continuing violence they suffered at the
hands of non-Jews in their home countries meant that the Jewish DPs
should not be sent back to their countries of origin. Rather, Harrison
recommended creating separate camps for the Jewish DPs and eventually resettling them in Palestine.

Harrison's report shook the U.S. military command in Germany. On
September 29, 1945, the day before the Harrison report was published
in the *New York Times*, President Truman ordered General Eisenhower,
commanding general of the U.S. Forces in Europe, to address the plight
of the Jews. The problem was in fact even deeper than the Harrison
report indicated, as Eisenhower soon learned. In Bavaria, the American
military governor, General George S. Patton Jr., was known to have
antisemitic attitudes. Even ordinary soldiers like Szajkowski learned
about the "incident" in early October in which he refused to implement
Eisenhower's order to improve the treatment of Jewish DPs and begin
the process of de-Nazification in Bavaria by removing known Nazis
from prominent positions.[25] Patton himself was removed from his post
on October 7, 1945. By the end of the year, across the U.S. Zone of
Germany, Jewish DPs were separated from non-Jewish DPs and began
to receive better treatment.[26] Rather than consider Polish Jews as Polish,
U.S. military authorities came to consider them as Jews and no longer
expected that they would return to their country of origin.[27]

The policy reversal effectively legitimized the often illegal actions
that Jewish GIs had been taking on behalf of Jewish DPs (and would

continue to take, facilitating illegal immigration to Palestine until an independent Israeli state opened its doors to the refugees). By the end of 1945, when Szajkowski was on his way home, U.S. policymakers were also becoming partisans of the Exodus.

A Jew in Germany could sense the moral high ground with regard to survivors of the Holocaust. But where was the moral high ground for the treatment of Jewish property looted by the Germans and uncovered in German castles, salt mines, and elsewhere? So many of the rightful owners had been murdered and their plundered schools and libraries destroyed. What was to be done with these remnants of European Jewish culture in the wake of a catastrophe that had irreparably changed Jewish demography?

The questions were divisive, even among the Allies. Although Allied leaders had sworn in the Inter-Allied Declaration of 1943 that they would return what had been stolen, they disagreed so fundamentally about the meaning of restitution that they could not coordinate or formulate policies. American military forces protected what they found from damage and theft by calling on the "Monuments Men" of the MFA&A (Monuments, Fine Arts and Archives Administration), a group of officers with backgrounds in museums and libraries assigned to work with the military on the ground. These officers identified, protected, collected, and centralized approximately 15 million looted items, of which 3.75 million originated from outside of Germany. The Monuments Men did not know much about Judaica, so their ability to deal with this loot was quite limited. Nevertheless, they knew rare books when they saw them and were able to protect them temporarily.[28]

MFA&A officers moved looted items to "collecting points" in Munich, Wiesbaden, and Offenbach for protection, identification, and sorting, awaiting their eventual restitution. The Munich collecting point was primarily for art looted from collections outside Germany; Wiesbaden, primarily for art looted from German collections; and Offenbach—a small town outside of Frankfurt—for Judaica. The Offenbach Archival Depot (OAD) was established in early 1945, after American forces found much of the collection of the Institute for the Study of the Jewish Question in nearby Hungen, where the Germans had stored it to safeguard it from Allied bombardment. Many more books remained in the former Rothschild Library in Frankfurt, and others were found in the sub-basement of another building destroyed in the bombing. The Hungen collection was large (estimated initially at somewhere between 1.2 million and 2.5 million volumes) and exclusively Jewish, so American military officials kept the collection intact where they had found it, supplying it with a military guard.[29] As they found other troves of Judaica elsewhere in Germany, they sent them to Hungen as well.

By July 1945, the depot for looted Judaica had outgrown the space in Hungen, and its collections were moved to an abandoned I. G. Farben warehouse in Offenbach. Books made up most of the collection, but there were also archives, ceremonial objects, and Torah scrolls. Unlike the Munich and Wiesbaden collecting points, which were run by the American military authorities for the *Länder* of Bavaria and Greater Hesse, respectively, the OAD was administered directly by the Office of Military Government in the U.S. Zone (OMGUS). OMGUS was little prepared to deal with the material. Throughout all of 1945 and into 1946, the OAD was poorly staffed, its materials completely unorganized, and looting was a common occurrence.[30]

A difficult Allied meeting in Paris in December 1945 ultimately led to the creation of separate restitution policies for each zone of Germany.[31] The French had always been the most fully committed to a broad conception of restitution. In France, the Nazis had looted extensively from both private citizens and public institutions, and the new government was committed to recovering whatever possible for the original owners or, if they could not be found, for the state. They established an agency, the Commission de Récupération Artistique, to recover cultural treasures, and within it, a Sous-Commission des Livres handled the restitution of books and archives.[32] The directors of these agencies knew that simply locating plundered goods would be impossible without full cooperation from the Allies, because much of what had been looted had been sent to Germany. French authorities, together with the Belgians and Dutch, believed that in addition to the return of unique items whenever possible, particularly looted works of art, Germany should also be asked to hand over other works of like value to compensate the conquered for their losses. This idea built on the legal precedent of the Versailles Treaty (reparations) and also reflected the long history of Franco-German struggles over cultural treasures.[33]

The Americans believed that stripping Germany's cultural patrimony would have potentially disastrous consequences for the peace. They restricted most restitution operations to easily identifiable items and rejected the substitution of items of like value when the actual looted items could not be found.[34] Furthermore, in keeping with their general commitment to race-blind policies, the Americans planned initially to treat "heirless" Jewish property as the property of the nations from which it had been looted. This included Poland, where there were few Jewish survivors, and the USSR, where few Westerners would have access to the material. Any unidentifiable property deemed heirless would be left to the German state governments. The British established similar policies in their zone of occupation.[35]

The Soviets had no interest in tracing the origins of the loot they found and returning it. Instead, they asserted that the victor had the right to take possession of any items of value that they found in Germany to compensate for their losses. This included cultural treasures, regardless of their origins. The so-called trophy brigades carried off treasures found in the conquered Reich to the Soviet Union, including art, books, and archives. Some of these items had originated in the East, some in Germany, and some elsewhere in Western Europe. No effort was made to determine the origins of these items at the time. In this way, materials that the Nazis had looted from the archives of, for example, the French army, the French postal service, the Paris Police Prefecture, and the private papers of many Jewish citizens of France such as Marc Bloch and Léon Blum made their way to the Soviet Union. Only in the 1990s, when scholars and investigators discovered the scope of Soviet postwar looting, could discussions begin about how to handle the materials that came to be known as "twice looted."[36]

Most of the materials looted by the Nazis and brought to the Reich were found in the U.S. and Soviet zones of occupation. Since the Soviets were not interested in restitution, only the Americans made a substantial effort to find appropriate owners of stolen loot. Procedures for the return of looted Judaica were established in February 1946, when Captain Seymour J. Pomrenze arrived to run the OAD. Pomrenze was a capable leader who had previously worked at the National Archives in Washington, D.C., and he was able to work with materials in German, Hebrew, and Yiddish.[37] Although he was only at the depot for six weeks, Pomrenze set in motion the processes that would lead to the return of 2.5 million of the 3 million items brought to the depot. Of these, about half were given to the representatives of the nations that had been pillaged. France received the largest number, 377,204 items, followed by the Netherlands with 334,241 items, the USSR with 273,645 items, and Italy with 252,068. Ten other nations—Austria, Poland, Czechoslovakia, Greece, Great Britain, Belgium, Yugoslavia, Norway, Switzerland, and Hungary—received smaller shipments. Conforming to U.S. policy, depot officials also gave 1.3 million volumes to German libraries, and American agencies took another 30,000 volumes. Most of this was accomplished by the end of 1946. Pomrenze estimated that in his six-week tenure alone, teams identified 30,000 items per day, and the pace remained steady under his successor, Captain Isaac Bencowitz, whose tenure lasted through October 1946.[38] Their operations show the commitment of U.S. military authorities to the principle of national sovereignty, and their reluctance, at least officially, to treat the looted Judaica any differently than other Nazi spoils.

Once the returned cultural treasures were handed over to national restitution officers, they were dealt with very unevenly, depending on the country.[39] The Soviet Union, for example, received the third largest number of books from the OAD, but it never established a restitution authority to return these materials to their original owners, even if they had survived the war, and instead kept the materials in state institutions, where very few people even knew of their existence.[40] In Poland, the returned Jewish cultural property was given to the Jewish Historical Institute, established in Warsaw in 1947.[41] France is one of the few countries that established a restitution agency specifically for books, run by librarians Camille Bloch and Jenny Delsaux. Of the estimated 10 million books that the Germans had looted in France during the war, Delsaux dealt with the return of the 1.2 million volumes found abandoned in depots across France (including 60,000 volumes still on the shelves of the Alliance Israélite Universelle library in Paris), as well as another 773,000 that their officers found in Germany, including 323,000 that were returned from Offenbach.[42]

While the official record of the OAD testifies to speedy work guided solely by official protocol, the experience of the French officials there tells a somewhat different tale. Across the board, French restitution authorities were suspicious of the Americans. Delsaux suspected that Americans were lax in their policies and that many items had been stolen under their watch. (Of course, the situation in the U.S. Zone was far better than what they faced in the Soviet Zone, where they were not even given permission to search.)[43] Reclaiming the materials from Offenbach was no simple task. Many of the books were in Hebrew, and the French feared that in their haste, the Americans and their German staff might not be able to identify them and would thus declare them heirless.

To assure the return of French books, Delsaux sent Rabbi Maurice Liber, head of the Ecole Rabbinique, to Offenbach in spring 1946, together with his student André Chekroum, as restitution officers representing the French state. There they found and identified some missing French items, including rare manuscripts looted from the Alliance Israélite Universelle. They also helped the staff at the depot read book titles since, according to their report, no personnel sorting books at that time read Hebrew. They also showed the Americans how to identify French bindings and book stamps to facilitate future restitutions.[44] In September 1946, Delsaux sent Paul Klein, the Hebraica librarian of the Bibliothèque Nationale, on a second mission. A third and final mission was undertaken in 1948 by Gershon Epstein, the head of the YIVO committee in Paris. Epstein's mission was the most productive of the three; he sent 40,000 volumes from the OAD to France, although some were lost in transit.[45] As a result of these three missions, the Alliance Israélite Universelle library was able to recover most of its prewar holdings, and the Ecole Rabbinique recovered a good portion of its collection as well.[46]

Jews outside of Europe and many on the ground with the Allied military forces found early American restitution policies better than no policy at all, but problematic nonetheless. Many Jewish leaders in New York and Palestine were beside themselves when they learned in 1945 that whatever could not be identified would stay in Germany. They criticized the plan to return so many materials to countries whose prewar Jewish populations had been wiped out by the Nazis. As with the Jewish DPs, Jewish cultural activists saw the race-blind, state-centered policies of the Americans as a major problem, for they did nothing to help the Jews reconstruct their lives collectively after so many had been killed.

Rabbi Maurice Liber, director of France's Ecole Rabbinique, in the Offenbach Archival Depot in 1946. *Courtesy National Archives and Records Administration, Washington, DC.*

A Jewish campaign to influence the fate of the looted Judaica took shape in late 1945, with Columbia University historian Salo Baron leading the most successful group, the Commission on European Jewish Cultural Reconstruction (JCR), founded in 1944 in New York. In a November 1945 *Commentary* article, he posited that the catastrophe had left European Jews leaderless. The survivors were few, he wrote, and without their elites, they would not know how to use these precious materials. The books should thus come to new homes in countries where Jewish elites remained intact.[47] Other groups in New York and Palestine competed with Baron's for influence. Judah Magnes, president of Hebrew University, argued that his institution alone was the "spiritual heir" of the Jewish books, manuscripts, and archives being found in Europe, writing, "We are to be the chief country for the absorption of the living human beings who have escaped from Nazi persecution. . . . By the same token we should be the trustee of these spiritual goods which destroyed German Jewry has left behind."[48] Despite internal competition, there was widespread Jewish agreement that orphaned

Jewish books should be sent out of Europe, to Palestine or the United States.

Meanwhile, a number of Jews in U.S.-occupied Germany acted on their own. Many even skirted the law to do what they thought was right with books and archives. Queens College history professor Koppel Pinson came to Germany at the end of the war as the Joint's education director. In late 1945, he made his way to Offenbach to see the looted Judaica for himself, and he was horrified at the thought that these price-less books, papers, manuscripts, and religious objects might return to the countries of origin, or worse, stay in Germany. From the moment he arrived there, he made the OAD his base and the fate of these mate-rials his cause. Like Baron and Magnes, Pinson believed that the looted Jewish property belonged to Jewish survivors collectively and should be put at their disposition in the new population centers, rather than sent back to the countries of origin.

Pinson had a significant impact on operations in Offenbach. He actively lobbied the U.S. military government to bring in a restitution officer trained in Judaica to handle the materials, resulting in Colonel Pomrenze's arrival in 1946. He also found ways to work around official policies to dispose of the books in the way he thought best. In 1945, he requested that some of the non-valuable Jewish books be loaned to the DP camps to help alleviate survivors' spiritual suffering. His initial request in late 1945 was for 25,000 books; a later request in 1947 for an additional 25,000 books was eventually denied because of improper recordkeeping on the part of the Joint. This last detail is telling. The fact that Joint leaders did not keep track of which books they took makes it clear that they saw the project less as a loan and more as a return of collective Jewish property to the Jewish people.[49]

In the same period, Max Weinreich sought to recover YIVO's library, looted from Vilna by the Nazis and uncovered in the OAD. He was frantic with worry that, given American restitution policies, these mate-rials might be sent back to Lithuania.[50] From Berlin, Szajkowski was able to confirm that the materials were indeed in the OAD and wrote to his friends at YIVO that an emissary should be sent to recover the materials as soon as arrangements could be made with the State Department.[51] In early 1946, the opportunity arose. Lucy Schildkret left her job as Weinreich's assistant at YIVO for a position with the Joint as an aid worker in the DP camps. Like Pinson, she made her way to the OAD, where she identified the remnant of YIVO's collection and, in 1947, helped to secure the return of almost 80,000 volumes found in the OAD to YIVO in New York. YIVO also managed to obtain many other items that had belonged to Vilna's pillaged Strashun Library.[52] Captain Pomrenze himself returned to Germany in 1947 to ship YIVO's materials to New York.[53] Although it went through official channels, this case was treated as an exception to the general rule that identifiable items were to be returned to their countries of origin, largely because Weinreich had convinced the authorities that YIVO in New York was the rightful heir of the Vilna libraries.

Hebrew University also boldly secured the transfer of some of the Jewish cultural treasures when the scholar Gershom Scholem traveled from Palestine to Europe in spring 1946 to seek out materials for the university's library. In Czechoslovakia, where the Nazis had sent a good deal of looted Judaica for a planned Jewish museum in Prague, he obtained valuable material.[54] Scholem then spent the month of July in Offenbach, carefully examining manuscripts and marking them with Roman numerals (I–V) indicating their value. Captain Isaac Bencowitz, then in charge of the OAD, had the manuscripts that Scholem had marked "I" and "II" placed in boxes and stored under lock and key.

At the end of December, after Bencowitz met with Scholem in Palestine, he prepared the paperwork for the Joint to take possession of five boxes of manuscripts, which were handed over to U.S. Army Chaplain Herbert Friedman, who signed for them with the name "Koppel Pinson." Friedman then drove the manuscripts to the Paris office of the Jewish Agency for Palestine. It would not take the stolen material, but Friedman was told that if he went to Antwerp, where Chaim Weizmann's personal library was being prepared for shipping, he might be able to send the boxes to Palestine. Friedman did just that, and the manuscripts ended up at the Hebrew University. Though Friedman remained proud of his actions for the rest of his life, it did cause a scandal that resulted in his dismissal from the army. Investigators also determined that Rabbi Philip Bernstein (the military government's advisor on Jewish Affairs, for whom Friedman worked), Koppel Pinson (who investigators claimed had thousands of books from the OAD in his personal library in New York), and Isaac Bencowitz had colluded in the theft.[55]

In his autobiography, Friedman depicts these transfers as justified. As he put it, "Saving those books amounts to saving the People of the Book."[56] Bencowitz associated them with the lost people who had owned them. As he wrote movingly in his diary at the time:

> I would walk into the loose document room [at the OAD] and take a look at the things stored there and find it impossible to tear myself away from the fascinating piles of letters, folders and little personal bundles.... [O]r in the sorting room, I would come to a box of books, which the sorters had brought together, like scattered sheep into one fold, books from a library which had once been in some distant town in Poland, or an extinct *Yeshiva*. There was something

Gershom Scholem in the Offenbach Archival Depot in 1946, sorting Hebrew manuscripts according to their value for scholars. Army chaplain Herbert Friedman would later be dismissed from army service for circumventing regulations in order to send Scholem some of the most valuable manuscripts found in the OAD for Hebrew University's collections. *Courtesy National Archives and Records Administration, Washington, D.C.*

sad and mournful about these volumes…as if they were whispering a tale of yearning and hope long since obliterated.

I would pick up a badly worn Talmud with hundreds of names of many generations of students and scholars. Where were they now? Or rather, where were their ashes? In what incinerator were they destroyed? I would find myself straightening out these books and arranging them in the boxes with a personal sense of tenderness, as if they had belonged to someone dear to me, someone recently deceased.

There were thousands of loose family photographs without any identification….[H]ow dear all these tokens of love and gentle care must have been to someone and now they were so useless, destined to be burned, buried or thrown away. All these things made my blood boil. How difficult it is to look at the content of the depot with the detachment of someone evaluating property or with the impersonal viewpoint of scholarly evaluation.[57]

In Offenbach, Bencowitz could not put aside his Jewishness any more than Szajkowski had been able to in Berlin. The piles of books and personal mementos could not be separated from the people who had owned them. He also referred to the specifically Jewish nature of the books, the libraries from which they had come, and the deaths of their owners ("In what incinerator were they destroyed?"). It is not surprising, then, that Bencowitz was sympathetic to Scholem. Like Friedman and so many others, he regarded these volumes as Jewish books and believed it would only make sense to put them in an institution outside of Europe, where Jews could continue to make use of them.[58] And like Scholem, he was willing to break army regulations in order to accomplish this goal.

There were many like them. Anecdotal evidence points to the surreptitious movement of countless quantities of materials outside of official channels in the same period. To take but one such example, a Megillat Esther now held at Temple Sinai in Washington, DC, was given in June 1945 to an army chaplain, Rabbi Eugene Lipman, in Pilsen, Czechoslovakia, by a survivor liberated from Terezin concentration camp. According to Lipman, the woman who entrusted the scroll to him insisted he return it to Leo Baeck, the German rabbi who had also been in the camp. Later, Lipman did meet Baeck at a conference in London and asked him what should be done with the scroll. Baeck asked him to take it to the United States, with the condition that it be used in an American congregation each year. Lipman's work with Jewish materials mirrored his work with Jewish DPs, whom he also helped to move from the zone of Soviet influence in Czechoslovakia to the U.S. Zone of Germany following liberation.[59] Many Jewish army chaplains have told such stories. Scores of synagogues across the United States now use the scrolls they salvaged.

Szajkowski also sent books and documents from Europe to the United States in 1945 without encountering problems from military authorities. The lack of a coordinated Allied restitution policy, the general sense among American Jews that an exodus of historic proportions was nearing completion, and military authorities' willingness to look the other way all created a climate conducive to unauthorized solutions. He could, and did, take what he wanted from Europe and dispose of it according to his own sense of what was right. Much like Poliakov and the CDJC historians in France, he found himself at the right place at the right time. Full of defiant confidence, he exploited the chaotic situation on the ground and amassed an impressive archive of materials from the abandoned Nazi ministries that documented their crimes against the Jews. Szajkowski took the material he collected for YIVO, where it would be appreciated by Jewish scholars, and where he hoped to find a job after he returned to civilian life.

In Berlin, Szajkowski's hunt for books became obsessive, driving him to trespass and carry off items to which he had no legitimate claim. He sent it all through the army post office. His interests were wide-ranging, including Nazi government documents, but also antisemitic books, newspapers, and pamphlets, as well as different types of items that survivors had saved from the camps and ghettos. He was not uninterested in Jewish books, and also found an entire run of the prewar German Jewish newspaper *Jüdische Rundschau*, as well as several issues of an underground Jewish newspaper from the Warsaw ghetto. But acquiring those Jewish periodicals was almost an afterthought.[60] Among the Germans, the papers of the perpetrators were in greatest abundance, and he collected them with relish.[61]

Taking these Nazi books and papers was contrary to regulations. According to a set of American directives in April and May 1945, troops were forbidden from acquiring any property previously belonging to Nazis or looted by them, including art, books, archives, and other cultural artifacts. Further, all Nazi party and German state archives were subject to confiscation by military units, particularly anything "devoted to the perpetuation of German militarism." Finally, all antisemitic books were deemed illegal and subject to confiscation or destruction.[62] Only the U.S. Library of Congress was exempt. Starting in 1946, its newly reestablished Mission in Europe was permitted to take quite a bit of antisemitica for future use and study.[63] The purpose of the directives was twofold: to rid Germany of Nazi influence and to prepare for trials against Nazi war criminals.[64]

Illegal as it was, collecting of the sort that Szajkowski did in Berlin in 1945 was in fact relatively widespread. All around him, American Jewish GIs were illegally taking supplies to help Jewish DPs. The Soviets were carting off tremendous quantities of loot—from art to archives to fine china to train tracks—to compensate for their wartime suffering. And goods of every sort were being traded on the black market for watches, chocolate, and cigarettes.[65] Szajkowski himself participated in a bit of speculation, having friends back home send him the noisy, black-faced watches that the Russians liked best. He sold them and used some of the proceeds to send his packages, keeping the rest for later. An immigrant several times over, he was not blithe to the fortunes of exile, and never forgot that the moment he returned home, he would be without a job.[66] In postwar Berlin, a soldier had ample room to operate, and when it came to collecting books and archives, Szajkowski's convictions provided the fuel.

It was easy for Szajkowski to find antisemitica in Germany in the summer and fall of 1945. In fact, he told Riva, you could find Nazi books in bookstores as late as July. Even after that, it was easy to barter with individuals.[67] Many things lay in abandoned buildings. He sent everything he could to YIVO. According to his own report, by the end of August 1945, he had sent fifty boxes. By the end of September, the number had grown to 250. In October, he reported sending five to ten boxes per day. Worried that things might get lost, confiscated by the capricious base censor, or pillaged in the U.S. mail, he repeatedly asked Riva if YIVO was receiving his packages. Even so, he sent more and more things.[68] By the time he left Berlin on November 9, 1945, to begin his long—but this time less dramatic—journey back through France to New York, he had sent hundreds of boxes to YIVO's New York address. He marked each and every package "To Shayke for YIVO" so that the base censor would be "absolutely sure what it's for" and let it go through. This was not booty; this was material for a library.[69]

His most important finds were official Nazi documents that he pilfered from the wrecked remains of the ministries themselves. After the Americans had arrived in the city, they had stationed guards outside some of the key Nazi ministries, such as Hitler's Chancery, to protect them from looting. Intelligence experts were often onsite, rummaging through the debris for material to use in the coming war crimes tribunals.[70] Despite this, Szajkowski did not have any difficulty getting in or hauling out the heavy materials. Indeed, his reports to Riva indicated how fully he was aided in his endeavors by authorities. "If I can get away from the Allied Command for a couple of hours, I take a car and go looking for books. On the day I send off the books I have to get up at 7:30 to be among the first at the post office (otherwise I sleep until 8:30.) The chauffeur of the Command Center arrives and the car is filled with bundles of books."

Szajkowski examining documents in the Nazi Propaganda Ministry, Berlin, 1945. He would send hundreds of boxes of these documents to YIVO, where they are now part of the Berlin Collection. *From the Archives of the YIVO Institute for Jewish Research.*

The work was backbreaking, but as much as he complained, he was not actually doing it alone. The Allied Command chauffeur and the guardsmen facilitated his task.[71] The army post office also helped. "You have to let the censor go through the things and not all the officers understand my quirkiness about sending books. First of course, you've got to schlep the books, pack them up, and then schlep them to the Post Office and there's never time to do it all."[72] With the help of these authorities, Szajkowski found the strength to persevere, returning frequently to the ruins of Goebbels's Propaganda Ministry after he found it in August, emerging time and time again "black as a chimney sweep and loaded down with books."[73] He also found Alfred Rosenberg's Riga archive, from his post as Reich Minister for the Occupied Eastern Territories.[74]

On one of his collecting jaunts, he found some blank sheets of Adolf Hitler's official stationery and wrote a letter in Yiddish to Riva on it. Crossing out the name and the title ("Adolf Hitler, Office of the Führer, NSDAP"), Szajkowski, the conquering Jewish GI, wrote the words, "May his name be blotted out forever."[75] Anything with Hitler's signature was actually quite valuable. Szajkowski reported trading some letters signed by Hitler for a ride in a jeep to haul out more papers from the Propaganda Ministry.[76] But this was not a financial investment; rather, it felt like a certain kind of justice, especially at this moment when he felt that the Allies were doing nothing to hold the Germans accountable. The Nazis had looted so much from the Jews; was it not only right that Jewish scholars gain access to the material remains of their evil plans?

The same attitude sometimes came into play in his always uncomfortable dealings with German civilians. "I often have the occasion to chat with Germans, because of my work...," he wrote to Riva. "As soon as they figure out that I'm a Jew, they begin talking about Jewish friends and even pull books off the shelves that are written by Jews. If it's possible, I'll take a few books for YIVO."[77] Aware that what he was doing was in fact a crime, he saw his petty theft of German property as a small way to begin to right the gigantic wrong that, to his way of thinking, was likely to go unpunished by the Allies.

Szajkowski's pace was relentless. Even though the base censor was willing to let his parcels through, there simply was not enough string in

Berlin to wrap all the parcels he was assembling for YIVO. It became something of a joke with him that he would use anything for string. He even drew a cartoon for Riva about it. The drawing shows two German women, standing over a backyard fence, hanging their laundry. The first says, "Every night, my laundry lines go missing. Poor people must be using them to hang themselves!" The other one responds, "You'd better ask our American neighbor about it—you know, the one with all the books."[78]

Szajkowski drew this cartoon and sent it to Riva Tcherikower from Berlin in October 1945, poking fun at his own obsessive hunt for string in the occupied city. He used the string to tie the parcels of books he was sending to YIVO. *From the Archives of the YIVO Institute for Jewish Research.*

Szajkowski's self-mockery reveals the depth of his compulsion to take everything possible and the unconscious meaning that stealing books had for him. His joke about the laundry lines turned on an association between his looting German books and German suicides—a primitive revenge fantasy generated by a Jew who was distraught that there was to be no real justice for the murderers of his family and his people.

The sadistic pleasure Szajkowski took in looting German books for Jewish scholarship was also apparent in several anecdotes he shared with Riva. On one occasion, frustrated over his inability to fit everything into the box he had found, Szajkowski ripped chapters of interest out of books in order to send them on to YIVO. In a haunting foreshadowing of his later ripping and cutting of documents from the French archives, he seemed to delight in taking vengeance:

> Am I barbaric to do that? Probably, but it's the only way. I simply can't send those books intact. They'd be lost in any case. So I'm doing my barbaric work with a clean conscience. Aside from that, is it barbaric to rip apart Nazi books? . . . Yesterday as I sat and tore pages out of a Nazi book . . . a German girl started crying. Her beastly Nazi soul couldn't bear seeing a Jew calmly tearing pages out of a German book. I told her to keep working and stop her games.[79]

The incident is telling on several levels. Szajkowski was not your usual collector; he did not prize his materials for their value as objects. A book in this condition was rendered practically worthless on the market. Primarily, Szajkowski wanted these books for their utility to Jewish knowledge. But his tone of sadistic triumphalism toward the German woman is unmistakable. Was she really crying about his ripping books? As with the woman who told him about killing her own child when the Russians came to Berlin, he refused to pity this crying woman. Since he yelled at her instead of finding out what was wrong, we will never know the reason for her tears. Instead, he imagined vengefully that *he* was making her cry with his "barbaric" act of ripping these books to pieces. Relishing his power as an American GI and conscious of his Jewishness, Szajkowski tore books like a barbarian to satisfy a deep psychological need to put the Germans in their place.

The materials Szajkowski sent from Germany became YIVO's RG 215, the "Berlin Collection," whose twenty-five linear feet contain fragmentary materials from a number of former Nazi ministries, particularly the Propaganda Ministry.[80] His efforts to collect this material did not go unrewarded. The materials he sent were received with much gratitude and were long remembered in the institution. Henia Berkovich, who worked at YIVO at the time, recalled in a letter to Lucy Dawidowicz in the mid-1980s that although she remembered very little from the era, "I do remember Shzkofsky [Szajkowski] slipping us cartons after cartons of commandeered books via the U.S. army."[81]

Max Weinreich was thrilled with the acquisitions. He even acknowledged Szajkowski's work in gathering these materials in his groundbreaking 1945 study of academic collaboration in Nazi Germany, *Hitler's Professors*, translated from the original Yiddish into English in early 1946 in the hopes of being useful to the prosecution of the Nazis. Weinreich pressured Szajkowski to stay in Europe beyond his expected return date in November 1945 so he could keep collecting. But Szajkowski just wanted to go "home"—that is, back to New York. He was depressed by all he was seeing (and also a little heartbroken about his English friend Elaine's reunion with her fiancé, an understandably jealous man who did not want the two to continue their intimate correspondence).[82]

Weinreich was pleased with the collecting nonetheless. He honored Szajkowski upon his return from service, inviting him to speak about his work at YIVO's twentieth annual meeting in January 1946. Readers of YIVO's newsletter, *Yedies fun YIVO*, would already have known of his exploits from the numerous articles about him in its pages throughout 1944 and 1945. The articles painted a portrait of a heroic rescuer of Judaica, contributing to the building up of YIVO's collection at a crucial moment of transition for the organization and for world Jewry, and helping scholars to document crimes against the Jews as the prosecution of the Nazis was beginning to take shape.[83]

Szajkowski's collecting—technically illegal—was tolerated because many among the Allied authorities thought that such actions were justified. For the same reason, authorities would also look the other way in Offenbach when many items slipped out the back. Even in the cases where priceless manuscripts were stolen—like the case involving Rabbi Friedman and Captain Bencowitz—the punishments were light, and U.S. authorities never tried to retrieve the stolen treasures from Scholem or Hebrew University. Authorities' leniency in these cases contrasts sharply with their treatment in other cases in which U.S. officers stole high-value items in occupied Germany. Although there too the thefts had been facilitated by lax policies on the ground, the State Department nevertheless made a sustained effort to find and return them. Criminals like Colonel Jack W. Durant and Captain Kathleen Nash, who stole the Crown Jewels of Hesse and sent them to the United States in January 1946, were tracked down within a few months, prosecuted, and sentenced to prison terms of five and fifteen years, respectively. In 1951, their booty was finally returned to the family from which it had been stolen.[84] This simply did not happen with the Judaica that was taken from Germany by Jews among the American occupation authorities, such as Friedman, Pinson, and Szajkowski.

American officials at all levels, starting with the White House, had a new view of the Jewish world. Indeed, even before military leaders had finished their work in the OAD in 1948, officials in both the U.S. military government and the State Department had become convinced that Jewish life in Europe was over and that any Jewish cultural property remaining in Europe really belonged elsewhere, in Jewish hands. In 1948, military government officials designated an independent Jewish body, the Jewish Restitution Successor Organization (JRSO), rather than the German states, as the heir to all Jewish property that had been seized by the Nazis and whose prewar owners had been killed. The money was to be used to help support Jewish refugees around the world. Analogous bodies were created in the British Zone (the Jewish Trust Corporation) and the French Zone (the Branche française of the Jewish Trust Corporation). For Jewish cultural activists, these decisions about heirless property represented a major victory. They had succeeded in persuading the Americans to look upon Jews as partners in their restitution efforts and to treat the surviving Jews and their property as something other than belonging to the European nations where they had originated. Szajkowski's worldview had prevailed: Even before there was a Jewish state, Jewishness had been recognized as equivalent to nationhood.

In the American Zone, the JRSO made Baron's JCR its "cultural arm," responsible for allocating the 500,000 heirless books, archives, and religious objects that had remained in the OAD after restitutions ceased at the end of 1948.[85] The scholars who led the operations—Baron, Columbia University law professor Jerome Michael, historian Joshua Starr, and philosopher Hannah Arendt—saw these cultural treasures as the collective property of the Jewish people. Just as they favored the exodus of the surviving Jewish DPs, they also favored the exodus of the plundered cultural treasures in order to keep them under Jewish custodianship. They turned time and again to the analogy between Jewish orphans and the looted cultural treasures. As Rabbi Bernard Heller of JCR later wrote,

> The repatriation of the identifiable books and articles resembled the return of kidnapped children to their former homes and the embrace of overjoyed parents who awaited them. The remaining unidentified books seemed like children whom the shock of war deprived of the power of recollection and awareness of identity. Even if they could manage to shake off the mentally petrifying grip of their amnesia, they would be confronted with the fact that the lands from which they came are now ravaged and their homes are demolished and their parents who would rejoice at their return are now no more alive. To these books and holy objects—the silent and stunned waifs of a horrible tragedy—[we] came not merely as a solicitous friend but … to provide them with a secure home and loving foster parents.[86]

Jewish Cultural Reconstruction began its work in February 1949. By that time, the organization had expanded to include representatives from the groups with which it had once competed for influence, including Hebrew University. Baron and other early leaders nevertheless maintained their leadership positions, and the organization remained in New York. In its certificate of incorporation of April 30, 1947, the organization committed itself to

locate, identify, salvage, acquire by gift or purchase or any other
lawful means, hold, preserve, repair, protect, catalogue and determine the disposition of, Jewish books and manuscripts and generally, Jewish religious and cultural objects and property of every sort
whatsoever anywhere in the world ... [and] to distribute the property
in such a way as to best serve and promote the spiritual and cultural
needs and interests of the Jewish people in particular and mankind in
general, and especially the spiritual and cultural needs of the victims
of Nazi or fascist persecution.[87]

Although they mention the needs of the survivors, the founders of JCR
did not intend to distribute this property to institutions in Europe.
Indeed, the initial roster of member organizations even excluded Cecil
Roth's organization in Great Britain, as well as the Alliance Israélite
Universelle in Paris, although the Alliance was added in December 1949.
Distributions instead proceeded on the basis of the aims articulated by
the group's executive secretary Hannah Arendt in 1946: "In view of the
wholesale destruction of Jewish life and property by the Nazis, reconstruction of Jewish cultural institutions cannot possibly mean mechan-
ical restoration in their original form, or in all cases, to their previous
location.... Ultimately it may ... seek to help redistribute the Jewish
cultural treasures in accordance with the new needs created by the new
situation of world Jewry."[88]

JCR's directors soon found themselves at odds with a few of the
surviving German Jews who preferred that some of their materials
remain in Germany. This was particularly the case in the British Zone,
where JCR had little influence and the authorities proved reticent
to remove property looted from Jews from the local authorities. In
1950, on a visit to the British Zone, Arendt reported that the small
number of surviving German Jews across the zone "frequently show
a deplorable tendency to make common cause with the German
government against the Jewish organizations." She persevered, iden-
tifying what cultural property still remained there and attempting to
make sure it landed in the hands of the Jewish Trust Corporation,
although she admitted temporary defeat in at least one case. In
Hamburg, she struggled unsuccessfully to convince Harry Goldstein,

Books deemed "unidentifiable" by U.S. restitution authorities in the Offenbach Archival Depot, 1946. Jewish Cultural Reconstruction would ultimately decide the fate of these heirless items. *Courtesy National Archives and Records Administration, Washington, DC.*

the president of the Hamburg Jewish Community, to give over its communal archives to JCR. He insisted they remain in the Hamburg state archives. "In his opinion," Arendt reported, "the Jewish organizations have not done a thing for the Hamburg Jews and as long as the international Jewish organizations do not help in the reconstruction of Hamburg community life, Mr. Goldstein will oppose every attempt to get Jewish things out of Hamburg." Believing Goldstein an honorable man, Arendt hoped he would eventually change his mind. JCR and the international Jewish organizations more generally believed that Jewish history in Europe had come to an end and was not worth rebuilding.[89]

Seen in a larger framework, Szajkowski's shipments to YIVO in 1945 were but small drops in a large river of books moving swiftly from Germany to America and Israel in the aftermath of the war. Although he worked outside laws and regulations in taking Jewish periodicals and Nazi papers from Germany to the new center of

Jewish scholarship in New York in 1945, his basic assumption found some echo among the American Jewish scholarly elite. With their help, an exodus of Jewish books from Germany was accomplished by the early 1950s, and the broader process bore the stamp of approval from the U.S. government.

6

The Fact Collector

WHEN SOLDIERS COME HOME FROM war, they are expected to return to normal. But what did that mean for someone like Szajkowski, a veteran twice over and a new immigrant, lucky to have escaped the fate of his siblings in Paris? The Holocaust refugees and survivors who made their way to America were met with the same expectations as the war veterans. They too were supposed to get on their feet financially, rebuild their personal lives, and come to terms with the past. The task was not easy. For refugees, "returning to normal" is never truly a return, since adapting to new circumstances also means transforming themselves. Szajkowski had done this once already when he moved to Paris in 1927. But there, he had the support of his older siblings who had landed there a few years earlier, not to mention the energy of a sixteen-year-old excited at the prospect of building a future in a country with a better outlook for Jews than Poland. Settling into America, Szajkowski had fewer resources. The savings he had managed to accumulate as a paratrooper would not go far. His emotional resources were especially taxed, and when he returned to New York in December 1945, he was depleted and had few friends. He had gotten close to a few people in New York before joining the U.S. Army, but when he returned, practically everyone he knew was in mourning. It made it hard to connect, particularly because after so many years in uniform, he had grown unaccustomed to the niceties of civilian life.

YIVO represented his best hope for establishing himself in America, both personally and professionally. Although many other refugees, far better credentialed than he, were also seeking YIVO's support, and its resources were stretched thin, he had reason to think that he would have a future there. He had made quite an impression with his daring exploits during the war. In addition to sending hundreds of packages to the institute for its collections, the generous soldier had also sent many personal gifts to his friends. There was the cigarette lighter he filched from a German soldier's corpse in Normandy for Symon Dawidowicz,[1] a few manuscripts from southern France for Max Weinreich,[2] a pair of antlers from Goering's hunting lodge for Weinreich's son Gabriel, as well as "an old saber with a sheath, with gold-encrusted Arabic writing on the blade,"[3] a smaller antique sword for Weinreich's other son Uriel,[4] and swatches of parachute, which he thought would make lovely shawls, for Riva Tcherikower, Regina Weinreich, Anya Gelernt, and Libe Schildkret.[5]

These were the unforgettable gifts of a man determined not to be forgotten. Through them, his friends at YIVO could share in the sweet feeling of revenge he had known in Berlin when, as a conquering hero, he had carted off Nazi property to even the score on behalf of his people. He kept the best of his loot for himself: a mummified female head, thousands of years old. Perhaps he found it in the Nazis' Kaiser Wilhelm Institute of Anthropology, Human Heredity, and Eugenics, which was not far from the Allied Command in Berlin's Dahlem district.[6] The immersion in Nazi stuff changed Szajkowski's sensibilities so much that he forgot to censor his macabre humor when he wrote to Riva about the female head. But the gifts, and particularly the documents for YIVO's collections, made an impression on Weinreich, who rewarded his younger friend's generosity by finding a way to employ him at YIVO shortly after his return.

Four years in uniform had changed Szajkowski, but he began to return to normal, at least on the surface. He found an apartment on Manhattan's Upper West Side and made some friends. In 1946, he started dating a Polish Jewish refugee, Chana Giterman. Eleven years Szajko's junior, Chana also had a YIVO connection. Her father Yitzhak

Giterman was a Warsaw-based historian who had worked closely with the institute in Vilna before the war. In the Warsaw ghetto, he had worked as director of the Joint and participated in the Jewish Combat Organization and in Ringelblum's Oyneg Shabes project. Although Chana's parents and brother ultimately perished in the ghetto, she herself escaped to Yokohama, Japan, from which she boarded a ship to San Francisco in 1941 and finally made her way to New York.[7]

Chana was interested in textile design, not scholarship. But family ties placed her firmly in the world of the Jewish cultural elite. The Gitermans were a secular branch of the extended Schneersohn family, and the orphaned Chana stayed in touch with her Paris cousin Isaac Schneersohn, the rabbi and industrialist who founded the CDJC in 1943 and ran the institution until his death in 1969. His brother, the Tel Aviv psychiatrist Fishel Schneersohn, was also a scholar interested in documenting the Jews' recent catastrophe. Other cousins were at the center of twentieth-century Hasidism. Her Brooklyn cousin Menachem Mendel Schneerson, was the seventh Lubavitcher Rebbe.[8] Another cousin was Schneour Zalman Schneersohn, the Hasidic rabbi who led the French Association des Israélites Pratiquants (Kehillat Haharedim), and in that context, protected ultra-orthodox Jews in France during World War II.

This was quite a pedigree, filled with spiritual and intellectual leaders, and contrasted sharply with Szajkowski's more humble one. But the extreme circumstances of the 1940s brought them together. After dating for a number of years, they married in 1953 in Paris, according to French custom, first at the mairie of the 11th arrondissement, then under a huppah in Isaac Schneersohn's apartment.[9] Three years later, they had a son Isaac, named for Chana's deceased father. The many congratulatory cards and letters the couple received from family and friends around the world, written in Yiddish, French, and English, testify to the love that surrounded them, and the sense that after a long delay, parenthood was finally giving these two orphans a fresh start at family.[10]

Szajkowski managed to get on his feet professionally too. With Weinreich's support, he was officially hired by YIVO in 1946 and put in charge of gathering materials from Europe.[11] His first project as a YIVO staff member involved arranging the materials he had sent from France and Germany in 1944–45. He also supervised the committees of *zamlers* in France and Belgium that he had helped to establish in 1945 and returned to Europe on several occasions to meet with them.[12] Over time, he arranged numerous other collections, including the papers of the immigrant aid organization HIAS-HICEM, the papers of the Joint, and the Tcherikower collection. He authored catalogues on YIVO's exhibitions on such diverse subjects as the Jews of Shanghai, Yiddish orthography, the shtetl, Simon Dubnow, and the poet Morris Rosenfeld.

He also established himself as a scholar. Many of his articles were in Yiddish, published in YIVO's scholarly journal *YIVO Bleter*, and in the Argentine journal *Davke*. He also published in English, forging close ties with the leading figures in Jewish studies in America, such as Salo Baron and the other editors of *Jewish Social Studies*, particularly its managing editor Abraham Duker, and Guido Kisch, editor of *Historia Judaica*. On a trip to Israel in 1953, he established a friendship with Israel Halperin of the Historical Society of Israel and later published articles, translated into Hebrew, in its journal *Zion*.

In the late 1940s and '50s, most of Szajkowski's articles concerned French Jewish history, and they were based on original archival research in France. Increasingly drawn to economic and social history, Szajkowski required access to sources that went beyond the texts available in libraries in New York. His "return to normal" thus, ironically, made him more peripatetic than ever. From 1947 to 1961, he frequently returned to France for long periods (including much of 1950–53), conducting research in archives and libraries across the country in search of documentation.

But despite these personal and professional accomplishments, Szajkowski did not entirely return to normal. Hints that something was amiss first surfaced at YIVO in 1949. For some time, nasty gossip had circulated among the staff about the packages Szajkowski had sent from Europe as a soldier and continued to bring in from France for YIVO's growing collections of material from Western Europe. In those years, the institute saw its share of drama, and such whispering campaigns were not unusual. Szajkowski had always tried to stay above it. He knew he had a difficult temperament and avoided confrontation when possible.[13] But things came to a head one day in December 1949 when, preparing for another trip to France, he spoke with Max Weinreich about his plans to meet with the YIVO *zamlers* there. Weinreich warned him not to take anything of questionable provenance, as he had in Berlin in 1945. The accusation stung, leaving Szajkowski speechless. Weinreich was suggesting—less gently than he might have—that Szajkowski's decision to cut ownership stamps off some of the Jewish books he had sent to YIVO from Berlin had been less than ethical.[14]

Humiliated, Szajkowski wrote an angry note reminding his supervisor that given the restitution policies being discussed in 1945, the cutting had been necessary to protect the books from being returned to Eastern Europe. But at least initially, Weinreich showed no sign of backing down and simply told him, "I got your note. We'll talk about it later." It was not enough to soothe Szajkowski's bruised ego. He retreated and addressed an angry letter of resignation to the whole YIVO staff. He was furious with everyone, he announced, but Weinreich most of all. How could he, of all people, call into question the heroism of Szajkowski's wartime collecting? "Without my shipment, Weinreich would not have been able to write *Hitler's Professors*," he wrote in the open letter, trying to recreate the moment when all YIVO honored him for his bold efforts on behalf of the Jewish people.[15] Back in 1945, they had all shared in the hope that scholarship would avenge Nazi crimes. Had they all forgotten that such scholarship depended on the efforts of intrepid *zamlers* at the front, willing to use unorthodox methods when needed?

But times were changing. Weinreich was probably not so worried about what Szajkowski had done in 1945, when the lines between legal and illegal were blurred and everyone understood that doing what was right could sometimes involve breaking the law. But now that the authorities had settled the question of where looted books would go—after all, that very year, American restitution efforts in occupied Germany had drawn to a close—it was time to reestablish clear policies. This meant having a talk with Szajkowski about what he was doing on his trips to France on behalf of YIVO. In establishing new acquisition policies that better suited the moment, Weinreich had to rein in his most zealous *zamler* who saw collecting as a way of reliving his glory days.

Returning to normal made sense for Weinreich, the director of a large scholarly institute determined to establish a strong presence in

America. But for Szajkowski, the psychological cost of the return to normal was too high to bear. For the refugee, survivor, and veteran, his basic sense of self-worth was bound up in his wartime heroism. If he was not a hero, what was he? The blow to his ego was intolerable. After he tendered his resignation, he left for France. There, a sympathetic Isaac Schneersohn had him over to dinner, listened to his story, and, without telling Szajkowski, wrote to Weinreich to try to repair the damage. "He's a capable man, despite his strong personality, and he has always shown great promise as an archivist and researcher. If you let him go, you will lose a good collaborator, and more importantly, he will be deprived of the guidance of an eminent supervisor who could have such a great influence on him and mold his talent," he wrote.[16] Szajkowski was still rough around the edges, but the talent was there; could Weinreich not give it another try? Plus, Schneersohn implied, without giving full voice to his worry, what would become of Szajkowski if he were left to follow his instincts?

As it turned out, it was Szajkowski who could not be budged. Weinreich he could forgive, but he found the whole atmosphere at YIVO poisonous. Besides, he still aspired to be a scholar, and YIVO had employed him only to work with the collections, leaving no time for his research.[17] So he set out to make it as an independent scholar. Schneersohn was having financial difficulties at the CDJC and was unable to hire him, although they stayed close and Szajkowski helped him find documents for CDJC projects on a number of occasions. Independent and courageous as ever, Szajkowski took advantage of the freedom to travel in search of new sources for his work, and threw himself into his research with all the ferocity of his early days as a journalist.

Only in 1952 did Szajkowski begin to mend the breach with YIVO. In France, he heard that YIVO was one of the institutions due to receive reparations money from the German government. Troubled as he was by the idea of YIVO supporting Jewish scholarship with blood money from the Germans, the news nonetheless moved him to write to his friend Moshe Kligsberg, the editor of YIVO's *Yedies*, to see about coming back. He needed money and, he said, "I am tired of exerting myself."[18] Likely the fact that he was about to marry weighed on his decision as well. By the end of 1953, it was all worked out and

Szajkowski returned from Paris, a newlywed, and went back to work at YIVO, his position funded by a YIVO-Yad Vashem cooperative project that hired refugees to work with collections documenting the recent catastrophe.[19] He quickly proved his worth as a *zamler* once again, returning to Paris in autumn 1955 to acquire for YIVO 400 additional pounds of documents from Isaac Schneersohn to supplement the UGIF collection.[20] Still, as valuable as his colleagues found his work, things were never quite the same. A few friendships were rebuilt—with Riva Tcherikower, Moshe Kligsberg, and Max Weinreich—but he remained largely alienated from his coworkers who found him strange and difficult. He was relegated to a fourth floor office and left alone to organize his collections.[21]

Although they later reconciled, Weinreich was right to suspect that Szajkowski had not forsaken his unorthodox collecting habits when he had returned home from the war. By 1949, rumors of his misdeeds in the archives had begun to follow the historian in France as well. French archivists' suspicions were later confirmed, although the scope of the thefts ultimately exceeded their wildest imaginations. As the extraordinary times of the war faded into memory, Szajkowski, once hailed as a book rescuer, became an archive thief. It was not so much the man who had changed as the world around him. Postwar conditions were making it more difficult to become a scholar than Szajkowski had imagined, but he was determined not to let that stop him. Holding fast to the ambition he had nurtured since the 1930s, he remained as willing to break the law in its service as he had been in wartime.

Between 1946, when he returned from his army service, and 1961, when he was caught stealing in Strasbourg and effectively barred from ever returning to France, Szajkowski published no fewer than a hundred journal articles and six scholarly books, an average of eight scholarly publications a year.[22] He was a leading expert in his field, publishing in the top Jewish history journals in English, Hebrew, and Yiddish. In most history departments today, he would be among the most accomplished and prolific professors on the faculty, and at the relatively young age of fifty, he still had many productive years ahead of him.

And yet his particular situation meant that he never achieved either the security or the status his scholarship would have earned him under different circumstances. His lack of degrees made a career as a university professor all but impossible. In this, he was not alone. YIVO in New York was filled with scholars unable to penetrate American academia, and many, such as Rudolf Glanz (who had earned a doctoral degree in law from the University of Vienna in 1918) and Isaiah Trunk (who had earned a master's degree in history in Warsaw in 1927), were quite successful at getting their work published and read. Still, even at YIVO, there was a clear pecking order. Yudl Mark, for example, was an accomplished linguist who had been Dubnow's private secretary as a young man in St. Petersburg, and later became the executive secretary of the Jewish National Council of Lithuania. The author of an important Yiddish grammar, he came to America in 1936, and in 1941, he became editor of the journal *Di Yidishe Shprakh*. Nevertheless, as his son remembers it, Mark was often made to feel like a *"shikyingl"* (errand boy) at YIVO because he lacked a university degree. In the institute, gradations in status were all the more marked and for some, quite painful to bear, precisely because scholars working there had come to scholarship through such diverse paths.[23]

Szajkowski's own professional insecurity never stopped him from pursuing his dreams. Although his articles were published in the best journals in the field, his books were self-published. Book publishing was different from journal publishing. With the exception of YIVO's publications, Jewish studies journals did not pay authors for their articles, while books offered the possibility for a historian to make some money.[24] It was an attractive opportunity and also offered more room to develop ideas, so Szajkowski gave it a try. But without the support of an institution—a publishing house or even a subsidy to cover the costs of publishing his books himself—it would be difficult. For the Yiddish-language studies he published in the late 1940s, he received some assistance from YIVO, but he had more trouble after 1949 once he quit his job and tried to make it on his own. Unable to find a printer for his longer studies in Yiddish, he decided to bring out his three major book-length studies in English. He created his own publishing house for the purpose, which he called Editions historiques franco-juives, and had three books printed in Paris in 1953. He and his new bride Chana saved on shipping by carrying them home to New York in their suitcases, and they kept the books in their apartment, selling them directly to scholars and libraries for five dollars each.[25] For the independent scholar, self-publishing represented an optimistic investment in his future as a Jewish historian writing in English.

The three studies printed in Paris in 1953 constituted Szajkowski's most rigorous work to date: *Agricultural Credit and Napoleon's Anti-Jewish Decrees; The Economic Status of the Jews of Alsace, Metz and Lorraine, 1648–1789*; and *Poverty and Social Welfare among French Jews, 1800–1880*. They succeeded in getting him recognition within the world of Jewish scholarship in English, so much so that he was able to secure a modest grant from the Alexander Kohut Memorial Foundation for his next project. The grant was administered by the prestigious American Academy for Jewish Research, which admitted him to its ranks in 1959, the one "Mister" on a long list of highly regarded "Doctors" and "Professors."[26] The study their grant supported, *Autonomy and Communal Jewish Debts during the French Revolution of 1789* (1959), was also published by the Editions historiques franco-juives. In the front matter of this later study, the better established Szajkowski could proudly thank the American Jewish scholarly establishment for its support. His scheme seemed to be working: Investing his own money in his scholarship might eventually pay off in terms of both recognition and support.

Judging from the reviews, however, Szajkowski's studies were not universally well received. The American-born, Harvard-educated historian Robert F. Byrnes wrote a mixed review of the first three of Szajkowski's self-published books in *Jewish Social Studies*. Byrnes was well qualified to assess Szajkowski's books. Although a Russianist, he had recently published a book on the history of French antisemitism that stressed its origins on the left, as well as on the right, a position Szajkowski had articulated in several studies of his own in the 1940s.[27] Moreover, few scholars were working on Jews in France at all. Considering that Szajkowski himself was the author of twelve of the twenty-one articles that *Jewish Social Studies* had published on France since the journal was founded in 1939, Byrnes was a natural choice simply because he was the author of the second greatest number, three.[28]

At first glance, Byrnes's review offers the kind of encouraging words a better established scholar can offer to a less well-established one, stressing Szajkowski's "genuine devotion to scholarship and thorough and detailed knowledge of the sources available." But it was also condescending. Byrnes intimated that the reason Szajkowski's prose was "inexact" and "unclear" was because it was translated from Yiddish, marking the author as a somewhat incompetent outsider. He also criticized the works as "suffer[ing] from the prevailing over-emphasis on specialization," making it hard to ascertain the studies' larger points. "I hope someday that Szajkowski will be able to produce a scholarly and readable volume on the economic status of the Jews in France from the 17th century until today. Such a volume would be most useful and he is the scholar most able to produce it."[29] Although Byrnes allowed that Szajkowski was erudite, his criticism was plain: These were narrow, badly written collections of obscure facts, the larger significance of which remained entirely unclear.

Byrnes was right. The studies were heavily documented, with extensive bibliographies, footnotes, and appendices in which exceedingly rare primary sources were reproduced. Although the prose was easily intelligible, it contained the kind of awkward formulations typical of non-native speakers. Finally, Szajkowski's arguments were limited, and conclusions were articulated weakly. This last problem in particular made it hard for even a knowledgeable reader like Byrnes to see their value for a wider audience, an important issue when so very few people anywhere knew much about French Jewish history. Byrnes hoped it was just a question of experience, and even suggested in his review a direction in which Szajkowski might go, to undertake a more general study of Jewish economic history in France over 300 years.

But given his situation, Szajkowski was unlikely to evolve in that direction. On the one hand, he, like Byrnes, was deeply committed to a scientific model for historical research, in which claims had to be derived from a thorough examination of evidence, a practice indicated within Szajkowski's text by extensive footnoting.[30] At the same time, however, Szajkowski's status outside the university system, and the financial problems that it caused, limited the extent of his research and thus the reach of his claims. In France, where Szajkowski spent much of the 1950s, this was the era of the hegemony of the *Annales* school, and social and economic historical studies were often completed by teams of researchers collaborating on large questions without compromising thoroughness or attention to detail. Szajkowski held himself to their scientific standards, but he had to work quickly, and alone.

Szajkowski was ever conscious of his comparative lack of resources, and it deterred him from designing the kind of study Byrnes was calling for. As he wrote in one of the studies Byrnes reviewed:

> If we have succeeded in bringing out some brand-new data in our study ... may it serve as a hint of how much could be accomplished if similar studies would secure proper moral and material support.... The work [of fully answering the large questions at stake in this study] is far beyond the powers of one individual, particularly if carried out without the financial and moral support of some Jewish institution. For this very reason the present analysis had to encompass merely a limited number of volumes in the mortgage archives, even though by far the largest that has ever been analyzed so far.[31]

But there was more to Szajkowski's style than professional insecurity and funding constraints. It was also a matter of principle. Having broken with the Communists and all forms of organized Jewish politics in disgust on the eve of the war, Szajkowski believed that Jewish history should be free of all ideology. In his apprenticeship with the Tcherikowers, he had come to believe that the only way beyond politics was to turn to the sources and defer big arguments until all possible remnants of the past were assembled and analyzed scientifically. For the moment, Szajkowski believed, the general arguments of the sort Byrnes might have liked him to produce were little more than "bombast" or "apologetics."[32]

If Szajkowski was a devotee of the fact, his choice to defer broad and far-reaching conclusions nevertheless made his work seem lacking. Since the nineteenth century, professional historians in Europe and the United States saw their work as a multistep process in which they found sources in hard-to-reach archives, paid careful attention to the most minute of details contained in the sources they read there, and used their training in foreign languages and deciphering difficult handwriting to do so. Szajkowski was a faithful practitioner of these skills. But most professional historians performed a final operation before publishing their work. From the mass of details found and analyzed, they would select only the most important to present as the "facts" upon which history could be written. The selection process was crucial. Limiting the facts allowed historians to arrange them into cogent narratives written with an authoritative voice.[33] It was this final, missing step that made Szajkowski's studies appear amateurish in the eyes of academics like Byrnes and dated in the eyes of most scholars working today.[34]

Szajkowski's refusal to pare down his evidence and construct a clear narrative was not simply a product of his professional situation. It was rather a conscious choice and had everything to do with the times in which he lived and worked. Szajkowski left Europe believing that Jews were at the start of a new moment in their history. Until many more sources were uncovered, it was impossible to know which facts were the most important, particularly for someone so disgusted with parties and their ideologies. This meant that truly scientific conclusions would have to be deferred.

Having taken such a stand on principle, Szajkowski peppered his work with the rhetoric of eschewing conclusions. He ended his 1958 article, "Population Problems of Marranos and Sephardim in France," by asking the reader to consider his findings "only as notes and not as a final study." He used similar terms in lieu of conclusions in other studies as well.[35] And yet, in spite of his protests to the contrary, obvious conclusions can be drawn by the interested reader. For "Population Problems," Szajkowski had examined the early modern civil registers of all births, marriages, and deaths found in the Bordeaux and Bayonne municipal archives. He noted that the list could be used to determine when and how the Spanish and Portuguese Jews who had been admitted to France in the sixteenth and seventeenth centuries as converts to Christianity of Jewish descent became the publically recognized Jews of the eighteenth. Working with the names themselves, long lists of which he published in the footnotes, he makes a plausible case that "almost all first generations of Marranos who arrived from Spain and Portugal were lost to the Jewish communities. Those who remained Jewish were Marranos who arrived at a later period and their number was small in comparison to those who had arrived earlier and remained Christians."[36] Historically speaking, this is a significant finding.

But Szajkowski insisted that it was impossible to generalize from his "notes" and deferred conclusions until work with many different types of sources was carried out. To judge from what he wrote, this might never happen. To go through all the lists of names contained in the

Bordeaux and Bayonne civil registers was a "task that would require a lifetime."[37] And even if one could complete that task, a "detailed monograph" on the subject could not rely on "scattered examples" from one or two sources, but had to compare many different types of evidence systematically. For example, on the question of Sephardic Jewish wealth, it would be easy to "cite a long list of Marranos and Sephardic Jews who were active in the field of maritime insurance." But what would that prove? If we wanted to know how wealthy these Sephardic Jews were, other sources would have to show what percentage of Jews was active in that field and what percentage of Jewish capital was involved in the transactions.[38] Research, as he conceived it, was a herculean task of assembly, a frantic run from one town to another, one library to another, taking notes on different types of documents and using them to answer specific questions.

Other works similarly pointed toward important and original conclusions, but there too, he refused to draw them explicitly, and focused on the wealth of facts he had collected. It can make for frustrating reading, particularly for readers who, like Byrnes, fail to see the points implicit in the evidence presented. Szajkowski's 1959 book *Autonomy and Communal Jewish Debts during the French Revolution of 1789* is an extreme example. The study offers the first comprehensive view of the dissolution of the old Jewish communal institutions during and after the Revolution. Looking beyond the laws of emancipation themselves, the study uses pamphlets, the press, published speeches, and communal documents like budgets, loan contracts, and copies of legal briefs and petitions to the government. These documents were held in public archives all over France: in Arles, Altkirsch, Avignon, Bordeaux, Carpentras, Cavaillon, Colmar, L'Isle-sur-Sorgue, Metz, Montpellier, Paris, and Strasbourg. Many had never been tapped. Most historians of the emancipation had confined themselves to the official record of the National Assembly, and those few who had used the types of sources Szajkowski examined had limited their inquiry to local questions rather than comparing the situation of Jews across France. To Szajkowski, even Ilya Tcherikower's results had been limited by insufficient and at times even sloppy research, an opinion he worked hard never to share publically, out of loyalty. Only careful attention to the sources could produce truly accurate findings.[39]

Despite the lack of a central narrative in *Autonomy*, the study nonetheless cast Jewish emancipation in an entirely new light by focusing not on political debates but on the shifting financial arrangements between Jews and the authorities who governed them. The Old Regime Jewish communities, Szajkowski shows, were state-controlled bodies whose main purpose was to collect and deliver taxes to the authorities. In their quest to create greater legal uniformity, Revolutionaries dissolved those communities, and Jews expected that, like the members of other dissolved groups with legal privileges, such as municipalities and craft guilds, they would no longer be held responsible for the debts the communities had contracted before the Revolution. But this would not be the case. The debts remained the responsibility of successor institutions, which thus became a tool for state discrimination even after Jews had nominally obtained equal rights. The study has thus served to temper the way emancipation has been conceived for American scholars previously inclined to celebrate it.[40] It was also an important corrective to those Yiddish-language historians who believed that abandoning the "ghetto," mistakenly imagined as a truly autonomous space, had been the cause of Jews' woes in modern Europe.

Indeed, despite his rhetoric to the contrary, across his studies on Jewish modernization in France, Szajkowski was developing a structural explanation for the persistence of anti-Jewish bias in modern France without romanticizing the days of semi-autonomous communal life destroyed in the Revolution. Although he never articulated it explicitly, his studies pointed toward an argument that emancipation had been left incomplete, just as the Revolution itself had been left incomplete. In *Autonomy*, he approached the question as a legal historian; in his 1954 book *Agricultural Credit and Napoleon's Anti-Jewish Decrees*, he approached the issue from an economic angle. Here, he used Napoleonic-era mortgage registers to understand what had sparked the explosion of anti-Jewish sentiment in Alsace at the beginning of the nineteenth century, just a decade after emancipation. Historians already knew that Napoleon thought the claims against the Jews were justified, and he had responded with harsh, discriminatory legislation: His "Infamous Decree" of 1808 banned Jewish money-lending for a period of ten years. But Szajkowski was the first to investigate the financial crisis that had provoked the situation. He began by locating what remained of the mortgage registers for rural Alsace, and learned that for the peasantry, it had been nearly impossible to obtain mortgages. Often, the only lenders they could turn to were Jews, who were generally poor themselves, and charged high rates of interest to guarantee their return. In the Revolution, these conflicts had been exacerbated as the lands of émigrés were broken into smaller plots and put up for sale. Entrepreneurial peasants attempted to take advantage of the situation, but in the absence of a public credit system, they had to borrow at high rates from Jewish creditors, and resented them for it. The study suggests that the Revolutionaries' failure to make agricultural credit available to the peasants in eastern France led to heightened antisemitism in the aftermath of emancipation. It points to social and economic, rather than purely ideological, bases for modern antisemitism.

In spite of the rigor, originality, and sheer volume of his work, however, Szajkowski's career was limited by both his marginal position and his unwillingness to synthesize. As Jewish studies entered the university system in the 1960s, his lack of credentials mattered more than ever. Beyond a brief stint teaching a course on "Archival Sources of Modern Jewish History" at Brandeis in 1973–74 and some guest lectures in a pioneering class about the Holocaust at Hampshire College that same year, he never taught.[41]

As an author too, the recognition he received was less than he would have liked. By the late 1960s, others, some of whom he perceived as less well qualified, were succeeding when he could not. Filled with bitterness, he grew more entrenched than ever in his historiographical approach. When he read the *New York Times'* review of Arthur Hertzberg's book *The French Enlightenment and the Jews* (1968), it was with impatience and envy. Hertzberg had once been a good friend. In fact, when Hertzberg was working on his doctoral dissertation under Salo Baron at Columbia in the 1950s, they had even traveled in France together. But now, Szajkowski fumed at what Hertzberg had written and how well it was being received. On the basis of evidence that Szajkowski had also written about, Hertzberg had earned the *Times* review with the provocative thesis that "modern, secular anti-Semitism was fashioned not as a reaction to the Enlightenment and the Revolution, but in the Enlightenment and Revolution themselves."[42] The book, Szajkowski believed, was a total waste of time. He wrote of Hertzberg's sweeping thesis:

> Such undocumented statements naturally arouse misgivings about the reliability of other assertions, but they still make serious scholarship more difficult because the rebuttals are sometimes unavoidable and they take up much valuable time. The richness of available material makes it possible to describe even in detail an imaginary anti-Jewish revolutionary society, especially among the intelligentsia. This is what some authors have tried to do. One can always cite a casual anti-Jewish expression by Jean-Paul Marat or another Jacobin, but conveniently omit Robespierre's strong statement in favor of Jews. My own studies contain hundreds of examples of both pro-and anti-Jewish statements by Jacobins and other partisans of the Revolution.... the question is, what was the source of the ... anti-Jewish convictions? In my opinion, it was the entire Christian anti-Jewish tradition. Those who think otherwise, who want to discover a secular source, should prove it by more than a mere similarity between the arguments of Voltaire and the anti-Jewish elements in Alsace.[43]

In his own mind if not in print, Szajkowski had an alternate interpretation of the French Revolution and the Jews. Ignoring the significance of some of his own research, he remained a partisan of the Revolution, and blamed the forces of reaction for antisemitic outbreaks.

But instead of taking on Hertzberg's provocative claims directly with a sweeping study of his own, he responded by publishing *Jews and the French Revolutions of 1789, 1830, and 1848* with Ktav in 1970. Generally considered to be his masterwork, the thick, red volume of more than 1,200 pages actually contains only reprints of English-language work he had published previously in journals, together with excerpts from his self-published books from the 1950s, plus a new sixty-page introduction describing each of the articles. Except for new page numbers, the work was not re-typeset, which gives it a strange appearance, its different fonts being those used by the different journals in which the pieces were originally published. The books had to be excerpted to fit into the volume, but they were not re-typeset either. One (*Poverty and Social Welfare among French Jews, 1800–1880*) even begins in the middle of a sentence, for which no explanation is provided. By 1970, even though Szajkowski had certainly gathered together enough data to build an argument about why Jews never achieved the full equality promised to them in the Revolution that could rival Hertzberg's 1968 study, he maintained his devotion to the written remains of the Jewish past in Europe and the close analysis of their contents, over and against grand argument.

Among his final publications was a three-volume *Illustrated Sourcebook on the Holocaust*, published by Ktav in 1977. This was a set of oversized books that contained photocopied reproductions of photographs and documents from the Holocaust across Europe. The texts reproduced—laws, posters, pages from newspapers, and so forth—were not translated from their original languages and, except in the index, they were not attributed to the institutions that held them. Each of the images was only briefly identified in captions, without the kind of explanatory narrative that usually accompanies images in this kind of publication, marketed as a sort of coffee-table book rather than a scholarly tome. No narrative told the story of the Holocaust or explained why these images were selected. There is no analysis of any sort, only the display of the sources themselves, many of which had come from Szajkowski's personal collection. The bare facts are meant to speak for themselves, even though in 1977, the public was not knowledgeable enough about the Holocaust to understand what was being presented to them.

All historians, to one degree or another, write their histories conscious that their knowledge is partial, limited to interpreting whatever wreckage of the past remains accessible despite the ravages of time.[44] But Szajkowski, who had made it his personal mission to salvage as much documentation as he could from the rubble of Europe in the dark days following the Holocaust, was perhaps more aware of those limits than most. From personal experience, he had seen how the most recent destruction had scattered the sources of Jewish history. Was it for that reason that he always put the remains of the past, in all their partiality and state of decay, at center stage in his works?

Whatever its cause, Szajkowski's devotion to the sources as the keys to history made archives and libraries absolutely central to his work. Much of what he cited in his articles from the 1950s was found in regional archives and libraries across France. The research involved in making studies such as *Autonomy* or *Agricultural Credit* was grueling. Two of the footnotes in *Agricultural Credit* give a sense of what the agenda entailed in a given locality as he hunted for the mortgage registers from the Napoleonic period:

> ... For the Lower Rhine we found the mortgage registries of the *arrondissements* of Strasbourg, Saverne, and Wissembourg; for Sélestat we utilized the registries of fees for registration, but they too belong to a later period. For the Upper Rhine we found registries of Colmar and Belfort only—all of a later period. The mortgage archives are much more complete in the *départements* of Moselle, Meurthe and Vosges.... In Meuse the mortgage archives had been lost. Under the law, copies of mortgage registries were to be sent to a certain location for security. But in 1951 we could not locate them....
>
> In 1939 a number of mortgage registers were evacuated to Altkirsch, from there to Huningue, where the author saw them in a half decayed condition in the cellar of the law court. It was impossible to handle them in that state. They were mainly transcription registers from Mulhouse.[45]

The pace of the investigation must have been exciting for the former journalist. Perhaps it even reminded him of his time in Berlin, when, time permitting, he dashed off to the wrecked Nazi Propaganda Ministry. Certainly the type of work he was doing in the archives resembled his sifting through piles of papers in Berlin. In order to publish at the rate of eight articles a year, he must have gone into the archives and libraries with a bibliographer's eye, not driven by a specific historical question, but simply looking for anything and everything pertaining to Jews, only later to sort his findings into articles by topic.

Indeed, Szajkowski was as accomplished a bibliographer as he was a historian. He published four major bibliographies on the history of Jews in France. Two article-length studies, "The Emancipation of Jews during the French Revolution" (1959) and "Judaica-Napoleonica" (1956), focus on some of the periods of greatest interest to scholars of modern Jewish history. A book-length study entitled *Franco-Judaica* (1962) gives detailed summaries of books, pamphlets, documents, and manuscripts pertaining to the history of Jews in France and Switzerland from 1500 to 1788, organizing them by topic and providing their institutional locations. The complete list of those locations covers four full pages in the large-format book, and reflects his remarkable nose for finding exceedingly rare material in state archives, the holdings of private institutions, and even the collections of individuals (e.g., the printer I. Bernas, Paris; Mr. A. Aron, New York; Rabbi N. Netter, Metz; Rabbi M. Ginsburger; the bookseller A. Rosenthal, Oxford; and the historian S. Posener, among others) in Europe, Israel, and the United States.

A final bibliographic work pertaining to the Jews in France is Szajkowski's *Analytical Franco-Jewish Gazetteer, 1939–1945* (1966), a study that he worked on for almost twenty years. He initially tried to publish it in *Historia Judaica*, but when Guido Kisch moved to Switzerland in 1962 and his journal was absorbed into the French *Revue des Etudes Juives*, that became impossible, as the *Revue*'s editor, Georges Vajda, was not interested in publishing reference works.[46] But the resilient Szajkowski was never one to give up. Instead, he published his *Gazetteer* himself and received modest sums from a couple of Jewish foundations (the Lucius Littauer and the Gustav Wurzweiler foundations) to defray printing costs. The result is perhaps Szajkowski's most significant work. In this geographical dictionary, Szajkowski lists every document he could find about Jews in France in World War II, organizing them by the town (*commune*) mentioned in the document. As such, it includes data on camps, places that Jews lived legally and illegally, resistance activities, arrests, executions, property confiscation, emigration, and self-help activity. It is an impressive feat of scholarship. Insisting in the narrative first section of the work that it was too soon to write a comprehensive history of the Holocaust in France, he instead offered scholars the tools to begin their research.[47]

Despite his protests to the contrary, the *Gazetteer* advanced a set of important insights that have shaped the way scholars have come to think about the high rate of Jewish survival in France compared to other countries under Nazi occupation. First, Szajkowski pointed to the unusual double role of the UGIF, which functioned as both a tool of Nazi oppression and an agent of resistance. With his unparalleled access to the UGIF's papers in New York, Szajkowski had had plenty of opportunity to ponder the organization. Indeed, he had been developing this theory in a number of articles since as early as 1947, even as he continued to tell others, often in a rather bullying way, that it was too soon to do a truly objective study about the Holocaust.[48]

A second important point was implied in the very geographical organization of the *Gazetteer* itself. Astoundingly, Szajkowski found documentation on Jews in more than 6,000 places in France, or one-seventh of all the towns and villages in the country. Considering how concentrated the Jewish population had been before the war, with one-half of France's Jews living in the capital, this was extremely noteworthy. As Szajkowski himself put it, "There is no doubt that this wide dispersion of the Jews living in France in World War II—about 350,000 in all—saved the lives of many thousands of them."[49] In the introduction, Szajkowski advanced general ideas about how the Jews managed to disperse themselves with the help of Jewish organizations and non-Jewish helpers, as well as how this dispersion foiled the attempts of the German and Vichy authorities to find them. But the conception of the *Gazetteer* is bibliographic rather than monographic. Every piece of evidence is identified and located but not analyzed; still, future researchers could and would build on Szajkowski's intuitions.[50]

Szajkowski's bibliographic approach to historical questions thus meant that his research had to be as broad as it was deep. The hunt for diverse sets of sources brought him to unlikely places. Finding many of these sources must have involved using many of the talents he had developed as an investigative journalist. Forming relationships with archivists was essential in this regard, since they were in a privileged position to know what existed and where. Only by such sleuthing could he find sources that had moved so many times over the years or had never been properly archived in the first place. Some of this investigation was done on-site, but much was done in advance, by writing to the archivists from New York. He seems to have forged particularly friendly relations with Jewish archivists, such as Georges Weill, whom he first met in the Archives Départementales du Bas-Rhin in 1955, and Gilbert Cahen, whom he met in the Archives Départementales de la Moselle in the same period. Happy to have met such a competent researcher interested in topics that they cared about as well, Weill and Cahen responded to his inquiries with useful information.[51]

Some of Szajkowski's research on sources about the Holocaust era in France was also done via correspondence. In 1955, he wrote to the archivists in each of France's departmental archives asking for copies of the Jewish census that had been conducted in 1941, and was informed of the government policy that had ordered these destroyed shortly after the war. He nonetheless persevered, eventually finding a census that covered eighty-seven of France's ninety administrative départements at the Institut de la Statistique et des Etudes Economiques. It was with this method that he found many of the other sources listed in the *Analytical Franco-Jewish Gazetteer* as well.[52]

He could be quite crafty in these letters. In 1952, he wrote to the archives of the French Foreign Affairs Ministry asking for permission to see the file on the 1840 Damascus Affair, in which the Jews of Damascus, then part of the Ottoman Empire, were accused of ritual murder. Because the case involved a French consul who was likely at least partially responsible for bringing the antisemitic charges, the file had never before been made available to researchers. An unsigned note of December 17, 1952, that Jewish historian Tudor Parfitt later found in the file itself shows how Szajkowski worked to gain access to it:

> M. Szajkowski/Frydman has let us know that he was able to procure photocopies in Berlin made by the Germans between 1940 and 1944. He presents three of these photocopies but refuses to reveal their number, simply stating that he does not believe he has the whole dossier.
>
> He notes that the dossier presents the role of Ratti-Menton and the Government of Louis-Philippe in an unfavorable light. In the confidence that other documents would allow M. Szajkowski to correct his conclusion in the favor of France he requests permission to see the rest of the file.[53]

Szajkowski's request was apparently refused, but in a 1954 article, he mentions the German photocopy of the file, and claims to have over a thousand pages of it in his possession without citing from them at any length. If he exaggerated how many pages he had from the file, it was only by a little. A file of this sort containing photocopies of documents on the Damascus Affair from the French Foreign Ministry stamped

"Französisches Aussenministerium," with pages numbered from 44 to 722, can now be found in the archives of YIVO in New York.[54]

The research technique was unusual and even daring. But it should not surprise us. Szajkowski had once been hailed as a heroic rescuer of endangered Judaica in the extraordinary times of World War II. After times returned to normal, he felt as passionate as ever about the remnants of the Jewish past, and so he threw himself into achieving his dream of becoming a successful scholar, even when support proved difficult to find. His craft, as he conceived it, depended on locating and interpreting as full a range of sources as possible. To find them, he would use every technique he could dream up, even if it meant he had to deceive a few archivists in the process.

7

French Losses

SZAJKOWSKI SEEMED ODD, EVEN SUSPICIOUS, to some of the archivists who worked in the institutions he visited in France in the 1950s. In fact, he gave a number of them reason to wonder if he'd been stealing from their collections. A few even investigated the matter, and concluded that it was likely that he had. But it was only in the Strasbourg Municipal Archives in 1961 that archivists actually turned to the police when they caught him red-handed. Even there, they were slow to decide to press charges. What made the French archivists hold back, thus unwittingly facilitating an untold number of additional thefts?

Making sense of archivists' decisions requires understanding the underlying tensions that shape their relationships with patrons. When an archival source is cited in a historian's work, the citation refers not only to a document, but to a relationship formed with an archivist. For most of the specialists who break ground in a new field, that relationship must be solidified even before they can forge the "facts" of history with their tools of interpretation. In this sense, the archivist's trust—guided by institutional policies but subject to individual judgments—is the key that unlocks the door to certain types of research. Historians must earn it with their credentials or, in exceptional cases, with their specialized knowledge. Often a collegial friendship forms between the historian and the archivist, based on their shared mission to make knowledge of the past public. It was this shared mission that earned Szajkowski such friendly relations with Gilbert Cahen, Georges Weill, and surely many other archivists in France in the 1950s. But even a cursory examination of how Szajkowski accessed the rare documents he cited demonstrates that relationships between historians and archivists can also be fraught. This is particularly the case for the historian on the hunt for information deemed "secret" by the authorities, as Szajkowski was when he tried in vain to get access to the Damascus Affair documents from the French Foreign Ministry archives.

If historians sometimes chafe at the limits archivists impose on their access, the relationship can feel even more strained from the perspective of the archivists. In democratic nation-states, archivists must maintain the proper balance between providing access to the documents in their charge and protecting them for posterity. The archival profession developed in the nineteenth century in places like France's Ecole des Chartes, and its practices were shaped by the gradual transition to democracy in the nation-state it served. In a practical as well as symbolic sense, archivists guarantee the state's transparency and accountability by making state papers available to citizens.[1]

But at the same time, archives also serve another, much older function. As the keeper of the state's laws and its records, the archives symbolize the state's wholeness, its continuity through time, its authority, and its reach. In *Archive Fever*, Jacques Derrida points out that the very meaning of "archive" comes from the Greek term *arkheion*, which referred to the home of the *archon*, or ruler. This was not just a private residence but also the house where official documents of public importance were domiciled. It is the task of the sovereign, he explains, to unify, identify, classify, and consign to the archives the documents deemed important for public memory.[2]

Modern French archives came into being in the tumultuous aftermath of the French Revolution, the Napoleonic wars, and the revolutions of the nineteenth century. Their creators saw them as a way to stabilize state power in a society shaken time and again by political and social upheaval. With their façade of completeness and order, the archives stood for the integrity of the sovereign itself, because it was in their stacks that the very stuff of the state's operations—its paperwork—was preserved. In this sense, in modern nation-states and particularly in France, archives remain a monument to state power even as they have also become a guarantor of democracy.[3]

And yet even though they stand for the state's ability to surmount the forces of disorder, archives and their guardians can never truly overcome disorder in practice. Behind the scenes, archivists constantly contend with chaos. They confront not only the rare political disruptions like war and revolution, but also the mundane facts of life in the archives: misplaced documents, crumbling paper, humidity, rodents, coffee stains, sunlight, and, of course, theft.[4] Maintaining the appearance of order is usually important enough that except in unusual circumstances, professionals are loath to publicize the losses they inevitably sustain.

Such was particularly the case in French archives after World War II. Following liberation, French authorities worked hard to find what the Germans had looted from public and private archives and libraries. Even so, many items could not be found. Authorities learned only decades later that much of the booty had been seized by the conquering Soviet "trophy brigades" in Germany. Nevertheless, archives and libraries returned to normal conditions after the war ended, and that meant restoring the façade of order. Rather than surveying their losses systematically and publicizing them, French authorities in the 1950s put the war years behind them by repressing the memory of wartime looting. In many of the government archives that had been looted by the Nazis, archivists chose not to call attention to the missing papers in the inventories and finding aids they prepared for researchers, even when many of the items in the newly inventoried series were missing. The *Gazette des Archives*, the premier scholarly journal for archivists in France, did not publish a single article on Nazi looting of French archives until 1973. The looting of libraries was not publicly memorialized by French Jewish institutions either, although internally, librarians were forced to deal with its effects.[5]

The phenomenon of forgetting the more painful aspects of the 1940–44 period was not limited to archives, of course. Following Henry Rousso, historians call it the "Vichy Syndrome."[6] In 1950s France, returning to normal was premised on ignoring the past. Indeed, this was also the era in which many convicted collaborators were granted amnesty. French Jews were not silent about their wartime losses, but in their Holocaust commemorations, they stressed their belonging to the French polity rather than the distinctiveness of Jewish suffering. The interpretive move helped them to reintegrate into the nation, but it also entailed repressing certain memories.[7] But even more than in other areas of French life, the archives were prone to such forgetting. The looting in World War II may have been vast, but professional sensibilities remained unchanged. As with all losses, archivists sought to minimize their impact, and in the research tools they prepared for researchers, they stressed their institutions' wholeness rather than their incompleteness and victimization.

The efforts to restore order in France's institutions of memory created a new reality that, paradoxically, perpetuated the disorder. Missing catalogues, lost documents, and changes in staff left these institutions vulnerable to new thefts. Without a systematic accounting of wartime losses, staff and patrons could only speculate when they found that certain documents were not in their proper places. In spite of the reestablishment of normal conditions, the disorder and losses sustained in the extraordinary times of the war cast a long shadow on the French archives. Obscured in its darkness, a thief could sometimes be hard to detect.

Two cases in which Szajkowski was suspected of stealing illustrate the conditions that made it difficult for archivists to turn to the police when they suspected Szajkowski of theft. One was discovered in 1953, in the Archives Départementales du Bas-Rhin, the state archives for the Bas-Rhin département located in Strasbourg, its administrative seat (not to be confused with the Strasbourg Municipal Archives). A local rabbi, Max Warschawski, visited the archives to consult the papers of the region's Jewish historical society, the Société d'histoire des israé-lites d'Alsace et de Lorraine (SHIAL).[8] The group had been very active before the war, and in 1936, it had donated papers of great historical interest to the archives.

Until Warschawski's effort to revive it in 1953, the SHIAL had been inactive since 1940, when its members fled Strasbourg for the unoccupied Southern Zone of France, even though many returned after 1945. Warschawski learned when he tried to see its collection that many items were missing. Worse, a number of pages had been cut and removed from some of the collection's bound registers. A quick look at the readers' log revealed that the last person to consult the collection was "S. Frydmann" [sic], on January 17 and 18, 1949. No one else had seen the papers since before the war. The archives staff thus had good reason to believe that Frydman—that is, Szajkowski—was the culprit.[9]

The staff at the archives knew Szajkowski well. Lucien Metzger, the archives' director, was Jewish himself and respected Szajkowski as a "serious scholar." As such, he had authorized him to look in the archives' stacks, normally off limits to researchers, when using materials that had not been catalogued. This was how Szajkowski got access to the materials from the archives' Q series ("Domaines nationaux," or National Property) that he cited in his 1952 article "Jewish Participation in the Sale of National Property during the French Revolution." In the article, the citations lack call numbers for these documents because they did not yet exist.[10]

The losses from the SHIAL's collection made the archives' staff nervous. To contain the damage, Metzger closed the collection to researchers. But he did not publicize the losses. Today the only explanation given to researchers for the missing items appears on the typed inventory for the collection, created in 1936 when it arrived at the archives. A handwritten note, undated and unsigned, reads simply, "Numerous items were removed by the Gestapo and the German police during the occupation of 1940–44."

On the surface, the claim about German looting seems plausible enough. Strasbourg was annexed directly to the Reich in World War II, and the Gestapo had been a presence in the town. The Germans had taken books from a number of Alsatian public libraries and sent them to libraries elsewhere in Germany. Other Alsatian libraries, such as the Colmar Municipal Library, had been closed to the public for the entire period of the occupation; its collections appear to have survived intact, but no one seems to really know for certain. Control of the Strasbourg University Library, with its world-class collection, was hotly disputed. Its French librarians had brought the collection to Clermont-Ferrand for safekeeping when the university had moved there in 1939, and the armistice agreement had guaranteed that the collection would remain in French hands. Nevertheless, in early 1941, its librarians were forced to give in to German demands for its return to the occupied city.[11] Seeing Alsace as an integral part of Germany, Nazi officials sought to integrate the region's libraries into the German system, and this sometimes meant moving things from Alsace to other parts of Germany.

And yet, the claim that the Gestapo removed the items that are now missing from the SHIAL's collection at the Departmental Archives is as dubious as it is vague. Why would the German authorities have taken some items and not others? Why would they have cut pages from bound registers rather than seize the volumes completely?[12] Cutting is a technique used by thieves eager to evade the watchful eyes of authorities. That was not the Germans' style. Accounts of the German military authorities' confrontation with the Strasbourg University librarian in 1940 depict men intent on flexing their muscles by *demanding* that books be transferred to their control, not surreptitiously stealing them.[13] But for postwar archivists in Strasbourg's Departmental Archives, blaming the Nazis for the missing documents served to explain as well as contain the damage. They protected the collection from further losses by restricting access, and a known villain—the Nazis—got the blame. The strategy also allowed the staff to maintain the appearance of order. As for dealing with Szajkowski, they chose surveillance over confrontation. They never accused him directly, but they monitored him closely on future visits. Georges Weill, who began work in the archives in 1954, recalls accompanying the scholar into the stacks himself, "never letting him out of my sight."[14]

A second case in which Szajkowski was suspected of theft is equally illuminating. Here too, library staff chose discretion and surveillance over confrontation. In this instance, it was the library of the Alliance Israélite Universelle (AIU) in Paris—a private and Jewish collection—that was Szajkowski's victim. That library had lost its entire collection to Nazi looting in 1940. Although it appeared that almost everything had been returned from Germany, it was in fact difficult to be sure, since the card catalogues never reappeared. Library staff spent much of the 1950s rebuilding the catalogues, a project that took until 1960 to complete. The scholars who used the collections in the late 1940s and '50s needed the expert help of the staff for the simplest of tasks. The anonymity some thieves depend on was not possible under these circumstances. Librarians were intimately involved in every patron's research, and the reading room contained just eight seats around a single large table.[15]

And yet, here too, there is evidence that Szajkowski stole materials in late 1948 or early 1949. At that time, disorder reigned in the stacks. The library's books had just been returned from Germany, thanks to the tireless efforts of Jenny Delsaux of the French book restitution authority and the Judaica experts she had employed to find them in Offenbach. Putting things back in order was a task entrusted to an able librarian, Paul Klein (who changed his name to Moche Catane when he moved to Israel in 1949), who came to the library from the Bibliothèque Nationale in 1948.[16] In addition to putting its own returned books back in order, the AIU had also been charged with returning the 60,000 books still left on its shelves by the Germans, who had used the institution as the center of their book-looting operations in Paris. The job was formidable, but French authorities' decision to empower the AIU librarians to serve as restitution officers eventually proved fortuitous for the library. When they had returned all the books they had been able to identity, Delsaux allowed them to keep the 30,000 books that remained on the shelves, a decision that not only helped them rebuild their collections, but restored the legitimacy of France's premier Jewish library.[17]

Nevertheless, the work meant that in 1948, the stacks were still in a chaotic state. At some point, Klein noticed that two valuable items he knew had come back from Germany had disappeared. The first was an important reference work, Heinrich Gross's 1897 *Gallia Judaica*, a German gazetteer that lists all French places that appear in rabbinic sources. A second item had not originated in the AIU's collection, but had been returned there in error nonetheless: the German photocopy of the French Ministry of Foreign Affairs' dossier on the 1840 Damascus Affair that Szajkowski later claimed to have seen "in Berlin" and that can now be found in YIVO's archives in New York. Klein pointed the finger at Szajkowski at the time, but then wavered in his judgment, so he hesitated to take action.[18] Saadia Cherniak, the head of the American Friends of the Alliance Israélite Universelle in New York, met with Szajkowski to discuss the matter at the behest of Eugène Weill, the AIU's general secretary in Paris. Szajkowski denied involvement and promised to speak to Weill about it on his next trip to Paris.[19]

Before that meeting could take place, however, Cherniak obtained more damning evidence. He learned that Szajkowski had sold several books to the New York Public Library (NYPL) and that the Jewish Division's librarian, Joshua Bloch, believed these items had come from the AIU library. Cherniak verified that this was likely the case after seeing three of the items, which were AIU reports from 1865, 1866, and 1867. In addition, Szajkowski had sold other books and pamphlets to the library of the Jewish Theological Seminary (JTS). Finally, the American Jewish Historical Society had informed Cherniak that Szajkowski had submitted an article about the early history of the AIU for publication in its *Proceedings*; when asked by the editors what sources he had used for the article, Szajkowski had shown them "a whole series of documents" that they believed must have come from the AIU's own collection.[20]

At that point, AIU leaders agreed that the time had come to deal with Szajkowski, although its president, René Cassin, believed this was best handled without involving the authorities. The AIU librarian Edmond-Maurice Lévy agreed that they should do everything possible to avoid a scandal. He had years of experience working at the Bibliothèque Sainte-Geneviève, where a librarian had been caught stealing valuable materials in the 1920s, and he drew on that memory in advising Cassin and Weill. In his estimation, formal legal proceedings were of little use to libraries in such cases, and it was better to work directly with the acquiring libraries, assuming that they had purchased these materials in good faith.[21] An additional reason was left unsaid: How would it look for a Jewish institution like the AIU to accuse a Jewish scholar of theft and selling the stolen goods to another Jewish library? The occupation was over and the AIU's legitimacy had been restored, but its leaders remained as careful as ever to avoid negative publicity for the Jews.

The AIU then obtained a list of titles that JTS had purchased from Szajkowski, with prices. Lévy had hoped that JTS would be willing to sell the AIU the items in question for the price they had paid Szajkowski. The list that JTS produced, however, was vague and completely disorganized, containing more than a hundred items described only in the most general terms. The prices paid for each item varied, but most had cost less than ten dollars. The JTS librarians did allow Cherniak to inspect twenty volumes more carefully, and he described them for Weill and Lévy in greater detail, noting where, for example, ownership stamps had been rubbed off certain books. In France, Lévy used the list to confirm that those items originated on the shelves of the AIU library.[22] For Lévy, some guesswork must have been involved; the AIU had no catalogue at the time, and JTS had provided incomplete bibliographic information. All involved, it seems, were feigning the use of formal procedures when, in fact, disorder in both libraries made it impossible to know with any real certainty whether the items in question were in fact stolen by Szajkowski from the AIU.

Things did not go quite as well at the NYPL where, despite the efforts of the Jewish Division's librarians, it proved difficult to obtain copies of the invoices of the purchases made from Szajkowski. It is not clear if that matter was ever resolved.[23]

AIU leaders chose a risky path by not involving the police. Even if they had been able to get everything back by dealing directly with the New York libraries, it would have solved only part of the problem. If Szajkowski were a habitual thief, he might strike again, and one could not be sure what he still had in his possession. Weill was also gravely worried about retribution in print. Szajkowski was a serious historian who could inflict harm on the organization's reputation in America at a time when the balance of power in the Jewish world was shifting to New York. The loss of French Jewish influence globally played an important role in Weill's decision to handle the matter with discretion. Having been made aware that Szajkowski had already published an article in Yiddish that painted the organization in a negative light, Weill believed that further alienating the scholar seemed dangerous.[24] He felt he needed to make further inquiries among people closer to Szajkowski.

The inquiries did nothing to ease Weill's fears about Szajkowski's character. He began by calling in the Paris YIVO representative Gershon Epstein for a meeting. Given that in 1961, Epstein would tell the Strasbourg police inspectors that he had broken with Szajkowski in 1948, it is not surprising that Epstein did not vouch for Szajkowski's integrity when Weill spoke with him in June 1950. Afterward, Weill had Cherniak contact Max Weinreich to inquire confidentially about the scholar's "morality."[25] Less than a year had passed since Weinreich had offended Szajkowski by calling his collecting ethics into question. Even so, Weinreich said nothing to Cherniak about the qualms he may still have harbored about his wayward protégé's character, assuring him that he had no reason to doubt Szajkowski's integrity. He did, however, admit that Szajkowski had recently left YIVO's employ, which left Cherniak and Weill wondering what Weinreich really thought.[26]

After careful consideration, Weill decided to confront the scholar directly about the books he had sold to JTS and NYPL and called him in for a meeting in September 1950. Szajkowski seems to have initially feared coming in and reacted defensively:

> ... I really am "hiding" in Paris.... Do I need to tell you the reason? ... I give no one my address, except Mr. Schneersohn, because the Jewish Communists will surely pay any price to compromise me, by any means necessary. And I assure you that they tried, not long ago. Surely you know why....
>
> To me, the story of the Alliance's books is very clear, but to prove it, I first have to be in New York. It will be easy to prove it to you with a letter, but I want to avoid a scandal.[27]

Szajkowski denied guilt, but only indirectly, and refused to confront his accuser in person. Szajkowski also gave Weill irrelevant information about being persecuted by the Communists to explain his refusal to come in. True or not, such information was beside the point. Perhaps the thief was using misdirection to draw attention away from his thefts and rehabilitate his reputation with mysterious references to another drama in which he himself was a victim.[28] Whether Szajkowski really believed he had anything to fear from the Jewish Communists in 1950, or whether it was merely a ruse to avoid confrontation with the AIU, we may never know.[29]

For the next few years, Weill worked with Cherniak to contain the damage. Like Metzger and his staff in the Departmental Archives in Strasbourg, they treated Szajkowski himself delicately and with respect. From 1950 to 1960, Szajkowski published four separate studies about the organization in respected American Jewish scholarly journals. None had the harsh tone of the Yiddish article from 1950, although they were not the glowing institutional histories that the AIU had itself produced. Cherniak obtained, read, and summarized each one in letters to Weill, highlighting Szajkowski's perspective on the organization.[30] Finally, librarians continued to allow Szajkowski access to the library, but as in the Departmental Archives in Strasbourg, they watched him closely. And when, in 1963, they heard through the archivist Georges Weill of Szajkowski's conviction in Strasbourg, they were greatly relieved. It meant that the thief would never return to their library again.[31]

French archivists in private and public institutions felt it necessary to respond with discretion to Szajkowski's thefts. They worried that a public airing of their grievances against the American institutions that had purchased stolen documents could backfire and bring additional harm. American leadership in the worldwide Jewish community meant that American institutions—Jewish newspapers, academic journals, and especially funding organizations—were in a position to shape Jewish opinion, and it made AIU leaders cautious. Their concerns were not unwarranted. Since the end of World War II and up until the present day, American Jewish leaders have repeatedly expressed doubts about the viability of Jewish life in France, which French Jewish leaders have generally considered exaggerated.

At the same time, French archivists also sought to avoid the negative publicity that the story of a Jewish thief in French archives might generate. The issue was particularly thorny in Alsace, where Szajkowski had stolen papers from Strasbourg's Departmental Archives and perhaps elsewhere. Alsatians, like other Frenchmen, stressed resistance rather than collaboration in their memory of World War II, and the effort involved minimizing discussions about the fate of the Jews in the war years. To cast the past in this light was particularly difficult in this region, which had been German rather than French in those years. Yet it was crucial for Alsace's reintegration into France. In early 1953, just before Metzger discovered Szajkowski's thefts in the SHIAL papers, Alsace's recent history dominated French news. A Bordeaux court heard the case of the Alsatian soldiers who, as conscripts in a German Waffen SS tank division, had massacred the citizens of the French town of Oradour-sur-Glane in June 1944 in retaliation for partisan activity in the region. The court exonerated the men, holding that they had acted against their will. The verdict effectively reaffirmed the region's belonging to France.[32]

Establishing Alsace's resistance credentials left little room to reckon with the region's long history of antisemitism. In this context, Metzger and Warschawski chose to avoid provoking the negative press that apprehending a Jewish criminal was likely to generate. Indeed, as late as 1961, when Szajkowski's thefts in the Strasbourg Municipal Archives became the subject of police investigation, Jewish archivists like Georges Weill cringed, certain that even then, the publicity would feed the flames of antisemitism.[33]

The only strategies that seemed viable under these circumstances were behind-the-scenes negotiations for the return of the stolen materials, coupled with attentive supervision of Szajkowski when he entered any archives. One may wonder if Szajkowski's thefts also explain the otherwise puzzling case of yet another collection in Strasbourg: the papers of the Strasbourg Consistory, the regional synagogue administration established in 1808, whose rabbi, Max Warschawski, was the one who discovered that the SHIAL papers were missing at the Archives Départementales du Bas-Rhin. The Consistory's papers were not made available to researchers from the early 1950s to 2001. Szajkowski himself provided this explanation: "The archives [of the Consistory in Strasbourg] were destroyed during World War II; only the minutes for the 1850s were saved."[34] We now know this was false. Was he purposely misinformed because he was a known thief? In any case, researchers would have found the explanation given to Szajkowski believable; Nazi looting was well known, even though the specifics were hazy.

What is most certain, however, is that French Jewish archivists cared deeply that their documents remain in France. The history of the SHIAL itself reveals as much. The historical society had been founded in 1905, over three decades after Alsace and Lorraine had been ceded to Germany following France's defeat in the Franco-Prussian War. A year before its founding, the German Jewish archivist Ezechiel Zivier had come to the region from Berlin to collect historical documents for the newly founded central archives for German Jews, the Gesamtarchiv der deutschen Juden. His visit worried Moïse Ginsburger, a rabbi who later became librarian at the Strasbourg University Library, when the region and the institution reverted to French control after World War I. In order to protect the regional Jewish patrimony from being sent to Berlin and "lost forever," he founded the SHIAL, and initially kept the papers it collected from the region's Jews in Strasbourg's Musée Alsacien, a decidedly local institution. They remained there until 1936, long after Alsace had reverted to French control, when the papers were transferred to the better funded Departmental Archives, then directed by Metzger, with whom Ginsburger enjoyed warm relations. Although he himself was German-trained and Jewish, Ginsburger preferred to see the region's Jewish patrimony preserved in a local institution rather than moved to a distant Jewish archive in the German capital.[35]

French archivists in public and private institutions viewed their Jewish collections in relation to French and local history, rather than as a chapter in the history of a lost Jewish past, as Szajkowski would have it. They protected Jewish collections not by calling in the police, but by housing them in French institutions and limiting access to them, and even, when they considered it necessary, lying to researchers about their availability and blaming the losses on Nazi looting.

And yet the problems with the Jewish collections required that the French archivists take some action to create order out of the chaos that made the thefts possible in the first place. In 1962, a small group of French Jewish historians and archivists formed the Commission Française des Archives Juives. Their purpose was to locate, classify, and make available the records of the French Jewish past for research. The records that interested them could be found in state institutions, as well as Jewish communal institutions.[36] As archivist Gilbert Cahen remembers it, the impulse for forming the group came from André Chamson, the new director of the French National Archives system, a historian of French Protestants who made the classification of the records of all the French religious groups an important priority.[37] This was part of a more general trend in the field to make records of interest to social historians more widely available.

But in addition, according to Georges Weill, Szajkowski's thefts also weighed on the minds of the commission's founders.[38] News of the thefts served to highlight a fact they knew all too well: In many public archives, records relevant to the study of Jews in France were unavailable and at risk because they had not been organized or classified. In some of such places, they knew from their own experiences with him, Szajkowski had managed to talk his way into the back of the archives where those materials were kept, having convinced archivists of his professionalism. They now knew that this had provided him with opportunities to steal.[39]

The founders of the commission were especially concerned that Szajkowski might have stolen documents in the 1950s in Jewish communal institutions, and particularly in the Paris Consistory. Unlike the Strasbourg Consistory, the Paris Consistory's files held documentation on Jewish religious life far beyond the surrounding region. Since its establishment by Napoleon in 1808, the centralized network of French Jewish regional consistories had made Paris its headquarters. All the regional consistories answered to a Central Consistory, which in turn, served as an intermediary in communications with the French state. Although the Central Consistory and the Paris Consistory were separate institutions, their papers were held in the same place, in the back of the consistorial synagogue on Rue de la Victoire.

The founders of the French Jewish archives commission knew that the materials held by the Paris Consistory had never been organized into an archive or transferred to the state archives, and that it would have been entirely possible for someone like Szajkowski to talk his way into its collections and take what he wanted. Ironically, the safest of the Consistory's papers were the documents from the World War II years. Schneersohn and Szajkowski had tried in vain to acquire this material for the Centre de Documentation Juive Contemporaine in 1948, but the Consistory's documentarian, Maurice Moch, dodged their requests.[40] He himself was working on a history of the Consistory during the war, a project that would occupy him for decades, and he kept the material in his home for that purpose.[41] As Szajkowski knew full well, having complete access to the documentation facilitates the historian's painstaking work of analysis, particularly with delicate subjects like this one.

But beyond the wartime materials, the Consistory's collection in Paris remained at risk. Indeed, much of the material now held in American Jewish research libraries likely originated in the papers of the Paris Consistory and the Central Consistory, and the materials were almost certainly purchased from Szajkowski in the late 1950s and 1960s. However, because nothing was ever documented about these losses at the Consistory itself, we cannot be certain how exactly these materials came into Szajkowski's possession. Yet as the archivists and historians of the commission already knew, the material that came from the Paris Consistory building was particularly vulnerable. Focusing their efforts on this institution from the very start, they began to catalogue its collections in the mid-1960s, after which time historians would have much better access to its holdings.[42]

In their work to bring to light the sources for the history of French Jews, the Commission Française des Archives Juives did not remove the material from the institutions that already housed it. Unlike the New York Jewish intellectuals who had brought European Jewish archives to new homes after World War II, these French historians and archivists were committed to protecting the traces of Jewish history in place. One exception to this general policy was historian Pierre Nora's mission, in April 1962, to Algeria. Commission leaders hoped Nora would recuperate the papers of the Algerian Jewish consistories left behind when entire communities of Algerian Jews fled to France in the concluding months of the Algerian war. But Nora was too late. Unable to find papers anywhere, he returned home empty-handed.[43]

Rather than building an archive of its own, the commission focused its modest resources on a massive bibliographic project beginning in 1972, under the direction of Bernhard Blumenkranz, to be known as the *Nouvelle Gallia Judaica*, after Heinrich Gross's 1897 gazetteer. Like Szajkowski—who was suspected of stealing the AIU's copy of Gross's *Gallia Judaica* in 1948—Blumenkranz admired the reference work and saw it as a model for a larger project, the *Nouvelle Gallia Judaica*, that would list every source in French archives that mentions Jews. They also completed a set of important bibliographies and geographical diction-aries about Jews in France.[44] Much like its cataloguing projects, the bibliographic projects speak to the faith the founders of the commis-sion had, and still have, in a future for Jews and for Jewish studies in France.

And yet, that future was not unthreatened, as their careful handling of Szajkowski showed. For French Jewish archivists, Szajkowski was a menacing figure, a historian who collected facts by stealing rare mate-rials from their collections. He had preyed on the chaos that Nazi looting had created in the AIU library and that neglect had created in the Paris Consistory, further victimizing a French Jewish community struggling to rebuild itself after the war. That community had been victimized primarily by the Germans, but now the rise of American Jewish power was also a problem in certain ways, making French Jewish leaders cautious about how to approach the issue of getting their stolen documents back from the libraries that had purchased them. Rather than involving public authorities, they had counted on the solidarity of Jewish librarians to return what had been stolen. As it turned out, there too, their trust was misplaced.

8

The Buyers

THE LEADERS OF THE ALLIANCE Israélite Universelle knew that Szajkowski had sold books and papers stolen from their collection to Jewish research libraries in New York as early as 1950. To get their books back, they had chosen the best strategy they knew: to confront the librarians directly and buy the purloined books and papers back. It cost money but it kept the matter quiet and, most important, it seemed that it would do the job of restoring their collection's wholeness. The strategy might have worked with a less dedicated thief, or with librarians more interested in questions of provenance. But these librarians did not investigate such questions, and Szajkowski knew it. Fortified with that knowledge, Szajkowski continued stealing rare materials from institutions around France until 1961, when he was caught red-handed in Strasbourg's city archives. His sales to libraries continued until his death in 1978. This was not a question of a few stolen books here and there. On the contrary, over the course of several decades, Szajkowski sold hundreds of thousands of pages of rare documents and a substantial number of published books and periodicals directly to a number of different research libraries specializing in Judaica.

It is hard to pinpoint exactly how many archival documents Szajkowski sold to libraries or when, because acquisitions records are scant. Inventories of collections at Brandeis University, Yeshiva

University, Hebrew Union College (HUC),[1] and the Jewish Theological
Seminary (JTS) indicate that these institutions purchased materials
from Szajkowski. HUC and JTS bought the largest sets. Both institutions made several purchases over time, but according to the inventories, the largest ones took place in the late 1950s and early '60s. JTS's
"French Jewish Communities Records Group" contains 11.2 cubic feet
of material housed in twenty-eight boxes, more than ten thousand
documents in all. The library probably purchased some of its related
collections from Szajkowski as well.[2] HUC first bought a large set of
materials from Szajkowski in 1955 or 1956; altogether, its collections
contain nearly ten thousand documents.[3]

Szajkowski also sold smaller collections to a few additional libraries.
Yeshiva University made its purchases in the late 1950s and early '60s.
Its "French Consistorial Collection" comprises five boxes of material
that came from the Paris and Central Consistories.[4] In the late 1950s,
the American Jewish Archives in Cincinnati purchased a small amount
of material, including documents pertaining to the Alliance Israélite
Universelle's work in the United States.[5] The Brandeis University library
reported in 1971 that it had acquired a collection of French Judaica,
though the exact date of the acquisition is unknown. The collection
contains 2,500 documents in seven boxes.[6] The materials are as diverse
in origin as in the HUC and JTS collections. The Central Archives
for the History of the Jewish People in Jerusalem also bought materials from Szajkowski over a period of many years, beginning in 1954.
It is likely that a number of other institutions also bought materials
from Szajkowski, but lack of documentation makes it hard to know for
certain.

In general, little remains by way of acquisition records from these
decades in any of these institutions. As a result, verifying information
about the origin of collections or pinpointing the dates and prices of
the purchases is all but impossible. The problem is a serious impedi-
ment for tracing the full extent of Szajkowski's crimes. At HUC, for
example, the French Miscellanea collection is comprised of about 1,000
items acquired at "various times from various sources," according to the
inventory prepared in 1979 by Jonathan Rodgers.[7] Although HUC's
librarian Herbert Zafren prepared annual reports that announced major
acquisitions, he rarely mentioned the sellers. So even though his 1956

annual report does announce obtaining a large collection on Jews in France from a single person, we do not know who that person was.[8] As such it has proved impossible to confirm information provided in the HUC collections' inventories that indicate the materials were purchased from Szajkowski from 1958 to 1960.[9]

The same problem makes it difficult to verify Roger Kohn's statement in the inventory for the JTS French Jewish Communities Record Group that "the collection was acquired by [JTS] from Szajko Frydman—a.k.a. Zosa Szajkowski—at an unknown date, probably during the late 1950s or early '60s."[10] Support for Kohn's claim can be found in what remains of the correspondence of librarians Nahum Sarna and Menahem Schmelzer with JTS alumnus Arthur Hertzberg from the early 1960s. Over a period of years, Hertzberg arranged for a philanthropist he knew to purchase materials from Szajkowski and donate them to the library. (The same correspondence also documents Hertzberg's unsuccessful efforts to find funds so that the library could hire Szajkowski as a librarian.[11]) Nevertheless, we cannot be exactly sure what JTS purchased from Szajkowski since the letters do not list particular items or sale prices.[12]

In all likelihood, detailed and accurate purchase records were never created in the first place in those years. According to an *Archives Manual* produced for JTS's internal use in 1978, information regarding provenance was often not recorded at all. Indeed, the *Manual* cites the library's "French Consistoire Central collection" (now the French Jewish Communities Record Group) as exemplary of the library's problem of inadequate recordkeeping. Even in the library's accession book, this collection's acquisition was described simply as "Napoleonic documents re Jews France 19th century. Printed and ms. Source—none."[13] Traces of the documents' dealer, much less a full description of the contents, cannot be found in the acquisition records.

In spite of the lack of acquisition records in both libraries, an examination of the materials themselves is sufficient to confirm that it was indeed Szajkowski who sold the JTS and HUC libraries these documents. At HUC, a small number of documents in the French collections are marked with Szajkowski's distinctive handwriting. The notes were the kind of thing you might expect a historian to write on *copies* of documents he made for his research, as a way to organize and analyze the evidence. On some pages, red or blue number stamps mark the documents according to a classification system in which an Arabic numeral is followed by a Roman one (e.g., 23-V)—a system that has nothing to do with how any of these libraries arranged their collections. Elsewhere, doodles in the same colored pencils are visible along the sides of the pages. On other documents, calculations in red, blue, or black pencil can be found, for example, on a communal tax roll produced in Metz in 1814, now held by the Central Archives for the History of the Jewish People in Jerusalem.[14] A final marking, visible on a few documents in these collections, links them to their dealer even more indisputably. This is the Yiddish name stamp "Z. Shaykovsky," a testament to the fact that the document was once the historian's personal property, but with no indication of where or how he had obtained it.[15]

In addition to these markings, some materials in these collections have been cut in various ways. To take but one example: At JTS, a 1790 bilingual excerpt from the deliberations of the Municipal Council of the city of Strasbourg is marked "XVI-126" in Szajkowski's handwriting. A rectangular piece is cut from the upper-right corner of the document, as if by a scissors. It is a neat cut, indicating deliberate removal, rather than decomposition.[16] The placement of the missing section on the page suggests the reason for the cut: This is precisely where institutions often stamped their documents to signify ownership.

Szajkowski transformed these documents not only by writing on them and cutting them, but also by rearranging them. Because he never described his personal classification system anywhere, we cannot be certain of his principle of organization. But we can be sure that he did not follow the principle of *respect des fonds* or one of its key elements, provenance. Since these principles were first elaborated in mid-nineteenth-century France, archivists around the world have come to embrace them as a guide in their work of classification, seeing them as a way to preserve the logic of the production of the documents and thereby help historians make sense of them. In compliance with these principles, archivists group documents together according to the body (institution, organization, family, or individual) that produced them and brought them to the archives. They also preserve the original order of the documents devised by the creators.[17]

As an archivist himself, Szajkowski was quite familiar with the principle of *respect des fonds*. Indeed, he used the principle to guide his work when he classified collections at YIVO, including the papers of the UGIF, the controversial French Jewish wartime umbrella organization. But he employed an entirely different schema with the papers he numbered and sold to other libraries. Those documents were grouped loosely by the subject they treated rather than the body that produced them. The JTS library still has the thirty-two-page description of the contents of what now comprise boxes 19 and 20 of the French Jewish Communities Record Group that Szajkowski prepared and gave them at the time of the sale. The documents all concern the same topic: "the conflicts between orthodox and reform, and on the separation between the church and the state (1905–1906)." This is an organization by research topic, not provenance.[18]

But Szajkowski's reorganization was but the first of two that these materials underwent in their journey from one collection to another. At some point after they acquired them, both HUC and JTS reordered the collections they had received. Working independently of one another, they came up against the same frustrating problems in arranging the documents. Keeping to the basic principle of provenance, JTS librarians attempted to keep the materials together whenever possible. But of course, the source for these collections was Szajkowski himself rather than the bodies that had produced the documents. Within the collections, the librarians recognized that the documents were arranged, somewhat artificially, by topic. Here, then, they broke with the principle of provenance and regrouped the documents in an attempt to restore order on the basis of well-known conventions in their field. They arranged some of the materials alphabetically by place name, although this was not done systematically, and much of the collection is still loosely grouped by topic.[19]

At HUC, librarians rearranged the documents sometime in the late 1970s. Here too, librarians attempted to respect the principle of provenance by keeping the materials from Szajkowski together, but they were frustrated that the grouping did nothing to reflect the institutional origins of the papers. They chose to deal with the problem by regrouping the papers into five separate collections: "Sephardic Jews of France," "Alsace-Lorraine," "Consistoire," "French Miscellanea," and the "Alsatian Jewish Inventories," which they named to reflect where they supposed the documents had originated. However, it proved impossible to know with certainty what bodies produced the documents, so like the librarians at JTS, they eventually retained certain aspects of Szajkowski's topical organization as well.

The result is a confusing hybrid schema. For example, HUC's "Alsace-Lorraine Collection" contains material on Jewish communal debts not only from Alsace-Lorraine, but also from the former Papal States of southeastern France. This is because when Szajkowski sold HUC these materials, they had all been grouped together for his study *Autonomy and Communal Jewish Debts* (1959), and it proved impossible to fully reorganize them according to the bodies that produced them. As a result, the documents about the Papal Jews are hidden within a collection the name of which does not reflect their origin. Although the librarians tried to facilitate the task of making sense of the documents in each collection by taking Szajkowski's topical organization and renaming it in the spirit of *respect des fonds*, in fact their work has had the opposite effect by further obscuring the logic of their creators.

HUC's Alsatian Jewish Inventories collection further illustrates the ramifications of the problem. This is a group of lists of household belongings, produced in the eighteenth and early nineteenth centuries, handwritten primarily in Ashkenazi cursive Hebrew and Western Yiddish, with a few items in German and French. They are the type of documents that the Société d'histoire des israélites d'Alsace et de Lorraine (SHIAL) had collected in the early twentieth century, and it is reasonable to assume that they might once have been found in their papers at the Archives Départementales du Bas-Rhin in Strasbourg, where Szajkowski was suspected of stealing in January 1949. The collection at HUC is composed of one hundred full lists and fifty fragments, and all the inventories were in a state of decomposition when they were processed.

Librarians had quite a difficult time putting the materials in order, and left them unprocessed for twenty years. On the inventory he produced in 1979, Jonathan Rodgers noted that "when [the materials] were unpacked, no order was discernible. Consequently, the collection was put into chronological sequence" and that "fragmentary inventories and supporting documents isolated from their respective inventories were also found throughout the collection. If it proved impossible to reintegrate them, they were placed at the beginning of the collection."[20] We cannot know if Szajkowski alone was responsible for the disorder, but Rodgers makes it clear how challenging it was, and still is, to make sense of these rare papers, given the state in which they arrived.

But Szajkowski himself felt no such confusion about the Alsatian Jewish inventories. He even authored a short study describing the collection, which appeared in print in a HUC journal right after he sold the documents to the library. In the article, he noted that the household inventories would be of great interest to anyone wishing to study the legal or economic history of the Jews of eastern France, since they show that Alsatian Jews were often indebted to Christian creditors when they died. This is an important piece of evidence for historians seeking to look beyond the inflammatory rhetoric about Alsatian Jews in the era of the French Revolution. Although Alsatian antisemites wrote only of poor Christian debtors driven to ruin by rapacious Jewish creditors who preyed on their need, these inventories reveal that the situation was often reversed.[21]

Yet Szajkowski's article tells us nothing about where he found the collection. Perhaps he feared blowing his cover, or perhaps he simply did not think it mattered. Even the collection's inventory, produced decades later, tells us only that these rare materials were purchased from Szajkowski in 1958 (around the time he completed his final study on the economic history of the Jews of eastern France). In his inventory, Jonathan Rodgers made the note in keeping with the principle of provenance.[22] But Szajkowski was only the intermediary. The new arrangement leaves unanswered the questions of who produced these documents, who first gathered them together, and why. Historians of Alsatian Jewry would certainly want to know the answers to these questions. They might tell us something about what Jews owned, how they transferred property, and what authorities were involved in those transactions. In state archives, and even in the private archives of the Jewish consistories in France today, materials are assigned their place according to the authority that collected them. As such, answers to these questions are clear. But in this case, the chain of theft and purchase has removed these rare materials from their sources. In the process, it has become more difficult to identify them and understand what they represent.

On the other hand, in spite of these difficulties, it was only because HUC acquired these documents that they were available at all to historians in the second half of the twentieth century. Five years before HUC acquired them in 1958, archivist Lucien Metzger had limited historians' access to the SHIAL papers in Strasbourg to protect the collection from further losses. In this sense, Szajkowski's sales to HUC mitigated the problem of access that his thefts had created.

Of course, Szajkowski probably had no intention of selling these documents when he first stole them from French archives, libraries, and synagogues. Much like cutting documents, writing on them greatly diminished their resale value. Arranging papers by topic was primarily useful in the writing process. The date of the sales is another important clue in this regard. The material Szajkowski used for *Autonomy and Communal Jewish Debts* was sold to HUC in 1958, just before the study was published.[23] The motive for the thefts was not the same as the motive for the sales, at least in this case. In a world before photocopies, let alone digital photography, this foreign scholar was stealing documents to make his research trips more efficient. Then, like a student selling back books at the end of the semester, once he finished the study for which he needed the documents, he turned around and sold them.

It is difficult to fully reconstruct the economy of Szajkowski's illegal document trafficking since so few traces of the sales remain. But we can glean enough to appreciate its financial significance for Szajkowski. The $3,400 he earned in 1961, when he sold stolen documents to the Oxford book dealer Albi Rosenthal, was not what a bank robber might rake in, but it was a substantial sum for a New Yorker living a modest lower-middle-class existence. In Szajkowski's case, it would have covered about three and a half years' worth of rent. His direct sales to American libraries yielded profits in the same range. In 1959, for example, Szajkowski sold three documents from the Alliance Israélite Universelle to the American Jewish Archives for fifteen dollars.[24] A 1957 sale of a run of the Alliance Israélite Universelle's *Bulletin* to Yeshiva University librarian Jacob Dienstag brought in $200.[25] In 1954, Israel Halperin bought a collection of newspaper clippings related to the Dreyfus Affair from Szajkowski for the Israeli Historical Society for $1,257.[26] In 1967, Szajkowski offered Frances Malino, then working on a dissertation at Brandeis, two microfilm reels of rare sources for her research on the

Sephardic Jews of Bordeaux for $200.[27] Szajkowski may have purchased rather than stolen some of what he sold, so there may have been costs involved. Even so, the sums he was paid were not negligible.

The money represented a much needed supplement to the scholar's income in the 1950s and '60s. His salary from YIVO was never quite enough to keep financial insecurity at bay, and he tried on several occasions to find employment in Jewish libraries and archives elsewhere, with no luck.[28] According to his IRS W-2 forms (only two of which are preserved in his papers at YIVO), he earned $5,488.56 in 1967 and $5,763 in 1968, worth about $38,700 in 2015 dollars. This was well above the poverty line, which in 1968 was set at $2,817 for a family of three with a male head of household, but also decidedly below New York City's average yearly household income of $7,918. Supporting a family on this income was by no means out of the question, and most people at this income level led honorable lives.

Nevertheless, it was not a salary that enabled Szajkowski to lead the comfortable, financially secure life of an educated, middle-class American. In the 1960s, Szajkowski shared a 700-square-foot one-bedroom apartment in a large building near Columbia University in Manhattan with his wife Chana and their son Isaac, born in 1956. Rents for apartments like heirs ran about $78 a month at that time, which was affordable on his YIVO salary.[29] But to live as Szajkowski might have aspired to—to get a larger apartment, to send his son to a private school or private college, to move to a safer neighborhood, to save for retirement, or to support his wife's desire to take college classes—would have put a strain on the family's finances. He and Chana separated for a number of years in the mid-1960s, which likely added to his expenses.[30] Szajkowski's friends in the 1970s remember him living very frugally, his modest lifestyle a testament to the difficulty of supporting a family of three as a scholar based outside the university system with no access to other resources.[31]

These continual financial struggles represented a psychological strain as well. Szajkowski's life had not turned out as he had hoped, and the disappointment was difficult to bear. He had come of age in the interwar years, the heyday of diaspora nationalism. Although Yiddish-speaking Jews had fought bitterly over political questions in those years, they nevertheless agreed that the Jewish world needed an elite class of intellectuals—journalists, literary writers, scholars, artists—much as other nations and aspiring nations did. As such, diaspora nationalism provided a new form of social mobility for poor Jews like Szajkowski. In the 1930s, he had poured his very soul into the effort to become a writer and a scholar. In those difficult years, the Jewish world seemed to promise that those who served their people in this way would also be able to make a respectable living. Never had these priorities seemed clearer to Szajkowski than during World War II when writers, scholars, and artists were treated as the Jews most worthy of the few coveted visas being issued in Marseilles in 1940 and 1941.

But diaspora nationalism had no place in the postwar Jewish world. Particularly in America, Jews no longer saw themselves as a nation that, scattered though it was, had its own intelligentsia to support. The Yiddish writers who survived the Holocaust found their opportunities greatly diminished, and those who, like Szajkowski, continued to pursue their dreams had to adapt to new circumstances. They published in new languages, supplemented their income with other work, and competed bitterly for scarce resources as their audience shrank. Like the Yiddish writers in Cynthia Ozick's 1969 story "Envy; or, Yiddish in America," Szajkowski lived in a world where alienation, competition, and mutual resentment reigned.[32]

Szajkowski was deeply embittered by the change. Gone was the sense of camaraderie and support he had found at the Tcherikowers' apartment in Paris in the 1930s. Still believing that scholarship was the cornerstone of a flourishing Jewish culture, the historian bemoaned this lost support in a 1954 publication.[33] The position was not purely theoretical: He had staked his future on that support and was insulted personally by the shift. The fact that the Jewish institutions with resources in the postwar world had closed this door to social mobility was as painful as any setback he had experienced in his life, and resentment reshaped his personality. By the late 1960s, he would write to Frances Malino that the reason his "friend" selling the microfilm could not be flexible about the high price he was demanding for its sale ($200) was that "he did spent [sic] a lot of time and money and could not do anything with the material because he could not obtain any help and instead of a historian he became a good [sic] manager of a large store."[34] The friend may have been invented, but Szajkowski's fiction spoke volumes about his self-perception. Szajkowski, the document dealer, justified his illegal commerce in his own mind by blaming the Jewish world for not having seen fit to support him as a scholar. Historian Richard I. Cohen put it best in his moving obituary when he explained that Szajkowski "felt that the Jewish world abandoned him on the wayside, without the means to support his life with dignity."[35]

Disillusioned with Jewish institutions in a general sense, Szajkowski had little compunction about deceiving them and even implicating them in his crimes if it provided the means to support his scholarship. Besides, he could see with his own eyes that there was money to be made from peddling rare Judaica. In the 1950s, the American market for the stuff was clearly on the rise. Albi Rosenthal, the Oxford dealer who unwittingly bought Szajkowski's stolen goods in 1961, was doing a booming business in Judaica in that era. Most of his acquisitions were from European collectors, and many of the buyers were American research libraries, then experiencing a period of remarkable growth.[36] With Szajkowski's inside knowledge of the business and his entrepreneurial spirit, the opportunities were obvious. Why not eliminate the middleman and go straight to the buyers?

The growth of the market for rare Judaica in the United States and Israel in the 1950s was fueled by a mythology of rescue that had taken shape during and just after World War II. This mythology was especially important in the particular institutions to which Szajkowski sold the largest collections. JTS and HUC were dedicated to training the next generation of America's rabbinate, and their leaders saw great libraries as the foundation upon which a learned elite could be trained. These librarians were guided by the same mentality that had shaped the work of Salo Baron and Hannah Arendt with Jewish Cultural Reconstruction, the organization that distributed the heirless cultural property found in postwar Germany. Knowing what they did about the destruction of European Jewish libraries and institutions of learning during the Holocaust, Jewish Cultural Reconstruction's directors saw themselves as saving their people's lost and scattered remnants from the vast graveyard of Europe and believed it a sacred task to salvage everything possible for the new centers of Jewish population and culture.

For the librarians who purchased materials directly from Szajkowski, the mythology of wartime rescue gave meaning to a far-reaching and aggressive program of acquisitions. Herbert Zafren at HUC and Nahum Sarna and Menahem Schmelzer at JTS saw their respective missions as building world-class institutions with unparalleled collections of historical documents useful to scholars in Jewish history. The offerings from Szajkowski represented a rare opportunity to acquire useful materials. Schmelzer, who had worked as Sarna's assistant in his first few years on the job, never asked Szajkowski directly where the materials came from, but he recalled hearing that the historian had brought "truckloads" of materials back from Europe after the war. Like Sarna before him, Schmelzer understood these materials to be part of the larger orphaned European Jewish heritage for which JTS, as a major Jewish research institution with solid resources, bore a special responsibility.[37]

A similar sense of mission informed the purchases at the Brandeis library. When he purchased materials from Szajkowski, Victor Berch was new to the job as special collections librarian, without professional training in library science. Nahum Sarna, who had recently become chair of the university's department of Near Eastern and Judaic studies, had recommended Szajkowski, and Berch took his recommendation seriously. He was also moved when Szajkowski told him that the materials had been "liberated from boxcars" he had found when he was in the U.S. Army during World War II. Berch had heard similar stories in the past and, like Schmelzer at JTS, was happy to get such rare materials for the library of his institution, a new university with world-class ambitions.[38]

Indeed, libraries had long been central to the identities of American Jewish research institutions. Even before the Holocaust, American Jews had begun to invest in Judaica libraries, archives, and historical societies as a way to affirm their belonging to a country that deeply valued such institutions. These collections were constructed in such a way as to defend Jews' patriotism and their Americanness.[39] At HUC, the library's expansion began in the aftermath of World War I, when librarian Adolph Oko saw how devastated Eastern European Jewish institutions had been in the war, and seized the opportunity to build the library by acquiring books from Europe.[40] The college was in a period of growth and Oko managed to raise $250,000 to build a new library building, a project completed in 1931.[41] Finding it possible to do substantial fundraising among American Jews for libraries, Oko also expanded the library's collections, and purchased manuscripts and rare books from the beleaguered communities of Eastern Europe, including the collection of Cantor Eduard Birnbaum of Königsberg.[42] Herbert Zafren's post-World War II program to expand the library collections was but a continuation of this earlier initiative.

The expansion of the JTS library also predated World War II. Since Alexander Marx's arrival in 1903, JTS had competed with the great European centers of learning by creating the world's largest Judaica library housed within a Jewish institution. For the seminary's leaders, building what supporter Mayer Sulzberger called a "national museum of the book" would demonstrate that American Jewry had finally come of age.[43] The quest to bring together as many Jewish books as possible in a single place was important enough to warrant sacralization. Bibliophile Harry Rabinowicz used the terminology of redemption when he marveled at the fact that on more than one occasion, the JTS library had been able to "reunite" previously separated parts of rare manuscripts. He called the phenomenon an "ingathering of the manuscripts," borrowing a concept from Jewish liturgy (*kibbutz galuyyot* or "ingathering of the exiles") in order to sanctify the library's acquisitions program.[44] His implication is clear. Centralizing the scattered fragments of the Jewish past was tantamount to reassembling the scattered Jewish people, restoring their coherence and wholeness. Like the official archives of modern nation-states, the modern Jewish library, even in America, was conceived of as a reflection of the people it sought to serve and represent. JTS library's mission was strengthened after the Holocaust under Chancellor Louis Finkelstein, but as at HUC, this was simply an expansion of a long-established program.[45]

It was this shared mission at JTS and HUC that helped both to become major beneficiaries of the heirless cultural property that Jewish Cultural Reconstruction distributed from 1949 to 1952. It was also out of this sense of mission that the libraries acquired many other rare books and manuscripts in more piecemeal fashion in the aftermath of the war from Judaica dealers and from individuals, including soldiers who had returned from Europe with Jewish cultural treasures. In a few cases at JTS, the library returned items to their owners upon learning that they had been acquired illegally.[46] These included at least some of the materials that JTS purchased from Szajkowski in 1950.

If building great libraries was understood to be an essential part of leading world Jewry after the Holocaust, the librarians themselves were well aware that the task before them was formidable. Nahum Sarna, JTS's chief librarian from 1957 to 1963, saw the pressures as impossible. On the one hand, the library was to keep up the breathless pace of acquisitions initiated by the indefatigable bibliographer Alexander Marx. On the other hand, library budgets were constrained, so that purchases threatened all the other library services.[47] In his article, "Building a Great Judaica Library—at What Price?" Sarna's successor Schmelzer wrote about these problems, laying out in detail the fundamental contradiction that plagued the library from the Marx era until his own day. The "one-sided, sometimes obsessive orientation toward expansion and acquisition" created an imbalance in library resources, resulting in poor classification, cataloguing, preservation, and accessibility.[48] One of the effects was ultimately quite tragic. Inadequate storage facilities for the collections—part of what Sarna in a moment of great anger and grief called "years of deliberate and criminal neglect"— contributed to the devastating effects of the fire of 1966 that destroyed or damaged 170,000 books housed in JTS's library. These included many irreplaceable items, among them the Torah scrolls that the Jewish community of Danzig had sent to JTS in 1938 for safekeeping when that city was taken over by the Nazis.[49]

The pressures facing librarians at the JTS library were immense. Fundamentally, they stemmed from the ambiguity lurking within the institution's very mission to replace the destroyed European centers of Jewish learning through aggressive acquisitions that far outpaced their ability to care for the materials they had acquired. Understanding their mission within a framework of "rescue" had paradoxically endangered the very materials it sought to preserve. The desire to centralize and protect the remnants of the Jewish past had not in fact been accomplished, in spite of the best intentions.

The situation was not unique to JTS and HUC. Even at YIVO, the library's expansion in the 1930s and '40s far outpaced its ability to catalogue and even store the materials. To get more space, the institute had to move several times in the years before, during, and after World War II, moves that Rabinowicz describes as a quest for "*lebensraum.*"[50] If the term seems ill-chosen, it nonetheless captures a certain aspect of the life of American Jewish research libraries in the mid-twentieth century. The directors of the most prestigious Jewish research libraries sought to acquire everything possible from the imperiled European Jewish communities, both as a rescue effort and in keeping with an older trend that might, in accordance with Rabinowicz's indelicate metaphor, be deemed imperial. Expansion for the sake of prestige, carried out in competition with other Judaica libraries, spurred the growth of these institutions just as much as the mission to save Jewish books from the forces of destruction in Europe.

Israeli institutions were guided by these same twin principles as they built up their own libraries and archives in the 1950s. The Central Archives for the History of the Jewish People (CAHJP) was founded in Jerusalem in the late 1930s as the Jewish Historical General Archives by the Historical Society of Israel (the name was changed in 1969, when the archives became independent of the Historical Society). Its first director Josef Meisl was the former archivist of the Berlin Jewish Community. He was succeeded at CAHJP in 1957 by Daniel Cohen, originally from Hamburg. These founders presented their institution as the "National Archives of the Jewish People in Diaspora," committed to bringing together the records of Jewish communities all over the world in a single, national framework.[51]

Although they had articulated CAHJP's mission before the Holocaust, in the war's wake, these German-born leaders were reenergized in their collecting efforts and dedicated the institution to gathering everything possible from the destroyed European Jewish communities.[52] Seeing "the redemption of the archives" from Europe as their institution's central goal, Meisl and Cohen sent representatives to scour Europe for any records that had been left behind and to make every effort to secure their transfer to Jerusalem. To this end, for example, Cohen engaged in a protracted battle for the records of the Hamburg Jewish community that Hannah Arendt had failed to secure on behalf of Jewish Cultural Reconstruction. Since the end of the war, the papers had remained in the city's municipal archives, where the archivist stubbornly refused to relinquish them. A compromise was finally reached in 1959: the CAHJP in Jerusalem received the records pertaining to the community's "internal matters," and the state archives in Hamburg retained materials relating to relations with the state.[53]

Although the CAHJP's directors have been limited in their efforts by inadequate funding over the years, their mission has not wavered. Seeing the institution as entitled "on moral grounds" to take possession of the records of the Jewish communities of the diaspora, they maintain that "the ingathering and housing of the archives in Jerusalem [is] a worthy act of commemoration for the destroyed communities."[54] Here again, we encounter an allusion to the "ingathering of the exiles." In Israel, the term had become ubiquitous in the mid-twentieth century, its meaning directly associated with the Zionist mission to build a nation. For the CAHJP's directors, as much as for their American counterparts, Jewish archives stand for Jewish people. Building the archives was thus imagined as a way to restore the nation's wholeness, threatened not only by the most recent catastrophe, but by the state of exile itself.

Given this mission, it is not surprising that the CAHJP purchased a number of original materials from Szajkowski over the years, beginning in 1953, when he first visited Israel. That year, Szajkowski was living mostly in France. He was about to be married and was deeply in debt, primarily from paying out of his own pocket to have his three book-length studies published. He was also investing in a potential future as an Israeli scholar, using his own funds to have articles translated for publication in the Israeli Historical Society's journal *Zion*. Through the society's director Israel Halperin, he sold the archives a number of documents pertaining to the Jewish delegation to the Malesherbes Commission from 1788, telling Halperin that he had bought the rare papers in a Bordeaux bookshop.[55] Over the next few years, he continued to sell rare materials to Halperin and another scholar associated with the group, Chone Shmeruk. An institution dedicated to accumulating and centralizing the records of Jewish life across the diaspora in one place, the society found it "worthwhile to do business" with its American friend.[56]

As late as 1967, the CAHJP continued to purchase papers from Szajkowski.[57] And as in the American libraries, the CAHJP arranged the materials they purchased by town of origin, since their exact institutional provenances had been obscured by the fact that they were acquired by an intermediary who was not in a position to truthfully explain exactly where he had obtained them. The decision to classify them this way fit well within the overall classification schema of the archives anyway. Conceived of as the archives of a single nation in diaspora, the CAHJP had arranged much of its material by country and town of origin, not necessarily by the bodies that created them. As such, here, even more than in the American Jewish institutions, the documents Szajkowski sold became part of a collection meant to represent the wholeness of the Jewish people, its persistence through time, and its indestructibility in spite of the persecution chronicled in so many of the papers in its boxes.

If these Jewish archives and libraries were working to centralize the remnants of the Jewish past as a kind of monument to the Jewish nation, Szajkowski's pattern of thefts and sales was having quite the opposite effect. For other scholars interested in French Jewish history, his document trafficking had created a strange and difficult situation. While some documents useful for studying a certain topic were now held in American and Israeli institutions, still others remained behind in France. To take one example, Szajkowski sold quite a bit of material—more than thirty boxes' worth—on French Jewish organizations in World War II to the Centre de Documentation Juive Contemporaine (CDJC) in Paris in late 1949 and early 1950, the period of his hiatus from YIVO. It is unclear whether these materials originated in the YIVO collection of UGIF materials, which Szajkowski was still in the process of gathering together from his sources in France. They do include documents from both the Comité de Coordination and the UGIF itself. They also included an intriguing set of materials on the mufti of Jerusalem, which Szajkowski must have picked up in Berlin.[58] The result: Both the CDJC and YIVO have incomplete collections of original source materials.

Another striking example can be seen in the footnotes of Szajkowski's 1959 book *Autonomy and Communal Jewish Debts*. Here, documents pertaining to the communal debts of Jews in the city of Metz are cited as held at HUC, in the Metz Municipal Archives, and in "Zosa Szajkowski's personal collection." The Jewish communal records of Metz, which are cited as providing information about who owed on these debts, are cited as residing at JTS, HUC, and the Metz Municipal Archives.[59] The documents had in effect been scattered by Szajkowski's trafficking in the late 1950s. They were far from their starting point and no longer grouped with the other documents of the same origin and type.

A third example is the most disturbing of all. It concerns one of Szajkowski's proudest finds, the Carpentras communal record book or *pinkas* known as the *Sefer ha-yakhas*, one of two such manuscripts he acquired in Carpentras in 1940 and gave to YIVO, and from which he published an excerpt in *YIVO Bleter* in 1943, shortly after he first arrived in New York.[60] Today, some of the *pinkas*'s pages are at YIVO, and others are at the CAHJP. Until historian Simone Mrejen-O'Hana discovered the split in the early 2000s, archivists in each of the two institutions believed they were in possession of the complete manuscript. In fact, although Szajkowski had indeed given the whole manuscript to YIVO in 1941, later, in 1958, he broke the manuscript apart and sold the pages that were in better condition to the CAHJP in Jerusalem. Today, while YIVO retains eleven rather deteriorated pages of the *Sefer ha-yakhas* (pages 1 and 49–58), the CAHJP has most of the others (pages 2–9, 11–48, and 59–97), which were in much better condition. Page 10 is now missing. Perhaps it fell apart, or perhaps it was enough of a treasure on its own that he was able to sell it elsewhere. On the top of the first page of the Jerusalem manuscript, Szajkowski's Yiddish-language signature is clearly visible, the mark of the owner who once gave it to YIVO, and then later, when he needed money, resold part of it to another institution halfway across the world. It would take decades for anyone to piece together what the dealer had done.[61]

Breaking up collections in this way helped Szajkowski stay in business. Stealing *everything* from an institution in France would have been risky, so he stole selectively. On the other end, selling by the piece allowed him to evade suspicion on the part of the buyers. It also netted him higher profits, since multiple buyers were likely to pay more for a collection sold by the piece than a single buyer would pay for a whole collection. To make his profit, Szajkowski sold not only to libraries, but to anyone who could pay, wherever they might live. This included a range of people and institutions in a variety of locations, not only the libraries in the United States and Israel, but also dealers like Rosenthal and a number of private collectors based in the United States.[62]

When he began to sell his stolen goods this way, Szajkowski compromised his commitment to making the remains of the Jewish past easily available for scholars. It was that belief that had motivated the collecting he did as a volunteer for YIVO during World War II. But something had changed within him. Instead of being a *zamler*, he became in time a kind of "good[s] manager of a large store" (to borrow his own words from his 1967 letter to Malino). Since his document theft and sale was a petty capitalist operation, profit was the goal. It did not matter whether the buyer was a library dedicated to making things available to other scholars or not. It did not matter where the library was located. Indeed, it did not matter whether the buyer was a library, an individual, or another dealer. The sales operation was not about reuniting scattered documents in a single collection and thereby making the Jewish people whole again, nor was it about making these documents available for study. It was about making ends meet, and it was devoid of any loyalties to institutions or ideological commitments. In the end, it resulted in a re-scattering of the documents to new locations.

Of course, without customers, even the most brilliant petty capitalist would have to close up shop. For the librarians who bought Szajkowski's wares, it was infinitely more plausible to imagine these documents as orphaned remnants of a murdered people than to imagine that one of their professional colleagues—himself an escapee from the European Jewish world that had been destroyed—was now an archive thief. It was not just a question of sympathy for a struggling survivor. The buyers' shared belief in reuniting the scattered, orphaned remnants of the Jews' diasporic past made them eager consumers of Szajkowski's wares.

In the wake of World War II, all Judaica librarians operated under the assumption that almost every old Jewish book, manuscript, or archival document that had been in Europe in the 1940s had passed through multiple hands in a chain of theft and rescue, a history that paralleled the destruction of the Jewish people in Europe and their rebuilding in America and Israel. For decades, it was simply not the practice in Israel or the United States to ask questions that could not be answered. More important to these postwar librarians was the goal of redeeming these stray treasures by incorporating them into the great Judaica libraries that they were building as a monument to the Jewish people, a symbol of their endurance and unity. But ironically, in their dogged competition with one another to fulfill that goal, they became as responsible for the new round of scattering as the dealer, who merely brought them the goods they so desired.

EPILOGUE

ON SEPTEMBER 26, 1978, Zosa Szajkowski was found dead. A few days earlier, he had been arrested outside of the New York Public Library in an organized police sting operation. The historian had been using the library for decades, and the staff there knew him well. One evening, when librarian Claire Dienstag was on duty at the reference desk, she noticed that Szajkowski had propped a large volume upright in front of him while he worked on other materials. Another patron caught Dienstag's eye and gestured at her to indicate that something was amiss. As it turned out, Szajkowski was stealing again, this time from a collection of pamphlets and ephemera, some of which were exceedingly rare, that had been bound together into volumes. Szajkowski had been working his way through the collection for quite some time. When the librarians checked the volumes Szajkowski had consulted previously, they saw that pamphlets had been removed systematically, as if by knife or scissors, throughout the entire collection.

The librarians were upset, but not wholly surprised. Szajkowski was a strange man, and he had been acting quite erratically. Moreover, over the years, they had heard talk of Szajkowski's sticky fingers in libraries and archives. Working with the library's security man, they called in the police. Two undercover officers were on hand to watch Szajkowski the next time he came to the library. They stopped the thief outside the door just after closing time and demanded to look inside his briefcase, where they found several of the rare pamphlets. The officers arrested Szajkowski and locked him up overnight at a local precinct.

In the morning, the police returned to the library and asked Dienstag to accompany them back to Szajkowski's apartment to search for additional materials from the library's collections. They found nothing they could identify as library property and quickly learned why: The document dealer had already sold his booty directly to the Harvard University library. In haste, Leonard Gold, chief of the Jewish Division, made his way to Cambridge, where he was able to recuperate the stolen materials—now mutilated, as Szajkowski had cut off the ownership stamps before selling the materials.[1]

The whole affair bore an uncanny resemblance to Szajkowski's capture in Strasbourg in 1961, but this time it ended differently. Even though the police had let him go after searching the apartment, the historian must have felt that there would be no escape, no chance of starting over. He could not hide what had happened from his wife, who had seen him come home with the police. He could not hide what had happened from his employers at YIVO, who would have to fire him once they got the news. And perhaps worst of all, he would lose his access to the libraries he needed most. Shamed, disgraced, and exposed as a thief, Szajkowski was utterly ruined. On September 26, 1978, he drowned himself in the bathtub of a room at the Hotel Taft in midtown Manhattan.[2]

Szajkowski's funeral would bring out many of the scholars and librarians among whom he had worked for three decades in New York. Abraham Duker, the long-time managing editor of *Jewish Social Studies*, arranged the service, and Arthur Hertzberg delivered the eulogy in Yiddish.[3] The American Jewish scholarly elite paid its respects to a man whose financial, professional, and psychological insecurities had driven him to steal from some of their most respected scholarly institutions, and to sell to them too.

Szajkowski had conducted his distasteful business with a passion that had grown increasingly pathological with the passing of the years. But his passion was not the kind of "archive fever" or irrational compulsion that Philippe Dollinger, the Strasbourg municipal archivist, had imagined when he confronted the thief in 1961. Szajkowski's thefts were carried out systematically over many decades, and the decision to undertake them was based on rational calculation. Indeed, Szajkowski profited from the thefts in more ways than one. They provided him with the documents he needed for his research and the money he needed to devote himself to it.

Of course, Szajkowski's business depended on the existence of buyers for his stolen books and documents and a readership for his scholarly work. His calculations were correct. The Jewish scholarly establishment was indeed appreciative of both the goods he had to offer and the scholarship he produced. Moreover, in most instances, they chose to look the other way when confronted with evidence of his misdeeds. The evidence was apparent to many who worked closely with him over the years. His YIVO colleagues had been whispering about him since the late 1940s. Librarians at the Jewish Theological Seminary (JTS) and the New York Public Library had been asked to return stolen documents to France in 1950 and yet continued to buy from him in later years. The American Academy for Jewish Research (then run by Salo Baron) had been informed of Szajkowski's thefts in Strasbourg in 1961, just a year after it had admitted him to its ranks. None of these institutions ever censured Szajkowski publicly. Even the Alliance Israélite Universelle in Paris—one of his earliest victims—never barred him from its library. Only two institutions, the Strasbourg Municipal Archives and the New York Public Library (notably, both public institutions), ever turned their cases over to the police.

For the private Jewish institutions, public relations issues played an important role in their decision-making. A Jewish criminal stealing from Jewish institutions might lead to the kind of bad press that is best avoided if at all possible. Pity for a poor man, a survivor and refugee who struggled to make ends meet, was an important factor as well. According to Ezekiel Lifshutz, Szajkowski's longtime supervisor at YIVO, librarians had long looked the other way when they realized what Szajkowski was doing in order to protect this "psychologically unbalanced person" and fellow Jew from disgrace.[4] But at the same time, most of these scholars and librarians appreciated what Szajkowski had to offer, to both Jewish scholarship and Jewish libraries and archives. Since World War II, the Americans and Israelis who supported

Szajkowski understood European Jewish life to be largely a thing of the past. As such, they were committed to rescuing whatever they could of its history for preservation, study, and the building of unparalleled collections of Judaica from all over the world.

The French historical materials Szajkowski studied and sold were of particular interest to American Jewish scholars in the postwar period. When assembled together, they offered a window onto an issue considered critical in modern Jewish history: political emancipation and its effects. Since the 1930s, Jewish historians had called into question whether emancipation, insofar as it had entailed abandoning communal autonomy, had ultimately benefited the Jews. Some, like Elias Tcherikower, went so far as to wonder whether emancipation and assimilation had left them even more powerless before their enemies, who grew more rabid and fierce with the passing of the years.

In the 1960s, scholars based in American universities began to examine the question as well. Like French Jews, American Jews had obtained equal rights earlier than Jews in most nations, and they had also achieved a high degree of social integration and success as individuals. During the 1960s, a broad ethnic revival in American culture led many American Jews to question whether that assimilation was ultimately a good thing for Jews or whether it would lead inevitably to the weakening of their identities and their capacity to defend themselves. Many of the American graduate students who turned to French Jewish history in the 1960s—Phyllis Cohen Albert, Arthur Hertzberg, Paula Hyman, Frances Malino, Michael Marrus, David Weinberg—were deeply concerned with these questions and turned to the French example to explore how these issues had played out in that setting.[5] For these younger historians, Szajkowski had facilitated their research by making new sources available. Yet he also confused them, as well as the scholars who followed in their footsteps, by moving those sources far from their points of origin, making it somewhat more difficult to understand the contexts in which they were produced.

In France too, interest in modern French Jewish history increased after the 1960s as new sources became available in the years following Szajkowski's thefts. The members of the Commission Française des Archives Juives (CFAJ) launched a number of different projects that facilitated the study of the history of Jews in France. These included archival classification projects, bibliographic projects, the publication of a journal, and the sponsoring of historical studies. In the early 1970s, the CFAJ also obtained microfilm copies of the large collections of French Jewish holdings that Szajkowski had sold to the libraries of HUC and JTS. A second copy of the microfilm was also produced for the Central Archives for the History of the Jewish People in Jerusalem. Although the originals were not returned, the existence of the microfilms did much to mitigate the damage caused by Szajkowski's thefts.[6] Thanks to the CFAJ's efforts, French scholars also became more engaged than ever before in the production of French Jewish history, and there too, the questions centered on the terms of emancipation and its long-term effects.

Szajkowski himself had produced scores of studies that attempted to understand the history of Jewish emancipation, assimilation, and antisemitism in France from every possible angle. His questions were driven by the sources themselves, which he ferreted out with the nose of an investigative journalist. Szajkowski's impact as an archive dealer was perhaps even more significant than his scholarship, opening the field to economic and social-historical questions. What he found expanded Jewish historians' view of emancipation and the social, political, and economic changes it wrought, particularly when it came to non-elites. Since the 1930s, he focused his eye on the documents that might reveal something about the lives of poorer and more obscure Jews, rather than great rabbis and wealthy lay leaders. Szajkowski may have quit the Communist Party, but he always remained fiercely anti-elitist. This meant that, unlike his mentor Tcherikower, he always rejected the idea of a French Jewish community sharing a single experience, and instead stressed its diversity and its internal conflicts.

Szajkowski's story resonates far beyond French Jewish history, because it forces us to reconsider our understanding of the very nature of archives. Typically, scholars tend of think of these institutions as a project of nation-building. This is true even for Jews, who have always lacked a single, unified nation-state to represent them. In describing their collections of books and papers in terms of "redemption" and "ingathering," Jewish archives and libraries in Israel and the United States have sought to restore Jewish unity symbolically by building and maintaining whole collections that bring together all the remnants of the Jewish past in a single place.

Telling Szajkowski's story forces us to confront the impossible grandiosity of those visions and the fundamental incompleteness of these and all archives. Even the ambitious microfilming projects carried out by the Central Archives for the History of the Jewish People in Jerusalem cannot create the coherent and complete archive that inspired their founders. To aspire to such wholeness is to work against time itself. It is itself a holdover from the world that was destroyed, a relic of its inhabitants' nationalist fantasies about the redemptive potential of history. It stems from a desire to restore what was lost, to produce order from disorder, and thereby avoid reckoning with the remnants as such.

The ambiguity that sits at the heart of the story of Zosa Szajkowski is in some ways extraordinary, but in other ways, it reveals an ambiguity in the very nature of archives. On the one hand, the creators of archives rescue the past for us. They gather together and preserve records from the past, making it possible for historians to study them and use them as evidence for our understanding of the past. On the other hand, there is also violence in the project of archiving. The very process of making an archive re-contextualizes documents and—in subtle and not-so-subtle ways—changes their meanings. While this is true of archives generally, it is particularly true of those that have been subject to the kinds of historical upheavals that have shaped the archives of European Jewry.

Our usual conception of what archives are is thus challenged by taking into account the historical factors that shaped them. Archives are not made by the powerful alone; the weak also play a role in their construction. If our understanding of archives in general is broadened to include all those who shaped their histories, these institutions look less and less like coherent monuments, and more and more like salvage heaps.

NOTES

Introduction

1. On German Jewish archives, see Daniel J. Cohen, "Jewish Records from Germany in the Jewish General History Archives in Jerusalem," in *LBI Year Book* 1, no. 1 (1956): 331–45; Sybil H. Milton, "Lost, Stolen and Strayed: The Archival Heritage of German-Jewish History," in *The Jewish Response to German Culture: From the Enlightenment to the Second World War*, ed. Jehuda Reinharz and Walter Schatzberg (Hanover, NH: Brandeis University Press, 1985), 317–35; and Denise Rein, "Die Bestände der ehemaligen jüdischen Geminden Deutschlands in den 'CAHJP' in Jersualem: Ein Uberblick über das schicksal der verschinedenen Gemeindearchive," in *Der Archivar* 4 (2002), 318–27.

2. The term "panoptical archive" is Eric Ketelaar's from his "Panoptical Archive," in *Archives, Documentation and the Institutions of Social Memory: Essays from the Sawyer Seminar*, ed. Francis X. Blouin and William G. Rosenberg (Ann Arbor: University of Michigan Press, 2006), 144–50.

3. This is not to say that *all* of the source material about French Jews in these massive collections was purchased from Szajkowski; the Jewish Theological Seminary Library in particular collected French Judaica from a number of different sources over the years, as documented in the *JTS Register*. For example, rare French pamphlets were acquired by the library in 1931, 1939, and 1940—years before Szajkowski began to sell materials.

4. Paula E. Hyman, "French Jewish Historiography since 1870," in *The Jews in Modern France*, ed. Frances Malino and Bernard Wasserstein (Hanover, NH:

Brandeis University Press, 1985), 327–46; and Lisa M. Leff, "L'Histoire des juifs de France vue des Etats-Unis," *Archives Juives* (March 2010): 126–36.

5. In the Jewish Theological Seminary's French Jewish Communities Record Group.

6. The term "ingathering of the exiles," an adaptation from Jewish liturgy, has been applied to Jewish archives in Israel and America; perhaps even more famously, it was applied to manuscripts by David Ben Gurion in a letter to Eliezer Kaplan, March 5, 1950, as cited in Ilan ben Zion, "Ingathering and Digitizing the Diaspora's Rare Hebrew Books," *Times of Israel*, October 14, 2013, www.timesofisrael.com/ingathering-and-digitizing-the-diasporas-rare-hebrew-books/.

7. The term is Antoinette Burton's, in her introduction to Burton, ed., *Archive Stories: Facts, Fictions, and the Writing of History* (Durham, NC: Duke University Press, 2005), 7.

8. Burton, *Archive Stories*, 5–7.

9. This is particularly the case in firsthand accounts, such as those of Lucy S. Dawidowicz, *From That Place and Time: A Memoir, 1938–1947* (New York: Norton, 1989); Herbert A. Friedman, *Roots of the Future* (Jerusalem: Gefen, 1990); and Seymour J. Pomrenze, "The Restitution of Jewish Cultural Treasures after the Holocaust: The Offenbach Archival Depot's Role in the Fulfillment of U.S. International and Moral Obligations (A First-Hand Account)" (Feinstein Lecture, National Foundation for Jewish Culture, June 4, 2002). Scholarly approaches adopt a more objective tone, but, with their focus on individuals more heroic than Szajkowski, they necessarily remain largely celebratory of the enterprise. See, for example, David E. Fishman, *Embers Plucked from the Fire: The Rescue of Jewish Cultural Treasures in Vilna* (New York: YIVO, 1996); and Samuel D. Kassow, *Who Will Write Our History? Emanuel Ringelblum, the Warsaw Ghetto, and the Oyneg Shabes Archive* (Bloomington: Indiana University Press, 2007).

10. For just a few examples, see Beth B. Cohen, *Case Closed: Holocaust Survivors in Postwar America* (New Brunswick, NJ: Rutgers University Press, 2007); Maud S. Mandel, *In the Aftermath of Genocide: Armenians and Jews in Twentieth-Century France* (Durham, NC: Duke University Press, 2003); and Tara Zahra, *The Lost Children: Reconstructing Europe's Families after World War II* (Cambridge, MA: Harvard University Press, 2011).

11. Lisa Leff, "Iraqi Jewish Archives Displayed in DC before Being Shipped back to … Iraq," *Tablet*, October 7, 2013, www.tabletmag.com/jewish-arts-and-culture/147736/iraqi-jewish-treasures; Avital Chizak, "Putin Refuses to Let the Lubavitcher Rebbe's Library Leave Moscow," *Tablet*, September 30, 2013, www.tabletmag.com/jewish-arts-and-culture/books/143902/moscow-putin-lubavitcher-library.

Chapter 1

1. Typescript copies of this confession (though sadly not the handwritten original) can be found in the thick file on the affair, held in the Archives de la Ville et de la Communauté Urbaine de Strasbourg (formerly Strasbourg Municipal Archives, hereafter AMS), Dossier "Frydmann" [sic], 202 NW 39. This translation is mine; emphasis added.

2. Dollinger to the Directors of the Alexander Kohut Memorial Foundation, New York, June 29, 1961, AMS, dossier "Frydmann."

3. Bonnie G. Smith, *The Gender of History: Men, Women, and Historical Practice* (Cambridge, MA: Harvard University Press, 1998), 121.

4. Dollinger to the Directors of the Alexander Kohut Memorial Foundation, New York, June 29, 1961. For Szajkowski's itinerary on April 14, 1961, U.S. Passport of Szajko Frydman, in YIVO RG 800.

5. The municipal archives in Strasbourg were still, in 1961, a division of the Strasbourg municipal library, and was therefore located in a different room in the same building.

6. Different accounts of this story were written up with slightly different details in the ensuing police investigation and trial. These details are from the court's final verdict, which contains a summary of the facts as accepted by the court; it is held in the Archives Départementales du Bas-Rhin, 1709 W 75: Jugement contre Szajkowski (Frydmann), January 14, 1963. The folders themselves can be found in AMS "Frydmann."

7. This list can be found in AMS "Frydmann."

8. Zosa Szajkowski, "The Discussion and Struggle over Jewish Emancipation in Alsace in the Early Years of the French Revolution," *Historia Judaica* 17 (1955): 121–42; Szajkowski, *The Economic Status of the Jews in Alsace, Metz and Lorraine (1648–1789)* (New York: Editions historiques franco-juives, 1954); "The Jewish Problem in Alsace, Metz, and Lorraine on the Eve of the Revolution of 1789," *Jewish Quarterly Review* 44 (1954): 205–43; Szajkowski, "The Jewish Status in Eighteenth-Century France and the 'droit d'aubaine,'" *Historia Judaica* 19 (1957); Szajkowski, *Autonomy and Communal Jewish Debts during the French Revolution of 1789* (New York: Editions historiques franco-juives, 1959).

9. From Christian Wilhelm von Dohm, "Concerning the Amelioration of the Civil Status of the Jews" (Berlin, 1781), as reprinted in excerpted and translated form in *The Jew in the Modern World*, 2nd ed. Paul Mendes-Flohr and Jehuda Reinharz (New York: Oxford University Press, 1995), 31.

10. For more on this topic, see Szajkowski, "The Jewish Problem," as well as Szajkowski, "Occupational Problems of Jewish Emancipation in France, 1789–1800," *Historia Judaica* 21 (1959); Arthur Hertzberg, *The French Enlightenment and the Jews: The Roots of Modern Antisemitism* (New York: Columbia University Press, 1968), esp. 113–32.

11. Walter Benjamin, "Unpacking my Library: A Talk about Book Collecting," in *Illuminations*, ed. Hannah Arendt (New York: 1968), 60–61.

12. Benjamin, "Unpacking My Library," 63.

13. Benjamin, "Unpacking My Library," 60.

14. "Une ténébreuse affaire: des documents disparaissent . . . ," *Dernières nouvelles d'Alsace*, April 23–24, 1961, 17.

15. "La presse israélienne satisfaite," in *Dernières nouvelles d'Alsace*, May 25 1960, 6.

16. Henry Rousso, *The Vichy Syndrome: History and Memory in France since 1944*, trans. Arthur Goldhammer (Cambridge, Mass.: Harvard University Press, 1991). On Alsace, see esp. 55–59.

17. Letters from Dollinger to Pierre Schmitt, Conservateur of the Municipal Library of Colmar, April 15, 1961; to H. Schiel, Director of Archives of Trier, April 15, 1961; and to A. Bruckner, the Director of the State Archives of Basel, April 17, 1961, all in AMS "Frydmann."

18. Notes from the police investigation (Division IV), July 7, 1961, and note to Fuchs of the AMS from Mayor Pflimlin, June 30, 1961; all in AMS "Frydmann."

19. Letter expressing surprise from Maurice Ettinghausen to Phillip Dollinger, June 28, 1961, AMS "Frydmann"; records of sales from Szajkowski, Roth, and many others were found in the firm's purchase records from the era, now held privately by his daughter Julia Rosenthal in London who kindly shared them with me in March 2008.

20. See letter from Dollinger to Rosenthal, June 20, 1961; and Ethinghausen to Dollinger, November 7, 1961, in AMS "Frydmann."

21. Records from the investigation of Szajkowski can be found in AMS "Frydmann." The court findings can be found in the Archives Départementales du Bas-Rhin, Strasbourg, 1709, W 75: Jugement contre Szajkowski (Frydmann) [sic]. I also benefitted from information shared with me in interviews with Georges Weill in fall 2007 and from reading the purchase records of A. Rosenthal, Ltd. from 1961.

22. François Joseph Fuchs to Prof. Franklin Ford, Harvard University, May 19, 1961, in AMS "Frydmann."

23. Letter from P. Rieber, Juge d'Instruction au Tribunal de 1ᵉʳ Instance à Strasbourg to M. le Procurer de la République, September 5, 1962, in AMS "Frydmann." Note that he could not have been referring accurately to Szajkowski's earlier emigration to France, since in 1927, Szajkowski's home country was Poland, not Russia.

24. See Franklin Ford's warm words about Fuchs in his *Strasbourg in Transition, 1648–1789* (Cambridge, MA: Harvard University Press, 1958), x–xi.

25. Dollinger to the Alexander Kohut Memorial Foundation, June 29, 1961, in AMS "Frydmann."

26. Interview with former librarians of the New York Public Library's Jewish Division (Claire Dienstag, Norman Gechlik, and Leonard Gold), October 30, 2008.

Chapter 2

1. Z. Szajkowski, "Destruction of Zaromb," *Le-zikaron olam; de Zaromber yidn vos zaynen umgekumen al kidesh-hashem* (*Yizkor-Book of Zaromb*) (New York: United Zaromber Relief Fund, 1947), available in English translation online at www.jewishgen.org/yizkor/Zareby/Zareby.html. On the history of the school, see Israel Steinberg, "The Yidishe Folkshul," *Le-zikaron olam; de Zaromber yidn vos zaynen umgekumen al kidesh-hashem* (*Yizkor-Book of Zaromb*).

2. Census figure cited in Szajkowski, "Destruction of Zaromb."

3. Szajkowski, "Destruction of Zaromb," 3–6.

4. See the various descriptions by former residents in *Yizkor-Book of Zaromb*.

5. Benedict Anderson, *Imagined Communities: Reflections on the Origin and Spread of Nationalism*, new ed. (London: Verso, 2006).

6. See Rebecca Kobrin, *Jewish Bialystok and Its Diaspora* (Bloomington: Indiana University Press, 2010).

7. On the Tcherikowers, see Joshua Karlip, *The Tragedy of a Generation: The Rise and Fall of Jewish Nationalism in Eastern Europe* (Cambridge, MA: Harvard University Press, 2013).

8. Cecile Kuznitz, *YIVO and the Making of Modern Jewish Culture: Scholarship for the Yiddish Nation* (Cambridge, UK: Cambridge University Press, 2013). For additional information, see Lucy S. Dawidowicz, *From that Place and Time: A Memoir, 1938–1947* (New York: Norton, 1984), chap. 4; and Zosa Szajkowski, "Der Yivo un zayne Grinders: Katalog fun der Oysshtelung tsum 50-yorikn Yovel fun Yidishn Visnshaftlekhn Institut," *YIVO Bleter* 46 (1980): 22–77.

9. Samuel D. Kassow, *Who Will Write Our History? Emanuel Ringelblum, the Warsaw Ghetto, and the Oyneg Shabes Archive* (Bloomington: Indiana University Press, 2007), 49–89; Kuznitz, *YIVO and the Making of Modern Jewish Culture*; and Lucjan Dobroszyki, "YIVO in Interwar Poland: Work in the Historical Sciences," in *The Jews of Poland between Two World Wars*, ed. Yisrael Gutman, Ezra Mendelsohn, Jehuda Reinharz, and Chone Shmeruk (Hanover, N.H.: University of New England Press, 1989), esp. 498.

10. Paula Hyman estimates that from one-third to over one-half of all Jewish immigrants in this period worked in the clothing trades. See her *The Jews of Modern France* (Berkeley: University of California Press, 1998), 120; for a closer look, albeit on an earlier period, see also Nancy L. Green, *The Pletzl of Paris: Jewish Immigrant Workers in the Belle Epoque* (New York: Holmes & Meier, 1986). On Szajkowski's brothers' trades, see, for Zilke (Uzyel, or Jules), his sister-in-law Myriam (Marjasza) Szuster Frydman Mitastein (Mitagsztejn)'s 1997 testimony in Spanish to the USC Shoah Foundation Video Archive, viewed at the United States Holocaust Memorial Museum, Washington, DC; and for more information on his other brother Syome (Zalmen) Frydman, see also the Yad Vashem Database of Shoah Victims' Names.

11. "Extrait du Registre d'Immatriculation," dated March 30, 1927, in YIVO RG 800. Friend's report is Abraham Duker, "Zosa Szajkowski," in the posthumously published Zosa Szajkowski, *Jewish Education in France, 1789–1939*, ed. Tobey B. Gitelle, Jewish Social Studies Monograph Series, no. 2 (New York: Conference on Jewish Social Studies, 1980), vi.

12. Archives Nationales, Fontainebleau, Fonds Moscou, 19940445, file 281. These are the Paris Police records looted by the Nazis, taken to Germany, then looted by the Soviets and returned in the 1990s to the Archives Nationales; and, among other things, they contain files on many foreign workers in Paris in the 1930s. Szajko Frydman's file also contains evidence that he applied for naturalization in 1933 but did not manage to obtain it and remained a foreign worker with Polish nationality until 1940 when the Polish consulate stripped him of his nationality. Many thanks to Daniel Lee for locating this file.

13. See Duker, "Szajkowski," vi. Upon his discharge from the U.S. Army in 1945, Szajkowski told U.S. Army officials that he had attended the Sorbonne for three years, from 1927 to 1930. I have many reasons to doubt that this is in fact true, although verification has proved impossible. But it seems highly unlikely for the following reasons: First, it would have him starting university education at a young age, with no prior secondary education; second, it's hard to see how he would have supported himself if he were a student in that period; third, he never mentioned this education elsewhere; and finally, he had every reason to pretend to have more education than he actually did in the interview used to compile this form, the "Separation Record," which was to be used as a kind of résumé for future employers. See the Separation Record of Szajko Frydman, serial no. 32 768 693, available from the National Personnel Records Center (St. Louis, MO), Military Personnel Records.

14. See Szajkowski's letter to Jacob Shatzky, December 29, 1936, in YIVO RG 356, Jacob Shatzky Papers, box 2, folder 22.

15. Information on Szajkowski's pseudonyms from entry "Shaykovski, Zosa," in Berl Kagan, *Leksikon fun Yidish-shraybers: mit Hesofes un Tikunim tsu Leksikon der nayer Yidisher Literatur un 5800 Psevdonimen* (New York: Aroysgegebn fun Raya Ilman-Kohen, 1986), 666.

16. Chaim Yankel's (who appears as Jakob on official documents) profession from "Destruction of Zaromb," 4; Duker writes, in contrast, that he "owned an iron supply store." I was not able to verify either story. Frydman's parents' names were verified on his 1953 French marriage certificate, a copy of which can be found in the Probate file of Szajko Frydman, in the archives of the Surrogate's Court, County of New York, file no. 5545, 1978. Nicknames discussed in Duker, "Szajkowski," vi.

17. An irony he seems not to have noticed, since it is not mentioned in the letter where he discusses reading *Martin Eden*. See Szajkowski's letter to Riva Tcherikower, June 12, 1945, in YIVO RG 81, folio 151982.

18. Jonathan Boyarin, *Polish Jews in Paris: The Ethnography of Memory* (Bloomington: Indiana University Press, 1991), 48.

19. On interwar Jewish associational life, see Paula Hyman, *From Dreyfus to Vichy: The Remaking of French Jewry, 1906–1939* (New York: Columbia University Press, 1979); Boyarin, *Polish Jews*, chaps. 1–3; and David Weinberg, *A Community on Trial: The Jews of Paris in the 1930s* (Chicago: University of Chicago Press, 1977).

20. On this point, see Shayke Fridman, *Etyudn tsu der Geshikhte fun ayngevandertn yidishn Yishev in Frankraykh* (Paris, 1936), 110–13; and Zaagsma, "Jewish Communists," 11.

21. Gerben Zaagsma, "Jewish Communists in Paris between Local and International," *Simon Dubnow Institute Year Book* 8 (2009): 1–19.

22. See, e.g., these articles in *Naye Prese* from Szajkowski's first year as a journalist: "Yidishe kleynhendler," November 9, 1934; "Zvishen di yidishe mebel-arbeter," November 27, 1934; "Zayn episeri iz a barometer," January 4, 1934; "In menerkonfektsie, der antrofrenar un zayne arbeter;" January 29, 1935. See also Hyman, *Dreyfus to Vichy*, 63–88.

23. See, e.g., these articles in *Naye Prese*: "15 yor Parizer-Kultur-lige," August 8, 1937; "Parizer yidishe bibliotekn un bukhhandlungen," October 24, 1934; "Zumer kolonie far undzere kinder," June 5, 1935; "Yidishe Arbeter-teater in Pariz far der milkhume," December 13, 1935. For more on cultural organizations in Jewish immigrant Paris, see Zaagsma, "Jewish Communists," 12n48; and Hyman, *From Dreyfus to Vichy*, 102–3.

24. See these articles in *Naye Prese*: "Mit der metro fun Pletsl bizn Belvil," April 27, 1935; "Kayn Nansi mitn Fiat," a six-part series in July 1935; "Fun Birobidzan tsu Pariz tsufus... ," November 22, 1934; "Vos zu zeyn in Pariz: Muzay Karnavalay," February 17, 1935; "Zumer kolonie far undzere kinder," May 6, 1935; "Katakombn afn Belvil," February 28, 1935.

25. See Nadia Malinovich, *French and Jewish: Culture and the Politics of Identity in Early Twentieth-Century France* (Oxford, U.K.: Littman, 2008), 219–23.

26. See, e.g., the six-part series in *Naye Prese* entitled "Di Yidn in Frankraykh: Biz der groyser franzeyzisher Revolutsye tsu der Geshikhte fun der Parizer Konsistorie," June 1934; and his seven-part series, "Tsu der Geshikhte fun der yidishe Arbeter Bavegung in Frankraykh," which focused especially on the hat-makers' union, August 1934.

27. Fridman, *Etyudn*.

28. These names are among those that appear in the early letters from Szajkowski to Tcherikower in 1939–40; see YIVO RG 81, folios 150906–151567.

29. M. Dobin, "Yidishe Emigrantn-arbeter in Pariz," *YIVO Bleter* 3, no. 4–5 (1932): 385–403; M. Dobin, "Di Profesies fun di Yidishe Emigrantn in Pariz," *YIVO Bleter* 4, no. 1 (1932): 22–42; A. Menes, "Di Yidn in Frankraykh," *YIVO Bleter* 11, no. 5 (1937): 329–55. Brutzkus also contributed to the *Yidn in Frankraykh* collection, ed. E. Tcherikower, and finally published by YIVO in New York in two

volumes in 1942, discussed below. On the work on the Historical Section more broadly, see Kuznitz, *YIVO and the Making of Modern Jewish Culture.*

30. The luggage the Tcherikowers themselves attempted to bring out of France, through Spain and Portugal, weighed in at 2250 kilos (see telegram from Tcherikower to YIVO-NY, August 29, 1940, in YIVO RG 81, file 2007); this excludes their library and much of their archives, which they left behind, mostly in Paris. On the Tcherikower Collection, see Fruma Mohrer and Marek Web, eds. *Guide to the YIVO Archives* (New York: YIVO, 1998), 269.

31. Szajkowski to Shatzky, May 15, 1936, in YIVO RG 356, box 2, folder 22, trans. Lillian Leavitt and Iosif Lakhman.

32. Szajkowski to Shatzky, December 29, 1936, YIVO RG 356, box 2, folder 22, trans. Leavitt and Lakhman.

33. Shayke Fridman, *Di Profesionele bavegung tsvishn di yidishe arbeter in Frankraykh biz 1914* (Paris: Tsuzamen, 1937).

34. *A Yor Arbet in der Aspirantur af Nomen fun der Tsemekh Tsabad baym Yidishe Visnshaftlekhn Institut* (Vilna, Poland: YIVO, 1937). For a wonderful description of the program, esp. in 1938–39, see Dawidowicz, *From that Place and Time,* 88–89 and *passim.*

35. Szajkowski to Tcherikower, March 31, 1936, in YIVO RG 81, folio 13180.

36. Szajkowski to Shatzky, October 9, 1938, in YIVO RG 356, box 2, folder 22; see also Duker, "Szajkowski," vii.

37. On the school, see Duker, "Zosa Szajkowski," vi, and Szajkowski, "Destruction of Zaromb," 4. Szyje Frydman's report card for 1923–24, on which he received mostly 3s and a few 4s on a scale of 1–5, can be found in YIVO RG 800. My thanks to Natalia Aleksiun, Brad Sabin Hill, and Samuel Kassow for help with research on the school, the *Państwowe Seminarium dla Nauczycieli Religii Mojżeszeszowej,* set up by Samuel Poznanski in 1918 at 9 Gęsia Street in Warsaw. Many thanks to Piotr Kosicki for help interpreting Szajkowski's grades.

38. Zosa Szajkowski, "1515 yidishe Mishpokhe in Pariz," *Yidishe Ekonomik* 2, no. 9–10 (1938): 471–80; "Fun Yidishn Arbeter-lebn in Pariz," *Yidishe Ekonomik* 2, no. 5–6 (1938): 232–49; and "Der Kamf kegn Yidish in Frankraykh: 19tn un 20tn Y.H.," *YIVO Bleter* 14, no. 1–2 (1939): 46–77.

39. "1515 Yidishe mishpokhe" uses data collected by the Colonie scolaire summer camp about its children, all from the poorer classes of the immigrant world. The flaw: Szajkowski treats each child as if he or she represents a different family, and does not recognize that some of the children may have been siblings from the same family.

40. The wide dispersion of the Historical Section can be seen in the locations of the authors listed in the collection of studies published together as E. Tcherikower, ed. *Historishe Shriftn* (*YIVO Studies in History*), 3 vols. (Vilna and Paris: YIVO, 1937–39).

41. Dubnow used these terms in his famous 1891 essay "On the Study of Jewish History," initially published in the Russian Jewish journal *Volskhod*, and translated into Hebrew the following year. For an excellent discussion of the essay, see Laura Jockusch, *Collect and Record! Jewish Holocaust Documentation in Early Postwar Europe* (New York: Oxford, 2012), 21–22.

42. Cf. Anderson, *Imagined Communities*; and Eric Hobsbawm, *Nations and Nationalism since 1780: Programme, Myth, Reality*, 2nd ed. (Cambridge, UK: Cambridge University Press, 1990).

43. Peter Fritzsche, "The Archive," *History and Memory* 17, no. 1/2 (2005): 18.

44. Lara Jennifer Moore, *Restoring Order: the Ecole des Chartes and the Organization of Archives and Libraries in France, 1820–1870* (Duluth, MN: Litwin, 2008).

45. See Kassow, *Who Will Write Our History?*, 49–88.

46. Elisabeth Kaplan, "We Are What We Collect, We Collect What We Are: Archives and the Construction of Identity," *The American Archivist* 63 (Spring/Summer 2000): 126–51. This citation, from the Minutes of the first meeting (held in the AJHS archives) appears on p. 127.

47. Denise Rein, "Die Bestände der ehemaligen jüdischen Gemeinden Deutschlands in den 'Central Archives for the History of the Jewish People in Jerusalem,'" *Der Archivar* 55, no. 4 (2002): 318–27.

48. See Kuznitz, *YIVO and the Making of Modern Yiddish Culture* on Eastern Europe; on Paris, see Szajkowski's letter to Elias Tcherikower, March 31, 1936, YIVO RG 81, folio 13180.

49. Jeffrey Shandler, *Awakening Lives: Autobiographies of Jewish Youth in Poland before the Holocaust* (New Haven, CT: Yale University Press, 2002).

50. Kassow, *Who Will Write Our History?*, 9–10. The results of the Paris survey were published by Zosa Szajkowski in "Di Yidishe Gezelshaftn in Pariz"; and by A. Alperin in "Dos Yidishe Gezelshaftlekhe lebn in Pariz," both in E. Tcherikower, ed., *Yidn in Frankraykh: Shtudyes un Materialn*, 2 vols., vol. 2 (New York: YIVO, 1942), 205–64.

51. On the complicated political situation in the region and the situation of Jews within it, see Oleg Budnitskii, *Russian Jews between the Reds and the Whites, 1917–1920*, trans. Timothy J. Portice (Philadelphia: University of Pennsylvania Press, 2011). This estimate of Jewish casualties appears on p. 406.

52. See Jockusch, *Collect and Record!*, 27–29; and Karlip, *Tragedy of a Generation*, 163–68.

53. The first volume of the pogrom study is E. Tcherikower, ed., *Antisemitizm un Pogromen in Ukraine, 1917–1918 (Tsu der geshikhte fun ukrainish-yidishe batzihungen)* (Berlin: Mizrakh-Yidishn Historishn Arkhiv, 1923); and on the Russian Revolution, E. Tcherikower, ed., *In der tkufe fun revolutsye: Memuarn, materialn, documentn; Zamlbikher* (Berlin: Idisher Literarisher Farlag, 1924).

54. Jockusch, *Collect and Record!*, 18–45. On the Warsaw ghetto efforts, see Kassow, *Who Will Write Our History?*

55. Hyman, *Jews of Modern France*, 151–52; Weinberg, *Community on Trial*, 121–36; Zaagsma, "Jewish Communists," 9.

56. See William Meyers, "Profiles in Combat," *New York Sun*, October 11, 2007.

57. On the dissolution or reorganization of the subsection, see Zaagsma, "Jewish Communists," 12–13.

58. See Meyers, "Profiles," and also Szajkowski's own ambiguous statement about leaving the PCF in his *Jews and the French Foreign Legion* (New York: Ktav, 1975), 62.

59. Szajkowski, *Jews and the French Foreign Legion*, 62.

60. See Karlip, *Tragedy of a Generation*, 176–234, about the history of this journal and the ideological crises of its contributors.

61. Szajkowski, *Jews and the French Foreign Legion*, 62–63; here he is citing an article by Tcherikower from the first issue of *Oyfn Sheydveg* (1939).

62. Szajkowski, *Jews and the French Foreign Legion*, 63.

63. Szajkowski, *Jews and the French Foreign Legion*, 62.

64. For a brilliant analysis of how this contradiction can be read in Glatstein's poem itself, see Anita Norich, *Discovering Exile: Yiddish and Jewish American Culture during the Holocaust* (Stanford, CA: Stanford University Press, 2007), 42–73.

65. Szajkowski, *Jews and the French Foreign Legion*, 62–63.

66. Elias Tcherikower, ed., *Yidn in Frankraykh: Shtudyes un Materialn*, 2 vols. (New York: YIVO-Section of History, 1942).

67. Paula E. Hyman, "French Jewish Historiography since 1870," in *The Jews in Modern France*, ed. Frances Malino and Bernard Wasserstein (Hanover, NH: Brandeis University Press, 1985), 331–33.

68. Cf. Guy Miron, *The Waning of Emancipation: Jewish History, Memory and the Rise of Fascism in Germany, France and Hungary* (Detroit, MI: Wayne State University Press, 2011).

69. Karlip, *Tragedy of a Generation*, 238.

70. See Tcherikower, "Di Frantseyzishe Revolutsye un Yidn (150 yor nokh der yidisher Emantsipatsie)," in *Yidn in Frankraykh*, 1: 109–52.

71. This reading from Karlip, *Tragedy of a Generation*, 241.

Chapter 3

1. Zosa Szajkowski, "Jews in the Foreign Legion," *Conservative Judaism* 21, no. 4 (1967): 28.

2. See his enlistment record in YIVO RG 800.

3. Szajkowski to Tcherikower, April 12, 1940, in YIVO RG 81, folio 151023.

4. Zosa Szajkowski, *Jews and the French Foreign Legion* (New York: Ktav, 1975), 61, 63. In a letter to the Tcherikowers, he told them that he hadn't lost the medallion and believed that it had saved him in battle; see Szajkowski to the Tcherikowers, July 19, 1940, in YIVO RG 81, folio 151104.

5. Szajkowski to the Tcherikowers, December 5, 1939, in YIVO RG 81, folio 150928. Another letter from Szajkowski to the Tcherikowers of April 12, 1940, in YIVO RG 81, folio 151023, suggests that Szajko may have left for the Foreign Legion in conflict with his family, especially his sister.

6. The friends he asked about included Avrom Menes, Henoch Gelernt, Daniel Charney, Joseph Bernfeld, and Franz Kursky.

7. Szajkowski to the Tcherikowers, November 28, 1939, in YIVO RG 81, folio 150914. This and all translations from the Yiddish letters in the Szajkowski-Tcherikower correspondence in YIVO RG 81, trans. Lillian Leavitt and Iosif Lakhman, unless otherwise noted.

8. Szajkowski to the Tcherikowers, December 5, 1939, in YIVO RG 81, folio 150925. A study of the slang was later published in New York: Zosa Szajkowski, "Argo fun Yidishe Soldatn in Frankraykh," *Yidishe Shprakh* 2, no. 3 (1942): 89–90.

9. These names appear in a letter from Szajkowski to the Tcherikowers, April 20, 1940, in YIVO RG 81, folio 151025.

10. Szajkowski's contributions to *Yidn in Frankraykh*, ed. Elias Tcherikower (New York: YIVO, 1942), were the following: Sh. Frydman, "Frantseyzishe Opklangen vegn Yidn in Poiln-Rusland fun 15tn biz Onhayb 19tn Y.H.," 1: 16–32; Sh. Frydman, "Di Revolutsye fun 1848 un di inevaynikste Kamfn in Frantseyzishn Yidntum," 1: 205–35; Z. Shaykovski, "150 Yor Yidishe Prese in Frankraykh," 1: 236–308; Z. Shaykovski, "Di Yidishe Gezelshaftn in Pariz: Dos Yidishe Gezelshaftlekhe Lebn in Pariz," 2: 205–47; Z. Shaykovski, "Yidn un di Parizer Komune fun 1871," 2: 93–154; Z. Shaykovski, "Yidn un di nokh-Napoleonishe Restavratsie in Frankraykh (1814–1815)," 1: 190–204; and E. Tcher-ski [Elias Tcherikower and Zosa Szajkowski], "Di Drayfus-Afere, di Arbeter-Emigrantn un di Frantseyzish-Yidishe Firers," 2: 155–92.

11. Zosa Szajkowski, "The Soldiers France Forgot," *Contemporary Jewish Record* 5 (1942): 593.

12. Szajkowski to the Tcherikowers, November 21, 1939, in YIVO RG 81, folio 150919.

13. Szajkowski to the Tcherikowers, June 7, 1940, in YIVO RG 81, folio 151067.

14. Szajkowski to the Tcherikowers, n.d. (mid-June 1940?), in YIVO RG 81, folio 151071. The translation from the French is my own.

15. Citation signed by Lt-Colonel Besson, Captain of the 12th Foreign Regiment, Infantry Division, July 27, 1940, reproduced in Szajkowski, *Jews and the French Foreign Legion*, 143. Original in YIVO RG 800.

16. Szajkowski to the Tcherikowers, June 25, 1940, in YIVO RG 81, folio 151078. Although he initially reported his lung hadn't been pierced, a doctor in Marseilles told him in September that his lung was wounded and would likely cause him pain for many years. See Szajkowski to Tcherikower, September 24, 1940, in YIVO RG 81, folio 151151. His French military medical file is also available; see Service des Archives medicales hospitalières des armées (SAMHA), Limoges,

France, file Szajko FRYDMAN. The initial report from the Bordeaux doctor, dated July 3, 1940, at the moment of evacuation to Carpentras, describes his injury as a "right arm and leg wound, by bullets" and does not mention the lung.

17. Szajkowski, "Jews in the Foreign Legion," 32. A fuller account of the battle and how Szajkowski got himself to safety is in a letter to the Tcherikowers, July 20, 1940, in YIVO RG 81, folios 151106–9.

18. SAMHA Archives, Limoges, file Szajko FRYDMAN.

19. Gelernt to Szajkowski, July 28, 1940, in YIVO RG 81, folios 151120–21. Szajkowski's earlier observations quoted, in agreement, in this letter.

20. Szajkowski, "Jews in the Foreign Legion," 33–34; and *Jews in the French Foreign Legion*, 76–82.

21. He became stateless when the Polish Consulate in Marseilles denied his Polish nationality; he had not been able to furnish sufficient proof. Certificate dated September 23, 1940, in YIVO RG 800.

22. Szajkowski to the Tcherikowers, August 6, 1940, in YIVO RG 81, folio 151125.

23. Szajkowski to the Tcherikowers, July 30, 1940, in YIVO RG 81, folios 151122–24.

24. Szajkowski to the Tcherikowers, August 9, 1940, in YIVO RG 81, folios 151088–89.

25. Szajkowski to the Tcherikowers, August 15, 1940, in YIVO RG 81, folios 151101–2.

26. Kursky to Weinreich, October 29, 1940, in YIVO RG 81, file 2007.

27. Szajkowski to the Tcherikowers, September 24, 1940, in YIVO RG 81, folio 151151.

28. See the documentation in YIVO RG 81, file 2008, for copies of the letters sent to support Szajkowski's immigration. Szajkowski reports that he got the immigrant visa "today" in a letter to Tcherikower, April 18, 1941, in YIVO RG 81, folio 151212.

29. Szajkowski to the Tcherikowers, July 25, 1940, in YIVO RG 81, folio 151116.

30. Szajkowski to the Tcherikowers, July 30, 1940, in YIVO RG 81, folios 151122–24.

31. Zosa Szajkowski, "Argo fun Yidishe Soldatn in Frankraykh," *Yidishe Shprakh* 2, no. 3 (1942): 89–90; Szajkowski, "The Soldiers France Forgot"; Szajkowski, "Jews in the French Foreign Legion, 1939–40," in *The Jewish Review: A Journal Devoted to the Study and Interpretation of Jewish Life and Thought* 5, nos. 1–4 (1948): 136–43; Szajkowski, "Incident at Compiègne," *Conservative Judaism* 21, no. 2 (1967): 27–33; "Jews in the Foreign Legion"; Szajkowski, "Jews in the French Army," in *Hayalim Yehudim Be-tzva'ot Europa* (Tel Aviv: Ma'arakhot, 1967), 30–41; and Szajkowski, *Jews and the French Foreign Legion*.

32. Szajkowski to the Tcherikowers, September 3, 1940, in YIVO RG 81, folio 151141.

33. Szajkowski to Weinreich, September 3, 1940, in YIVO RG 81, folio 151140.

34. Szajkowski to Weinreich, September 3, 1940, in YIVO RG 81, folio 151140.

35. Szajkowski to the Tcherikowers, July 25, 1940, in YIVO RG 81, folio 151116.

36. Szajkowski's numbers, presented in a table he compiled based ostensibly on the Marseilles Consistory records (many of which are now held at the Jewish Theological Seminary, New York), in which population statistics for the entire Vaucluse

département are broken out by commune. See Zosa Szajkowski, "The Decline and Fall of Provençal Jewry," *Jewish Social Studies* 6 (1944): 116.

37. Szajkowski, "Decline and Fall"; Z.S., "Dokumentn fun di arbe Kehiles in 18tn Y.H.," *Yidn in Frankraykh,* 1: 304–16; *Dos Loshn fun di Yidn in di arbe Kehiles fun Komta-Venesen* (New York: YIVO, 1948); "Materialn un notitzn: di Geshikhte fun Karpentraser Beyt-Haknesses in 18tn Y.-H.," *YIVO Bleter* 23 (1944): 149–52; "Pinkassim fun Karpentras, 18tn Y.H.," *YIVO Bleter* 21, no. 3 (1943): 351–55; "Vi Azoy Men Hot Opgeshemdt Tsemakh Karmi in Karpentras," *YIVO Bleter* 24 (1944): 123–30; and "Yidishe Motivn in der Folkskultur fun Komta-Venesen in 17tn-19tn Y.-H.," *YIVO Bleter* 20 (1942): 312–41.

38. A French version, translated by Michel Alessio as *La Langue des Juifs du Pape,* was published by Vent Terral in Valence, France, 2010.

39. See Szajkowski, *La Langue,* 34.

40. See the hearty endorsement by Weinreich in the preface to the 1948 book.

41. Szajkowski to the Tcherikowers, August 12, 1940, in YIVO RG 81, folios 151129–30.

42. In his preface to Szajkowski, *Dos Loshn.*

43. Michel Alessio, introduction to the French translation of Szajkowski's study, *La Langue,* 12. Translation into English is mine. For another critique, see René Moulinas, *Les Juifs du Pape en France, les communautés d'Avignon et du Comtat Venaissin au XVIIe et XVIIIe siècles* (Paris: Privat, 1981), 191.

44. Moulinas, *Les Juifs du Pape en France,* 191, as cited in Alessio's introduction to Szajkowski, *La Langue,* 14.

45. Szajkowski, "Decline and Fall," 118.

46. Szajkowski to the Tcherikowers, August 12, 1940, in YIVO RG 81, folios 151129–30.

47. Szajkowski, "Decline and Fall," 133.

48. Szajkowski to the Tcherikowers, August 12, 1940, in YIVO RG 81, folios 151129–30.

49. Szajkowski to Tcherikowers, September 24, 1940, in YIVO RG 81, folio 151151. Henoch and his wife Hannah (Anya) Gerlernt sometimes used the names Hochgelernt and Hochgelernter, spelled in a variety of ways.

50. Szajkowski to the Tcherikowers, April 22, 1941, in YIVO RG 81, folios 151158–61.

51. Szajkowski, "Decline and Fall," 131.

52. Szajkowski, *Jews and the French Foreign Legion,* 80.

53. Szajkowski to Weinreich, September 3, 1940, in YIVO RG 81, folio 151140; and Szajkowski to the Tcherikowers, September 2, 1940, in YIVO RG 81, folios 151138–39.

54. Szajkowski to Weinreich, September 3, 1940, in YIVO RG 81, folio 151140.

55. Z.S., "Dokumentn fun di arbe Kehiles in 18tn Y.H."; and Szajkowski, "Pinkassim fun Karpentras, 18tn Y.H."

56. Simone Mrejen-O'Hana, "Les Pinqassim de Carpentras au regard du Saint-Siège," *Bulletin du Centre de recherche français de Jérusalem* 16 (2005): 47–52. Information about the inventories at the AADV from my email correspondence with Mrejen-O'Hana dated August 10, 2012. The current inventory is available online: http://e-archives.vaucluse.fr/ead.html?id=FRAD084_paroissiaux#!{%22c ontent%22:[%22FRAD084_paroissiaux_de-7670%22,false,%22%22]}.

57. Mrejen-O'Hana, "Les Pinqassim," 45–47.

58. The full text of this other communal record book can be consulted online: http://e-archives.vaucluse.fr/ead.html?id=FRAD084_paroissiaux#!{%22c ontent%22:[%22FRAD084_paroissiaux_tt3-171%22,false,%22sdx_q19%22],%22f ragment%22:%22ead-fragment.xsp?c=FRAD084_paroissiaux_tt2-90&qid=sdx_ q19%22}.

59. Szajkowski to the Tcherikowers, September 2, 1940, in YIVO RG 81, folios 151138–39.

60. Szajkowski to Weinreich, September 3, 1940, in YIVO RG 81, folio 151140.

61. For an insightful analysis, see Elliott Colla, *Conflicted Antiquities: Egyptology, Egyptomania, Egyptian Modernity* (Durham, NC: Duke University Press, 2007).

62. See Noah S. Gerber, "The Cultural Discovery of Yemenite Jewry: Between Ethnography and Philology" (Ph.D. diss., Hebrew University, Jerusalem, 2009).

63. Adina Hoffman and Peter Cole, *Sacred Trash: The Lost and Found World of the Cairo Geniza* (New York: Nextbook, 2011).

64. Jason Kalman and Jacqueline S. du Toit, *Canada's Big Biblical Bargain: How McGill University Bought the Dead Sea Scrolls* (Montréal: McGill-Queen's University Press, 2010).

65. See, e.g., Weinberg, *A Community on Trial,* xiii, for one version of these stories, which abound among archivists and researchers.

66. On the deal with the IISH, see their website: http://www.iisg.nl/collections/yid-dish/yidhis.php. On the history of the Bund archive, see Marek Web, "Between New York and Moscow: The Bund Archives," in *Jewish Politics in Eastern Europe: The Bund at 100,* ed. Jack Jacobs (New York: New York University Press, 2001), 243–54. On Gelernt's involvement, see Gelernt to Szajkowski, July 28, 1940, in YIVO RG 81, folios 151120–21.

67. Szajkowski to the Tcherikowers, June 9, 1941, in YIVO RG 81, folio 151232. Reference to "Had-Gadio" (his transliteration) in letter (in French) dated June 10, 1941, in YIVO RG 81, folio 151233. No French archive, to the best of my knowledge, contains information about the little-known camp at Oued Zem. Some information about the fate of the *Wyoming* and its passengers, including many frantic cables from Oued Zem, can be found in YIVO RG 245.5, HICEM Main Office in Europe, folder France II, 155.

68. Szajkowski, "The Soldiers France Forgot," 596.

69. Szajkowski to the Tcherikowers, June 26, 1941, in YIVO RG 81, folio 151235.

70. Szajkowski to the Tcherikowers, August 4, 1941, in YIVO RG 81, folio 151239.

71. HICEM may have purchased the ticket for him. On the price of tickets and many other details about the ship, see the colorful description in Victor Brombert, *Trains of Thought: Memories of a Stateless Youth* (New York: Norton, 2002); this price quoted on page 209.

72. Ship manifest, Ancestry.com, New York Passenger Lists, 1820–1957.

73. Frydman reported the four deaths in a letter to the Tcherikowers from the stop in Bermuda, August 29, 1941, in YIVO RG 81, folio 151241. Contemporary coverage of the *Navemar* can be seen in articles in the *New York Daily News*, September 15, 1941; and articles in the *New York Times, New York Post,* and *New York Herald-Tribune* of September 19, 1941. Other accounts can be found in Brombert, *Trains of Thought*, chap. 9, and in a marvelous interview by Paul Sigrist Jr. of passenger Renée Chneour (daughter of the famous Yiddish and Hebrew writer, Zalmen Shneur) on January 5, 1994, for the *Ellis Island Oral History Project*, series EI, no. 424. This partial list of accidents and health problems is from a Letter to the Claimants, January 1942, from Saul Sperling, their representative in a class-action lawsuit. See the Saul Sperling Collection, Leo Baeck Institute, New York, AR 3857.

74. The JDC's assessment can be found in YIVO RG 335, American Jewish Joint Distribution Committee papers, file 376. On the ensuing lawsuit, see the Saul Sperling Collection.

75. Brombert, *Trains of Thought*, 215.

76. Telephone interview with René Bravmann by the author, December 2008.

77. Szajkowski to the Tcherikowers, August 29, 1941, in YIVO RG 81, folio 151241.

Chapter 4

1. Chaim Yankel Frydman to Szajko Frydman, April 23, 1941, in YIVO RG 800. Thanks to Laura Jockusch for help in reading the Polish.

2. Szajkowski's family had moved to Warsaw in the interwar years, perhaps even as early as 1923 but certainly by the mid-1930s. His mother had died there shortly before the war. See Szajkowski to Riva Tcherikower, September 7, 1944, in YIVO RG 81, folio 151670; and testimony of Myriam Mitastein to the USC Shoah Foundation, October 1997.

3. YIVO Archives, Records of YIVO-NY, RG 100A-69, *aspirantur* program 1941–42, 1942–43.

4. Hans F. Loeser, *Hans's Story* (New York: iUniverse, 2007), 98–99; and Victor Brombert, *Trains of Thought: Memories of a Stateless Youth* (New York: W.W. Norton, 2002), 245–58.

5. Szajkowski to the Tcherikowers, February 21, 1943, in YIVO RG 81, folio 151263.

6. Szajkowski to the Tcherikowers, July 21, 1943, in YIVO RG 81, folio 151412. On the Ritchie Boys, see Christian Bauer's documentary *The Ritchie Boys* (Alliance Atlantic Communications, 2004); and Brombert, *Trains of Thought*, 258–66.

7. *Boche* is a derogatory French term for German. Szajkowski to the Tcherikowers, July 22, 1943, in YIVO RG 81, folio 151413.

8. Szajkowski to R. Tcherikower, August 31, 1943, in YIVO RG 81, folio 151432.

9. Szajkowski to R. Tcherikower, March 28, 1944, in YIVO RG 81, folio 151516.

10. Szajkowski to R. Tcherikower, April 18, 1941, in YIVO RG 81, folio 151212.

11. Szajkowski to R. Tcherikower, April 1, 1945, in YIVO RG 81, folio 151893; June 2, 1945, folio 151968.

12. Szajkowski to R. Tcherikower, July 26, 1944, in YIVO RG 81, folio 151626.

13. Szajkowski to R. Tcherikower, October 8, 1944, in YIVO RG 81, folio 151704.

14. Szajkowski to R. Tcherikower, August 8, 1944, in YIVO RG 81, folio 151648.

15. Szajkowski to R. Tcherikower, September 25, 1944, in YIVO RG 81, folio 151689.

16. Szajkowski to R. Tcherikower, March 16, 1944, in YIVO RG 81, folio 151505.

17. Benjamin Harshav, *Language in a Time of Revolution* (Stanford, CA: Stanford University Press, 1993), 52.

18. Szajkowski to R. Tcherikower, March 16, 1944, in YIVO RG 81, folio 151505.

19. Szajkowski to R. Tcherikower, March 16, 1944, in YIVO RG 81, folio 151505.

20. Dana Herman, "Hashevat Avedah: A History of Jewish Cultural Reconstruction, Inc." (Ph.D. diss., McGill University, 2008), 39.

21. Cecil Roth, "The Restoration of Jewish Libraries, Archives and Museums," *Contemporary Jewish Record* 7, no. 3 (June 1944), 257. The article is based on an address delivered at a Jewish Historical Society of England Conference in London in April 1943.

22. Elizabeth Simpson, ed., *The Spoils of War: World War II and Its Aftermath: The Loss, Reappearance, and Recovery of Cultural Property* (New York: Bard Graduate Center for Studies in the Decorative Arts, 1997); Lynn H. Nicholas, *The Rape of Europa* (New York: Vintage, 1994); and Patricia Kennedy Grimsted, *Trophies of War and Empire: The Archival Heritage of Ukraine, World War II and the International Politics of Restitution*, Harvard Papers in Ukrainian Studies (Cambridge, MA: Harvard University Press, 2001).

23. Sophie Coeuré, *La Mémoire spoliée: les archives des français: butin de guerre nazi puis soviétique* (Paris: Payot, 2007), 17–58.

24. Leslie Poste, "The Development of U.S. Protection of Libraries and Archives in Europe during World War II" (Ph.D. diss., University of Chicago, 1958), 33–34.

25. Coeuré, *Mémoire spoliée*, 164–65. On Napoleonic looting, see also Ernst Posner, "Some Aspects of Archival Development since the French Revolution," in Ken Munden, ed., *Archives and the Public Interest: Selected Essays by Ernst Posner* (Washington, DC: Public Affairs Press, 1967), 27, and his "Effects of Changes of Sovereignty on Archives," in the same volume, 174.

26. Lara Jennifer Moore, *Restoring Order: The Ecole des Chartes and the Organization of Archives and Libraries in France, 1820–1870* (Duluth, MN: Litwin, 2008), 12–13 and passim. See also Posner, "Effects," 168–81.

27. Coeuré, *Mémoire spoliée*, 164.

28. Posner, "Effects," 173.

29. Coeuré, *Mémoire spoliée*, 166.

30. "Hague Treaty of 1907," reprinted in Simpson, ed., *Spoils of War*, 278–79.

31. Postwar treaties, reprinted in Simpson, ed., *Spoils of War*, 282–285.

32. "Treaty of Peace with Germany," reprinted in excerpted form in Simpson, ed., *Spoils of War*, 280–81.

33. On art plunder, see Nicholas, *The Rape of Europa*; and Simpson, ed., *Spoils of War*.

34. Jean-Claude Kuperminc, "La Reconstruction de la Bibliothèque de l'Alliance Israélite Universelle, 1945–1955," *Archives Juives* 34, no. 1 (2001): 98–113.

35. Among the smaller collections were those of the Fédération des Sociétés Juives de France; the Paris Consistory; the Paris branch of YIVO; the Paris branch of the World Jewish Congress; the Palestine Jewish Colonization Association; the Dubnow Fund; and the Eclaireurs Israélites de France (the Jewish Scouts). See Nicholas Reymes, "Le Pillage des bibliothèques appartenant à des juifs pendant l'occupation: les livres dans la tourmente," in *Revue de l'histoire de la Shoah: Le Monde Juif* no. 168 (2000): 31–56.

36. On the ERR, see Joseph Billig, *Alfred Rosenberg dans l'action idéologique, politique et administrative du Reich Hitlérien: Inventaire commenté de la collection de documents conservés au C.D.J.C. provenant des archives du Reichsleiter et Ministre A. Rosenberg* (Paris: CDJC, 1963); Jean Cassou, ed., *Le Pillage par les allemands des oeuvres d'art et des bibliothèques appartenant à des juifs en France* (Paris: CDJC, 1947); Coeuré, *Mémoire spoliée*; Patricia Kennedy Grimsted, "Road to Ratibor: Library and Archival Plunder by the Einsatzstab Reichsleiter Rosenberg," in *Holocaust and Genocide Studies* 19, no. 3 (2005): 390–458.

37. Herman Kruk, *The Last Days of the Jerusalem of Lithuania: Chronicles from the Vilna Ghetto and the Camps, 1939–1944*, ed. Benjamin Harshav, trans. Barbara Harshav (New Haven, CT: Yale University Press, 2002).

38. Herman, "Hashevat Avedah," 10.

39. David E. Fishman, *Embers Plucked from the Fire: The Rescue of Jewish Cultural Treasures in Vilna* (New York: YIVO, 1996).

40. Michael J. Kurtz, *America and the Return of Nazi Contraband: The Recovery of Europe's Cultural Treasures* (New York: Cambridge University Press, 2006), 47.

41. The Monuments Men were limited to protection efforts, not restitution, except for items seized illegally. This limitation was implied in American Military Law no. 52, in spring 1945; specific policies for restitution were developed along those lines beginning in December 1945. For a full discussion of the policies, see Poste, *Development*, 66, 69.

42. On the Monuments Men, see Nicholas, *Rape of Europa*, chap. 9–11, and Robert Edsel, *The Monuments Men: Allied Heroes, Nazi Thieves and the Greatest Treasure Hunt in History* (New York: Center Street, 2009).

43. Kurtz, *America*, 62.

44. Kurtz, *America*, 61.

45. Nichols, *Rape of Europa*, 320–26; and for the most extensive discussion of the meetings and agreements prior to 1946, see Poste, "Development," chapter 1.

46. Szajkowski to R. Tcherikower, June 26, 1944, in YIVO RG 81, folios 151588–91. A good description of the perilous river landings of the paratroopers from the 82nd Airborne can be found in Stephen Ambrose, *D-Day, June 6, 1944: The Climactic Battle of World War II* (New York: Simon & Schuster, 1991): 212–15.

47. Szajkowski to R. Tcherikower, July 5, 1944, in YIVO RG 81, folio 151599; and August 4, 1944, folio 151637.

48. Szajkowski to R. Tcherikower, July 5, 1944, in YIVO RG 81, folio 151599.

49. Szajkowski to R. Tcherikower, July 7, 1944, in YIVO RG 81 folio 151601; and June 20, 1944, in YIVO RG 81, folio 151582.

50. Szajkowski to R. Tcherikower, July 22, 1944, in YIVO RG 81, folio 151620.

51. Szajkowski to R. Tcherikower, October 14, 1944, in YIVO RG 81, folio 151713.

52. Szajkowski to R. Tcherikower, June 20, 1944, in YIVO RG 81, folio 151582.

53. Szajkowski to R. Tcherikower, July 20, 1944, in YIVO RG 81, folio 151618.

54. Szajkowski to R. Tcherikower, July 5, 1944, in YIVO RG 81 folio 151599.

55. Szajkowski to R. Tcherikower, November 9, 1944, in YIVO RG 81, folio 151768; and Myriam Mitastein testimony. Zilke was a nickname for Uzyel; he also went by Jules in France.

56. Szajkowski to R. Tcherikower, November 9, 1944, in YIVO RG 81, folio 151768.

57. Szajkowski to R. Tcherikower, December 28, 1944, in YIVO RG 81, folio 151808.

58. Szajkowski to R. Tcherikower, January 26, 1945, in YIVO RG 81, folio 151820.

59. Szajkowski to R. Tcherikower, March 10, 1945, in YIVO RG 81, folio 151878.

60. Szajkowski to R. Tcherikower, October 3, 1945, in YIVO RG 81, folio 152139. Information about Szajkowski's relatives cross-checked against the Myriam Mitastein testimony, as well as the testimony of Michelle Frydman Mitastein Haydenblit, both given in Spanish in 1997 in Mexico, to the USC Shoah Foundation.

61. Myriam Mitastein testimony.

62. Szajkowski to R. Tcherikower, April 23, 1945, in YIVO RG 81, folio 151914.

63. See Monique and Michelle Mitastein's letters to Szajkowski in February 1956, in YIVO RG 800.

64. Szajkowski to R. Tcherikower, November 9, 1944, in YIVO RG 81, folio 151768.

65. Szajkowski to R. Tcherikower, November 15, 1944, in YIVO RG 81, folio 151774.

66. Szajkowski to R. Tcherikower (in English), November 8, 1944, in YIVO RG 81, folio 151763.

67. These figures from Annette Wieviorka, "Despoliation, Reparation, Compensation," in *Starting the Twenty-First Century: Sociological Reflections and Challenges*, ed. Ernest Krausz and Gitta Tulea (New Brunswick, NJ: Transaction, 2002), 205–6. On wartime experiences of Jews in Paris, see Renée Poznanski, *Jews in France during World War II*, trans. Nathan Bracher (Hanover, NH: Brandeis University Press, 2001).

68. Szajkowski to R. Tcherikower, November 9, 1944, in YIVO RG 81, folio 151768.

69. Szajkowski to R. Tcherikower, November 15, 1944, in YIVO RG 81, folio 151774.

70. On the despoliations and their indemnifications, see the report of the Mattéoli Commission: Annette Wieviorka and Floriane Azoulay, *Le Pillage des appartements et son indemnisation* (Paris: Documentation française, 2000); and Maud S. Mandel, *In the Aftermath of Genocide: Armenians and Jews in Twentieth-Century France* (Durham, NC: Duke University Press, 2003), 52–85.

71. On the whereabouts of goods at the end of the war more generally, see Leora Auslander, "Coming Home? Jews in Postwar Paris," *Journal of Contemporary History* 40, no. 2 (2005): 237–59. On apartments, see David Weinberg, "The Reconstruction of the French Jewish Community after World War II," in *Proceedings of the Sixth Yad Vashem International Congress: She'erit Hapletah, 1944–1948: Rehabilitation and Political Struggle* (Jerusalem: Yad Vashem, 1990), 171.

72. On Marjasza's property, Szajkowski wrote: "There's no work and no apartments to be had. The French moved into the majority of Jewish homes and now they won't leave. My sister-in-law was lucky in that respect, but her apartment is empty. The Germans took everything. So the French neighbors say" (Szajkowski to R. Tcherikower, November 15, 1944, in YIVO RG 81, folio 151777). It is interesting to compare Szajkowski's relatively negative attitude toward the neighbors with Marjasza/Myriam's relatively positive and grateful one, at least as she recalled it in 1997; see Myriam Mitastein testimony.

73. See Mandel, *Aftermath of Genocide*, 52–85.

74. Szajkowski to R. Tcherikower, November 29, 1944, in YIVO RG 81, folio 151785.

75. Szajkowski, *Jews and the French Foreign Legion* (New York: Ktav, 1975), 62–63.

76. Szajkowski to R. Tcherikower, December 28, 1944, in YIVO RG 81, folio 151808.

77. Szajkowski to R. Tcherikower, February 12, 1945, in YIVO RG 81, folio 151851.

78. Szajkowski to R. Tcherikower, France, February 29, 1945 [sic], in YIVO RG 81, folio 151836; and July 6, 1945, in YIVO RG 81, folio 152006.

79. Szajkowski to R. Tcherikower, September 30, 1945, in YIVO RG 81, folio 152129. For more on the schisms within the French Jewish community (particularly those involving the Communists) in the immediate postwar commemorations, see Simon Perego, "Commémorations," in *Dictionnaire du Judaïsme français depuis 1944*, ed. Jean Leselbaum (Paris: Armand Colin, 2013), 175–77.

80. This information from a letter sent by Jacoubovitch to Szajkowski, October 1, 1945, and passed on to Riva Tcherikower, in YIVO RG 81, folio 152137. Szajkowski urged Riva to have the letter published or at least circulated in America.

81. Szajkowski to R. Tcherikower, February 3, 1945, in YIVO RG 81, folio 151845.

82. Szajkowski to R. Tcherikower, January 26, 1945, in YIVO RG 81, folio 151820; and November 20, 1945, in YIVO RG 81, folio 152192.

83. On Jarblum's compromises with the Bundists and the Communists, see, e.g., Szajkowski to R. Tcherikower, April 12, 1945, in YIVO RG 81, folio 151900;

and November 20, 1945, in YIVO RG 81, folio 152192; on Belgium, see letter in English, May 14, 1945, in YIVO RG 81, folio 151942.

84. See for example the letter he received from Jacoubovitch and sent on to Riva Tcherikower for circulation in America, dated October 1, 1945, in YIVO RG 81, folio 152137.

85. See, e.g., Szajkowski to R. Tcherikower, February 2, 1945, in YIVO RG 81, folio 151833; and February 7, 1945, in YIVO RG 81, folio 151851; in Belgium, things seemed just as bad to him; see April 28, 1945, in YIVO RG 81, folio 151917; and May 24, 1945, in YIVO RG 81, folio 151950.

86. Szajkowski to R. Tcherikower, December 27, 1944, in YIVO RG 81, folio 151812.

87. Szajkowski to R. Tcherikower, November 28, 1944, in YIVO RG 81, folio 151791; November 29, 1944, in YIVO RG 81, folio 151785; January 1, 1945, in YIVO, RG 81, folio 151817; January 11, 1945, in YIVO RG 81, folio 151820; and February 12, 1945, in YIVO RG 81, folio 151851. See YIVO's report on this in *Yedies fun YIVO* 6 (December 1944): 7. The papers are now part of RG 81, the Tcherikower Collection.

88. Szajkowski to R. Tcherikower, October 18, 1945, in YIVO RG 81, folio 151253.

89. Szajkowski to R. Tcherikower, November 9, 1944, in YIVO RG 81, folio 151768; November 16, 1944, folio 151777; November 29, 1944, folio 151785; February 12, 1945, folio 151851.

90. Szajkowski to R. Tcherikower, March 28, 1945 (in English), in YIVO RG 81, folio 151853; and May 1, 1945 (in English), in YIVO RG 81, folio 151922. The French one was published as "The Jewish Press in France, 1940–44," in *Yedies fun YIVO* 9 (July 1945), 3; the Belgian equivalent does not appear to have been published.

91. Szajkowski to R. Tcherikower, May 29, 1945, in YIVO RG 81, folio 151958.

92. Szajkowski to R. Tcherikower, August 1, 1945, in YIVO RG 81, folio 152071.

93. Szajkowski to R. Tcherikower, February 29, 1945 [sic], in YIVO RG 81, folio 151865; April 1, 1945, in YIVO RG 81, folio 151893; and n.d., folio 151912.

94. Szajkowski to R. Tcherikower, August 1, 1945, in YIVO RG 81, folio 152071.

95. Szajkowski to R. Tcherikower, July 15, 1945, in YIVO RG 81, folio 152039.

96. Szajkowski to R. Tcherikower, May 2, 1945, in YIVO RG 81, folio 151924. Epstein's collecting eventually produced much of what now forms a marvelous collection at YIVO, RG 128, Rabbinical and Historical Manuscripts. Weinreich's correspondence with Epstein through the 1950s testifies to the difficulties Epstein had securing funds from the organization. See YIVO RG 584, file 545b.

97. Szajkowski to R. Tcherikower, March 8, 1945, in YIVO RG 81, folio 151878. On his thinking that these materials were most useful for a historian, see Szajkowski to R. Tcherikower, April 1, 1945 (in English), in YIVO RG 81, folio 151898.

98. Now in YIVO Archives, New York, UGIF papers, RG 210, folders 92.10–92.14.

99. Szajkowski to R. Tcherikower, April 12, 1945, in YIVO RG 81, folio 151900. The donor may have been Jacoubovitch (given his close friendship with Szajkowski at the time) who was publicly accusing one wartime Jewish leader, the Russian-born

Elie Krouker, of collaboration when he headed the Comité de Coordination des Oeuvres Juives de Bienfaisance. See Simon Perego, "Jurys d'honneur: The Stakes, Modes, and Limits of the Purges among the Jews in Post-Liberation France," in Gabriel Finder and Laura Jockusch, eds., *Jewish Honor Courts: Revenge, Retribution and Reconciliation in Europe and Israel after the Holocaust* (Detroit, MI: Wayne State University Press, forthcoming 2015).

100. On France not being a "secure spot for Jewish archives," see Szajkowski to R. Tcherikower, March 8, 1945 (in English), in YIVO RG 81, folio 151881.

101. See Perego, "Jurys d'honneur." These intra-Jewish commmissions were extralegal bodies that heard cases related to Jewish collaboration with the Nazis and their allies during the war.

102. Szajkowski to R. Tcherikower, April 12, 1945, in YIVO RG 81, folio 151900. It was impossible to ascertain whether the copy was indeed sent; the CDJC now has copies of all of YIVO's UGIF papers.

103. YIVO Archives, New York, UGIF papers, RG 210, Finding Aid.

104. See the entry for "Union Générale des Israélites de France," in Fruma Mohrer and Marek Web, eds., *Guide to the YIVO Archives* (New York: YIVO Institute for Jewish Research, 1998), 286–87. YIVO has additional materials from France under the German occupation in the Tcherikower papers (RG 81), folders 1649–57, "Materials from France under the German occupation (from Jakoubovitch)."

105. This is RG 343; see Mohrer and Web, *Guide*, 238.

106. Zosa Szajkowski, *Analytical Franco-Jewish Gazetteer, 1939–1945, with an Introduction to Some Problems in Writing the History of the Jews in France during World War II* (New York: n.p., 1966), 13; see also Renée Poznanski, "La Création du Centre de Documentation Juive Contemporaine en France (avril 1943)," in *Vingtième siècle* 63 (1999), 62, where Szajkowski is lauded for saving these records from destruction in compliance with the circulars.

107. Sonia Combe, *Archives interdites: l'histoire confisquée* (Paris: La Découverte, 2001), 194–232.

108. Quoted in Szajkowski, *Gazetteer*, 13n1.

109. Samuel D. Kassow, *Who Will Write Our History? Emanuel Ringelblum, the Warsaw Ghetto, and the Oyneg Shabes Archive* (Bloomington: Indiana University Press, 2007).

110. On the creation of the CDJC, see Poznanski, "Création," 51–63.

111. Poznanski, "Création"; and Laura Jockusch, *Collect and Record! Jewish Holocaust Documentation in Early Postwar Europe* (New York: Oxford University Press, 2012), 56–62.

112. Léon Poliakov, *L'Auberge des Musiciens: Mémoires* (Paris: Jacques Grancher, 1981), 184–91; Poznanski, "Création"; and Annette Wieviorka, "Du Centre de Documentation Juive Contemporaine au Mémorial de la Shoah," *Revue de l'histoire de la Shoah* no. 181, (2004): 10–36.

113. See Jockusch, *Collect and Record!*, 66.

114. Schneersohn to Weinreich, August 6, 1947, in CDJC Archives, Paris, MDXXXVI-5: Conférence Européenne des Commissions Historiques et des Centres de Documentation Juives, 1947, Box 6.

115. Szajkowski to R. Tcherikower, August 9, 1945, in YIVO RG 81, folio 152081.

Chapter 5

1. Szajkowski to R. Tcherikower, June 2, 1945, in YIVO RG 81, folio 151968. Military assignments confirmed by consulting Szajko Frydman's military personnel records, held at the National Personnel Records Center, Saint Louis, Mo.

2. Szajkowski to R. Tcherikower, June 3, 1945, in YIVO RG 81, folio 151968; and reiterated on July 6, 1945, in folio 152006.

3. Many Jewish observers of the Nuremberg Trials agreed with Szajkowski even after the trials began. For them, the emphasis on war crimes made the genocide less central an issue than they would have liked and left some crimes unpunished, such as crimes against German Jews who were persecuted within Germany rather than as part of aggressive war. See Lawrence Douglas, *The Memory of Judgment: Making Law and History in the Trials of the Holocaust* (New Haven, CT: Yale University Press, 2001), 11–64.

4. Atina Grossmann, *Jews, Germans, and Allies: Close Encounters in Occupied Germany* (Princeton, NJ: Princeton University Press, 2007), 49.

5. Szajkowski to R. Tcherikower, August 14, 1945, in YIVO RG 81, folio 152091.

6. Szajkowski to R. Tcherikower, July 9, 1945, in YIVO RG 81, folio 152025. Szajkowski used the word "patronization" here.

7. Szajkowski to R. Tcherikower, July 11, 1945, in YIVO RG 81, folio 152031.

8. Szajkowski to R. Tcherikower, July 12, 1945, in YIVO RG 81, folio 152037 (ellipses in original).

9. Szajkowski to R. Tcherikower, September 1945, in YIVO RG 81, folio 152113; and November 20, 1945, in YIVO RG 81, folio 152192. For more on the extent of American fraternization, see Grossmann, *Jews, Germans, and Allies*, 71–77.

10. Szajkowski to R. Tcherikower, May 29, 1945, in YIVO RG 81, folio 151958.

11. Szajkowski to R. Tcherikower, September 12, 1945, in YIVO RG 81, folio 152115.

12. Szajkowski to R. Tcherikower, July 21, 1945, in YIVO RG 81, folio 152046.

13. Daniel B. Silver, *Refuge in Hell: How Berlin's Jewish Hospital Outlasted the Nazis* (Boston: Houghton Mifflin, 2003).

14. Grossmann, *Jews, Germans, and Allies*, 31.

15. All these citations are from the same letter: Szajkowski to R. Tcherikower, July 25, 1945, in YIVO RG 81, folio 152068.

16. Szajkowski to R. Tcherikower, July 25, 1945, in YIVO RG 81, folio 152068.

17. Szajkowski to R. Tcherikower, August 9, 1945, in YIVO RG 81, folio 152081. The Yiddish phrase I'm rendering as "supporter of the Exodus from Europe" is "an onhenger fun yitzias Eyrope."

18. Szajkowski to R. Tcherikower, August 9, 1945, in YIVO RG 81, folio 152081.

19. Szajkowski to R. Tcherikower, August 4, 1945, in YIVO RG 81, folio 152076.

20. Szajkowski to R. Tcherikower, September 25, 1945, in YIVO RG 81, folio 152125.

21. Szajkowski to R. Tcherikower, October 3, 1945, in YIVO RG 81, folio 152139; October 4, 1945, in YIVO RG 81, folio 152140; and October 8, 1945, in YIVO RG 81, folio 152150.

22. Grossmann, *Germans, Jews, and Allies*, 142–45.

23. Abraham Klausner, *A Letter to My Children: From the Edge of the Holocaust* (San Francisco: Holocaust Center of Northern California, 2002). See also Avinoam Patt, "The People Must Be Forced to Go to Palestine: Rabbi Abraham Klausner and the She'erit Hapletah in Germany," *Holocaust and Genocide Studies* 28, no. 2 (2014): 240–76.

24. On this issue, see Grossmann, *Germans, Jews, and Allies*, 142–53 and passim; and Lewis Barash, ed., *Rabbis in Uniform: The Story of the American Military Chaplain* (New York: J. David, 1962).

25. Szajkowski to R. Tcherikower, October 2, 1945, in YIVO RG 81, folio 152140. "Incident" is the term Szajkowski used.

26. See Grossmann, *Germans, Jews, and Allies*, 138–39.

27. On the Harrison report and its effects on Allied policy, see Dan Diner, "Elements in Becoming a Subject: Jewish DPs in Historical Perspective," in *Jahrbuch zur Geschichte und Wirkung des Holocaust* 2 (1997): 229–48.

28. These numbers are presented as "conservative" estimates of booty found in the U.S. Zone by Leslie Poste, in "The Development of U.S. Protection of Libraries and Archives in Europe during World War II" (Ph.D. diss., University of Chicago, 1958), 333. Poste himself was a librarian who had been part of the MFA&A and then became an OAD officer; he later completed a dissertation on the OAD's work at the University of Chicago. On the Monuments Men more generally see Kathy Peiss, "Cultural Policy in a Time of War: The American Response to Endangered Books in World War II," *Library Trends* 55, no. 3 (2007): 370–86; Lynn H. Nicholas, The *Rape of Europa:* The Fate of Europe's Treasures in the Third Reich and World War II (New York: Vintage, 1994), chaps. 9–11; and Robert Edsel, *The Monuments Men: Allied Heroes, Nazi Thieves and the Greatest Treasure Hunt in History* (New York: Center Street, 2009).

29. Poste estimates that, given the eventual number of restitutions, the 1.2 million volumes estimate is a better one, and is probably even a little high, though it is hard to know since the collection went unguarded for so long, and reports of looting were widespread. Eventually, the OAD returned 2,832,893 volumes; this represented a majority of the 3,475,568 volumes the Americans restituted in total following the war. Poste, "Development," 333–35.

30. Michael Kurtz, *America and the Return of Nazi Contraband: The Return of Europe's Cultural Treasures* (New York: Cambridge University Press, 2006), chap. 3; see also Poste, "Development"; and Seymour J. Pomrenze, "The Restitution of Jewish Cultural Treasures after the Holocaust: The Offenbach Archival Depot's Role in the

Fulfillment of U.S. International and Moral Obligations (a First Hand Account)," National Foundation for Jewish Culture, Feinstein Lecture 2002, www.jewishlibraries.org/ajlweb/resources/feinstein/pomrenze.html.

31. Kurtz, *America*, 95–103.

32. Jenny Delsaux, *La Sous-Commission des livres à la Récuperation Artistique, 1944–1950* (Paris: Ruoms, 1976).

33. Poste, "Development," chapter 1; and Kurtz, *America*, 94–102.

34. These disagreements can be traced back to at least the middle of the war, and inhibited the establishment of clear, coordinated policies. For a full discussion of this history, see Poste, "Development," 66, 69.

35. Kurtz, *America*, 95–103.

36. Patricia Kennedy Grimsted is the acknowledged expert on these "twice-looted" archives; see, e.g., her "The Road to Minsk for Western 'Trophy' Books: Twice Plundered but Not Yet 'Home from the War,'" *Libraries and Culture* 39, no. 4 (2004): 351–404; and the collection of essays she co-edited with F. J. Hoogewoud and Eric Ketelaar, *Returned from Russia: Nazi Archival Plunder in Western Europe and Recent Restitution Issues* (Builth Wells, UK: Institute of Art and Law, 2007). See also Sophie Coeuré, *La Mémoire spoliée: les archives des Français, butin de guerre nazi puis soviétique* (Paris: Payot, 2007).

37. Poste, "Development," 339–40.

38. These numbers were assembled from the monthly reports of the OAD, by Poste, "Development," 351–69, 392–93.

39. Comparisons have been done regarding the restitution of non-cultural Jewish property after the war, but not regarding restitution of Jewish property. See Martin Dean, Constantin Goschler, and Phillip Ther, eds., *Robbery and Restitution: The Conflict over Jewish Property in Europe* (New York: Berghan Books, 2007).

40. See Grimsted, "The Road to Minsk"; and her "Road to Ratibor: Library and Archival Plunder by the Einsatzstab Reichsleiter Rosenberg," *Holocaust and Genocide Studies* 19, no. 3 (2005).

41. For a good summary and scholarly bibliography regarding the disposition of Jewish cultural property in Poland, see http://forms.claimscon.org/Judaica/poland.pdf.

42. Numbers are estimates from Martine Poulin, *Livres pillés, Lectures surveillés: Les bibliothèques françaises sous l'Occupation* (Paris: Gallimard, 2008), 419. The discrepancy between the number of books the French report having gotten back from the OAD (323,000) and the number the Americans report returning to them (377,204) is striking and too large to be accounted for by the number of books on the shipment lost in transit in 1948.

43. Delsaux, *Sous-Commission*.

44. Folder, "Mission Liber," in Archives Nationales, Paris, F/17/17980.

45. Delsaux, *Sous-Commission*, 16.

46. Kuperminc, "Return," 142. For an assessment of the impact of book restitutions in France, see Lisa Moses Leff, "Post-Holocaust Book Restitutions: How One State Agency Helped Revive Republican Franco-Judaism," in Seán Hand and Steven T. Katz, ed., *Post-Holocaust France and the Jews, 1945-55* (New York: New York University Press, forthcoming 2015).

47. Baron, "The Spiritual Reconstruction of European Jewry," *Commentary*, November 1945, 4–12. This quotation appears on page 6. I pull here from Dana Herman's analysis; see her "Hashavat Avedah: A History of Jewish Cultural Reconstruction, Inc." (Ph.D. diss., McGill University, Montréal, 2008), 48.

48. Letters to L. G. Pinkerton, American Consul-General in Jerusalem, January 28, 1946, and to Koppel Pinson (a senior official at the American Jewish Joint Distribution Committee based in Frankfurt at the time and a member of Baron's Commission), May 3, 1946; both cited in Herman, "Hashavat Avedah," 61–62.

49. Herman, "Hashavat Avedah," 166–71. Lucy Schildkret (later Dawidowicz), who arrived in Germany in 1946 to work for the Joint as well, did much to solve the problem by reconstructing records of the books; but she recommended that the second request be denied in order to repair the relationship between the Joint and the military officials in Offenbach. On this story, see also Dawidowicz, *From That Place and Time*, 312–13.

50. He voiced these concerns in a letter to Cecil Roth in 1944; see Herman, "Hashavat Avedah," 63.

51. Szajkowski to R. Tcherikower, August 1, 1945, in YIVO RG 81, folio 152073; and Szajkowski to YIVO friends, August 29, 1945, and September 1, 1945, in American Jewish Historical Society Archives, New York, papers of Lucy Dawidowicz, box 51, folder 6.

52. Dawidowicz, *From That Place and Time*, 313–19; Herman, "Hashavat Avedah," 159–66.

53. For an account of the fate of the YIVO library during and after World War II, see David Fishman, *Embers Plucked from the Fire: The Rescue of Jewish Cultural Treasures in Vilna* (New York: YIVO, 1996).

54. Herman, "Hashavat Avedah," 60.

55. See Herman's excellent account of the affair in "Hashavat Avedah," 171–79. For the investigation results regarding Friedman and ordering his dismissal for this theft, see the "Administrative Admonition" in his papers at the American Jewish Archives, Cincinnati, OH, MS763, box 1/13. Friedman received no punishment beyond this administrative admonition and his subsequent dismissal from the military.

56. Friedman, *Roots of the Future*, 112.

57. Cited in Poste, "Development," 394.

58. Letter of Richard Howard of the MFA&A to Joseph Horne, February 12, 1947, in NARA RG260 ("Ardelia Hall Collection"), box 66, file Jewish Cultural Property 1947–50, as cited in Herman, "Hashavat Avedah," 177–78.

59. Suzanne Pollack, "Megillah Comes Back Home," in *Washington Jewish Week*, March 7, 2012, http://washingtonjewishweek.com/main.asp?SectionID=4&Sub SectionID=4&ArticleID=16772.

60. Szajkowski to R. Tcherikower, August 4, 1945, in YIVO RG 81, folio 152076.

61. Szajkowski to R. Tcherikower, October 7, 1945 in YIVO RG 81, folio 152146.

62. Poste, "Development," 64–67.

63. This was by order no. 4 of the Allied Control Council, dated May 22, 1946, cited in Poste, "Development," 22. On the Library of Congress Mission in Europe, see Robert G. Waite, "Returning Jewish Cultural Property: The Handling of Books Looted by the Nazis in the American Zone of Occupation, 1945–1952," *Libraries and Culture* 37, no. 3 (2002): 215.

64. These measures laid the groundwork for the U.S. military to confiscate Nazi archives and use the documents for war crimes trials. After those trials were over, the captured German documents remained in British and American hands, and became the subject of a protracted effort on the part of the West German government to get them back, seeing the ownership of these archives as an important symbol of their sovereignty. Astrid M. Eckert, *The Struggle for the Files: The Western Allies and the Return of German Archives after the Second World War*, trans. Donna Geyer (New York: Cambridge University Press, 2012); and Gerhard L. Weinberg, "German Documents in the United States," *Central European History* 41 (2008): 555–67.

65. Grossmann, *Germans, Jews, and Allies*, 25–31.

66. Szajkowski to R. Tcherikower, July 24, 1945, in YIVO RG 81, folio 152058.

67. Szajkowski to R. Tcherikower, July 2, 1945, in YIVO RG 81, folio 152002.

68. Szajkowski to R. Tcherikower, August 27, 1945, in YIVO RG 81, folio 152104; September 21, 1945, in YIVO RG 81, folio 152122; and October 13, 1945, in YIVO RG 81, folio 152147. On the losses, see August 9, 1945, in YIVO RG 81, folio 152081.

69. Szajkowski to R. Tcherikower, August 27, 1945, in YIVO RG 81, folio 152104.

70. Hans Loeser, *Hans's Story* (Lincoln, Nebr.: iUniverse, 2007), 136.

71. Szajkowski to R. Tcherikower, October 23, 1945, in YIVO RG 81, folio 152157.

72. Szajkowski to R. Tcherikower, August 14, 1945, in YIVO RG 81, folio 152091.

73. Szajkowski to R. Tcherikower, August 19, 1945, in YIVO RG 81, folio 152095.

74. Szajkowski to R. Tcherikower, October 4, 1945, in YIVO RG 81, folio 152140.

75. Szajkowski to R. Tcherikower, October 5, 1945, in YIVO RG 81, folio 152144.

76. Szajkowski to R. Tcherikower, August 19, 1945, in YIVO RG 81, folio 152095.

77. Szajkowski to R. Tcherikower, August 9, 1945, in YIVO RG 81, folio 152081.

78. Szajkowski to R. Tcherikower, October 27, 1945, in YIVO RG 81, folio 152159.

79. Szajkowski to R. Tcherikower, June 22, 1945, in YIVO RG 81, folio 151993.

80. Mohrer and Web, *Guide to the YIVO Archives*, 28–29.

81. Letter dated August 25, no year but probably mid-1980s, from Lucy S. Dawidowicz's uncatalogued private personal correspondence. I am grateful to Nancy Sinkoff for sharing this letter with me.

82. Szajkowski to R. Tcherikower, October 18 and 29, 1945, in YIVO RG 81, folios 152153 and 152163. On Elaine's fiancé, see Szajkowski to R. Tcherikower, August 9, 1945, in YIVO RG 81, folio 152081.

83. On Szajkowski's role in providing source material for *Hitler's Professors*, see Max Weinreich, *Hitler's Professors: The Part of Scholarship in Germany's Crimes against the Jewish People* (New York: YIVO, 1946), 2, as well as the article about the book in the newsletter, which likewise mentions Szajkowski, "Role of German Scholarship in Annihilation of Jews Analyzed," *Yedies fun YIVO*, no. 10 (September 1945): 1–2. See also the Program of the 20th Annual Conference of the YIVO, in *Yedies fun YIVO*, no. 12 (December 1945): 6–7.

84. On this story and a number of other high-profile cases, see Kenneth D. Alford, *The Spoils of World War II: The American Military's Role in the Stealing of Europe's Treasures* (New York: Birch Lane Press, 1994).

85. Bernard Heller, "The Homecoming," in *Liberal Judaism*, September 1950, 24–25.

86. Heller, "Homecoming," 28.

87. Cited in Herman, "Hashavat Avedah," 131.

88. Commission on Jewish Cultural Reconstruction, "Tentative List of Jewish Cultural Treasures in Axis-Occupied Countries," supplement to *Jewish Social Studies* 8, no. 1 (1946): 6.

89. See the field reports of JCR, e.g., Hannah Arendt's "Field Report no. 18," February 15–March 10, 1950, a copy of which is held in the Alliance Israélite Universelle (AIU) Library, Paris, Fonds Edmond-Maurice Lévy, AP1/76. JCR's distributions from July 1, 1949, to January 31, 1952, when it concluded its operations, reflect the mentality described above. A total of 431,745 books was given to institutions in the countries where Jewish populations were now largest, with Israel receiving 44 percent of the total, the United States 37 percent, West Germany 3 percent, Great Britain 4 percent, and France 2 percent. Taken together, Switzerland, South Africa, Argentina, Australia, and Brazil received 6 percent, and the remaining 4 percent was divided among twelve additional countries. See Herman, "Hashavat Avedah," 226–29.

Chapter 6

1. Szajkowski to R. Tcherikower, July 15, 1944, in YIVO RG 81, folio 151612.

2. Szajkowski to R. Tcherikower, February 2, 1945, in YIVO RG 81, folio 151833; and February 7, 1945, in YIVO RG 81, folio 151856.

3. Szajkowski to R. Tcherikower, September 21, 1945, in YIVO RG 81, folio 152122; author's email correspondence with G. Weinreich, July 27, 2011. Weinreich recalls the sword, but not the antlers, which may not have arrived at their destination.

4. Szajkowski to R. Tcherikower, August 14, 1945, in YIVO RG 81, folio 152091.

5. Szajkowski to R. Tcherikower, June 26, 1944, in YIVO RG 81, folios 151588–91.

6. Szajkowski to R. Tcherikower, November 5, 1945, in YIVO RG 81, folio 152168.

7. Passenger list of the *Asama Maru*, arriving in San Francisco May 11, 1941, *California, Passenger and Crew Lists, 1882–1957* [online database] (Provo, UT: Ancestry.com Operations Inc, 2008). Giterman's name appears on microfilm roll M1410:360. See also Ezekiel Lifshutz, "Notes about the Writer I Knew: Zosa Szajkowski/Shayke Frydman," unpublished Yiddish manuscript, 1983, in Ezekiel Lifshutz papers, Central Archives for the History of the Jewish People, Jerusalem, P130. Lifshutz, YIVO's archivist, was Szajkowski's supervisor from 1954 until Lifshutz's retirement in the early 1970s.

8. Indeed, in the 1950s, the rebbe and his wife were occasional visitors in the Frydmans' Upper West Side apartment and spoke warmly of their hospitality. Isaac Schneersohn to Szajkowski, March 25, 1955, in CDJC, MDXXXVI-13: Correspondence internationale, folder Amérique, 1948–54 [sic].

9. Szajkowski to R. Tcherikower, October 27, 1953, in YIVO RG 81, folder 2009.

10. A whole file of these cards and letters is in YIVO RG 800, Zosa Szajkowski papers.

11. Max Weinreich to Elliot E. Cohen, December 25, 1947, in YIVO RG 584, folder 592; and Max Weinreich to Leibush Lehrer, July 20, 1946, in YIVO RG 584, folder 595. Many thanks to Nancy Sinkoff for sending these to me.

12. Interview with Chana Mlotek by author, June 5, 2012.

13. See Szajkowski to Moshe Kligsberg, March 10, 1943, in YIVO RG 719.

14. Copy of Szajkowski's letters to Max Weinreich, December 14 and 19, 1949, in CDJC, MDXXXVI-13, Correspondance internationale, folder Amérique, 1948–1954.

15. Szajkowski to Weinreich, December 14, 1949, in CDJC, MDXXXVI-13, Correspondance internationale, folder Amérique, 1948–1954. Translation by Solon Beinfeld.

16. Isaac Schneersohn to Max Weinreich, December 28, 1949, in CDJC, MDXXXVI-13, Correspondence internationale, folder YIVO, 1947–53. The translation from the French draft is mine.

17. Szajkowski to Weinreich, December 19, 1949, in CDJC, MDXXXVI-13, Correspondence internationale, folder Amérique, 1948–54.

18. Szajkowski to Moshe Kligsberg, August 23, 1952, in YIVO RG 719.

19. Lifshutz, "Zosa Szajkowski."

20. On the same trip, he acquired for YIVO the HICEM and Colonie Scolaire collections. See Szajkowski to Ezekiel Lifshutz, October 22, 1955, October 27, 1955, and November 7, 1955, Lifshutz papers, CAHJP, P130.

21. See Lifshutz, "Zosa Szajkowski."

22. The journals in which he published most frequently were *Hebrew Union College Annual, Historia Judaica, Jewish Social Studies, Jewish Quarterly Review, The Proceedings of the American Academy for Jewish Research*, and *Publications of the*

American Jewish Historical Society. He also published frequently in Yiddish in the *YIVO Annual of Jewish Social Science,* the *YIVO Bleter,* the Argentine journal *Davke,* as well as the more popular *Yidishe kemfer* and *Kiyoum* (Paris). He also sometimes published in Hebrew in *Zion, Yad Vashem Studies,* and *Horeb,* and had a few short articles in Italian and French. The best of his English-language articles were gathered and republished as a collection: Zosa Szajkowski, *Jews and the French Revolutions of 1789, 1830 and 1848* (New York: Ktav, 1970).

23. Author's telephone interview with Emmanuel Mark, December 4, 2009. Many thanks to Abe and Riva Kriegel for putting me in touch with Mr. Mark. Biographical information confirmed by cross-referencing Gennady Estraikh, "Yudl Mark," in the *YIVO Encyclopedia of Jews in Eastern Europe,* consulted online at http://www.yivoencyclopedia.org/article.aspx/Mark_Yudl.

24. Lifshutz, "Zosa Szajkowski."

25. On difficulties publishing in Yiddish and his plans to distribute his work himself, see Szajkowski to R. Tcherikower, October 27, 1953, in YIVO RG 81, folder 2009. On selling his books himself, see also the receipt Jacob Dienstag made out to Szajkowski, January 7, 1960, for a $5.00 copy of his 1959 self-published book, in Yeshiva University Archives, collection S. Frydman, cab. 25, drawer 2. On carrying the books home, see the unusually high number of suitcases Chana and Szajko Frydman brought with them on their trip home from Le Havre, landing in New York on November 12, 1953. See Ancestry.com, New York Passenger Lists, 1820–1957. Many extra copies of the books were found in the Frydman apartment in 2012 after Chana's death; see YIVO RG 800.

26. Szajkowski's membership card is archived among lists of members from 1960–62, in Archives, Jewish Theological Seminary of America, ARC 9, papers of the AAJR, folder 6, box 13.

27. Robert F. Byrnes, *Antisemitism in Modern France* (New Brunswick, NJ: Rutgers University Press, 1951); Zosa Szajkowski, *Antisemitzm in der Frantseyzisher Arbeter-Bavegung: fun Furierizm bizn sof Drayfus-Afere* (New York: published privately, 1948); and "Socialists and Radicals in the Development of Antisemitism in Algeria (1884–1900)," *Jewish Social Studies* 10, no. 3 (1948): 257–80.

28. The other authors were Edmund Silberner (one), Henri Sinder (one), Salomon Posener (two), Léon Poliakov (two), and Hannah Arendt (one).

29. In *Jewish Social Studies* 17, no. 4 (October 1955): 338–39. The works under review were Zosa Szajkowski, *Agricultural Credit and Napoleon's Anti-Jewish Decrees* (New York: Editions historiques franco-juives, 1953); *The Economic Status of the Jews in Alsace, Metz and Lorraine (1648–1789)* (New York: Editions historiques franco-juives, 1954); and *Poverty and Social Welfare among French Jews (1800–1880)* (New York: Editions historiques franco-juives, 1954).

30. Anthony Grafton, *The Footnote: A Curious History* (Cambridge, MA: Harvard University Press, 1997), 8–9.

31. Zosa Szajkowski, *Agricultural Credit,* 19–20.

32. Szajkowski, *Agricultural Credit*, 19.

33. Smith, *The Gender of History*, 137.

34. See, e.g., Jonathan Sarna, "Recalling Arthur Hertzberg: Public Intellectual," *Jewish Week*, April 21, 2006.

35. Zosa Szajkowski, "Population Problems with Marranos and Sephardim in France, from the 16th to the 20th Centuries," *Proceedings of the American Academy for Jewish Research* 27 (1958): 83–105; "Jewish Participation in the Sale of National Property during the French Revolution," *Jewish Social Studies* 14, no. 4 (1952): 292.

36. Szajkowski, "Population Problems," 23.

37. Szajkowski, "Population Problems," 5.

38. Zosa Szajkowski, *Jews and the French Revolutions of 1789, 1830 and 1848* (New York: Ktav, 1970), xxxvii–xxxviii.

39. As Szajkowski wrote to Israel Halperin of the Israeli Historical Society, he believed Tcherikower's work about French Jews in the Revolution of 1789 was "a weak compilation of work and suffers from a lot of imprecise facts," though out of love and gratitude for him and especially for his widow Riva, he never criticized his mentor in print. Szajkowski to Halperin, September 22, 1952, in CAHJP, Papers of the Israeli Historical Society, P127, file "Halperin."

40. Zosa Szajkowski, *Autonomy and Communal Jewish Debts during the French Revolution of 1789* (New York, n.p., 1959). His work clearly influenced Hertzberg, whose *The French Enlightenment and the Jews: The Origins of Modern Anti-Semitism* (New York: Columbia University Press, 1968) is usually cited as the first English-language book to openly attack the triumphalist narrative of Jewish emancipation.

41. On Brandeis, Jonathan Sarna, who took the course as an undergraduate, email with author, November 18, 2008; on Hampshire, Aaron Lansky, *Outwitting History: The Amazing Adventures of a Man Who Rescued a Million Yiddish Books* (New York: Algonquin Books, 2005), 9.

42. Hertzberg, *French Enlightenment and the Jews*, 7.

43. Zosa Szajkowski, *The Jews and the French Revolutions*, xxiv–xxv.

44. Grafton, *The Footnote*, 89.

45. Szajkowski, *Agricultural Credit*, 76 n.193 and n.195.

46. Guido Kisch to Szajkowski, November 3, 1963, in Archives of the Leo Baeck Institute, New York, Guido Kisch papers.

47. Zosa Szajkowski, "The Emancipation of Jews during the French Revolution: A Bibliography of Books, Pamphlets and Printed Documents, 1789–1800," in *Studies in Bibliography and Booklore* (Cincinnati, OH: Hebrew Union College-Jewish Institute of Religion Library, 1959); *Franco-Judaica: An Analytical Bibliography of Books, Pamphlets, Decrees, Briefs and Other Printed Documents Pertaining to the Jews in France, 1500–1788* (New York: American Academy for Jewish Research, 1962); "Judaica-Napoleonica: A Bibliography of Books, Pamphlets and Printed Documents, 1801–1815," in *Studies in Bibliography and Booklore* 2 (1956), 107–52;

and *Analytical Franco-Jewish Gazetteer, 1939–1945, with an Introduction to Some Problems in Writing the History of the Jews in France during World War II* (New York: published privately, 1966).

48. See, e.g., his "The Organization of the 'UGIF' In Nazi-Occupied France," *Jewish Social Studies* 9, no. 3 (1947): 239–56. On Szajkowski's "misgivings about historical truth," see the description of Szajkowski's remarks at a dinner party at Isaac Schneersohn's, reported in a letter to Max Weinreich, December 1, 1948, in CDJC, MDXXXVI-13, Correspondence internationale, folder YIVO, 1947–53.

49. *Gazetteer*, 16.

50. On the importance of Szajkowski's insights in the *Gazetteer*, see, e.g., Michel Laffitte, *Juif dans la France allemande* (Paris: Tallandier, 2006), 373–75.

51. I thank archivist Georges Weill for sharing with me evidence that shows how one such relationship worked. Weill provided me with photocopies of his correspondence with Szajkowski over the years 1956–58. Evidence of both men's friendship with him can be found in their letters sent to him in 1956, in YIVO RG 800.

52. Zosa Szajkowski, "Glimpses on the History of Jews in Occupied France," *Yad Vashem Studies on the European Jewish Catastrophe and Resistance* 2 (1958): 151–52; and *Analytical Franco-Jewish Gazetteer*.

53. As cited in Tudor Parfitt, "'The Year of the Pride of Israel': Montefiore and the Damascus Blood Libel of 1840," in *The Century of Moses Montefiore*, ed. Sonia and V. D. Lipman (London: Littman, 1985), 136.

54. Zosa Szajkowski, "Goral ha-tiḳim, be-minisṭeryon ha-ḥuts ha-tsarfati ha-nog'im la'alilat dameseḳ" ("The Files on the Damascus Affair [1840] in the Archives of the French Foreign Ministry"), *Zion* 19, no. 3–4 (1954): 167–70. See the Damascus Affair file at YIVO, which is part of RG 116, France Territorial Collection 1, box 91.

Chapter 7

1. Two excellent histories of the French archives are Jennifer S. Milligan, "Making a Modern Archive: The Archives Nationales of France" (Ph.D. diss., Rutgers University, 2002); and Lara Jennifer Moore, *Restoring Order: The Ecole Des Chartes and the Organization of Archives and Libraries in France, 1820–1870* (Duluth, MN: Litwin, 2001).

2. Jacques Derrida, *Archive Fever: A Freudian Impression*, trans. Eric Prenowitz (Chicago: University of Chicago Press, 1996), 2–3.

3. Milligan, "Making a Modern Archive"; and Moore, *Restoring Order*.

4. Milligan, "Making a Modern Archive"; and Moore, *Restoring Order*. On monumentality, see the many fine articles in Francis X. Blouin and William G. Rosenberg, eds. *Archives, Documentation and the Institutions of Social Memory: Essays from the Sawyer Seminar* (Ann Arbor, MI: University of Michigan Press, 2006), esp. Penelope Papailias, "Writing Home in the Archives: 'Refugee Memory' and the Ethnography of Documentation," 402–16. On paperwork and

the modern state, see Ben Kafka, *The Demon of Writing: Powers and Failures of Paperwork* (New York: Zone Books, 2012).

5. Sophie Coeuré, *La Mémoire Spoliée: les Archives des Français: butin de guerre Nazi puis Soviétique* (Paris: Payot, 2007), 182 and passim.

6. Henry Rousso, *The Vichy Syndrome: History and Memory in France since 1944*, trans. Arthur Goldhammer (Cambridge, MA: Harvard University Press, 1991).

7. See Simon Perego, "Les commémorations de la destruction des Juifs d'Europe au Mémorial du martyr juif inconnu du milieu des années cinquante à la fin des années soixante," *Revue d'histoire de la Shoah* no. 193 (2010): 471–507.

8. Papers related to the founding of the SHIAL can be found in Archives Départementales du Bas-Rhin (ADBR), 64J15. On the history of the SHIAL and its collections, see Peter Honigmann, "Les Archives de la Société d'histoire des israélites d'Alsace et de Lorraine au cours de la première moitié du XXe siècle," paper presented at the XXIIIe Colloque de la Société d'histoire des israélites d'Alsace et de Lorraine (Strasbourg, 2001); and Georges Weill, "Le Sort des archives de la Société d'histoire des israélites d'Alsace et de Lorraine: quelques observations à propos de la communication du Dr. Honigmann," paper presented at the XXIIIe Colloque de la Société d'Histoire des Israelites d'Alsace et de Lorraine (Strasbourg, 2001). Szajkowski's thefts in Strasbourg are discussed in both articles.

9. Peter Honigmann, correspondence with the author, December 2, 2007. Honigmann is the director of the Central Archives for Research on the History of Jews in Germany in Heidelberg, who began classifying the archives of the SHIAL, as well as those of the Consistoire Israélite du Bas-Rhin in Strasbourg in 1998. In our correspondence, Honigmann sent me a copy of his October 1998 correspondence with Rabbi Warschawski (who died in 2006), which tells this story. Honigmann confirmed Warschawski's story by consulting the now-destroyed *registre des lecteurs* of the ADBR himself, which confirmed that Szajkowski was the last person to order the papers (in January 1949) before Warschawski asked for them in 1953. An abridged version of this story is published in Honigmann's "Les Archives."

10. Zosa Szajkowski, "Jewish Participation in the Sale of National Property during the French Revolution," *Jewish Social Studies* 14, no. 4 (1952): 305 nn.53-54. For Metzger's view of Szajkowski, I have quoted here the recollections of Georges Weill, in "Le Sort," 168.

11. All this information is taken from questionnaires filled out by librarians in response to a 1961 inquiry conducted by Jacques Feller on French libraries during the war, held at the Archives Nationales (AN), Paris, Comite d'histoire de la 2ᵉ Guerre Mondiale, Sous-commission d'histoire culturelle, questionnaire pour les Bibliothecaires, 72-AJ-253. On Strasbourg University library, see the 47-page report of L. A. Fouret, "L'Université pendant l'occupation, 1940–41, Vol. 1, La Bibliothèque de l'Université de Strasbourg. I also relied on information provided

by Pierre Schmitt of the Municipal Library of Colmar and Monsieur Haby of Gubewiller in their responses to the same 1961 inquiry, also in AN, 72-AJ-253.

12. Honigmann, "Les Archives," 160.

13. Fouret, "La Bibliothèque de l'Université de Strasbourg," in AN, 72-AJ-253.

14. Weill, "Le Sort des archives," 168.

15. On the Alliance Israélite Universelle library during and after the war, see Jean-Claude Kuperminc, "La Réconstruction de la bibliothèque de l'Alliance israélite universelle," *Archives juives* 34, no. 1 (2001): 98–113. Much of my information on the AIU library in the 1950s was learned in my interview with Madame Yvonne Lévyne (who personally took part in the library's reconstruction), November 6, 2007.

16. Archives of the Alliance Israélite Universelle (AIU), *Registre des Procès-Verbaux du Comité Central de l'Alliance*, PV 14, report of February 25, 1948.

17. Letter from Edmond-Maurice Lévy to the Sous-Commission des Livres, November 26, 1945, AN F17/17977. See also Lisa Moses Leff, "Post-Holocaust Book Restitutions: How One State Agency Helped Revive Republican Franco-Judaism," ed. Seán Hand and Steven T. Katz, *Post-Holocaust France and the Jews, 1945-55* (New York: New York University Press, forthcoming 2015).

18. Letter from Paul Klein to Noé Richter, October 17, 1949, in AIU, fonds Lévy, AP1/76; handwritten note from 1950 regarding the Damascus Affair file in AM SG019a.

19. Letter from Saadia Cherniak to Eugène Weill, February 24, 1950, in AIU, file AM SG019e.

20. Cherniak to Weill, May 19, 1950, in AIU, file AM SG019e.

21. Edmond-Maurice Lévy to Weill, May 29, 1950, in AIU, file AM SG019e.

22. Cherniak to Weill, June 9, 1950; and Weill to Cherniak, June 26, 1950, in AIU, file AM SG019e.

23. Cherniak to Weill, July 5, 1950, in AIU, file AM SG019e.

24. Zosa Szajkowski, "Di Kamf fun Yahudism vegn Tsionizm," *Yidisher Kemfer*, no. 821, September 23, 1949. Joseph Millner translated the article into French and sent it to the AIU on February 9, 1950, where it is archived in AIU, AM SG019b. The article argues that the AIU actively opposed Zionism in the 1920s and '30s.

25. Weill to Cherniak, June 29, 1950, in AIU, AM SG019e.

26. Cherniak to Weill, July 14, 1950, in AIU, AM SG019e.

27. S. Frydman to Weill, September 18, 1950, in AIU, AM SG019d. This translation from the French is my own.

28. The pattern is strikingly similar to how he would handle his conversation with Albi Rosenthal in 1961, explored in chapter 1. There too, he would refuse to confront his accuser directly or in person, explaining that he was about to undergo surgery for an old war wound. Experts say that this kind of reaction—conscious or not—is typical of someone who is lying, particularly when a clear pattern is discernible. See

James B. Stewart, *Tangled Webs: How False Statements Are Undermining America: From Martha Stewart to Bernie Madoff* (New York: Penguin, 2011).

29. My research has fallen short of being able to explain why Szajkowski was so certain in 1950 that he was in danger from the Jewish Communists, although many years later, he did tell journalist William Meyers and his wife, the scholar Nahma Sandrow, that he had changed his name from Frydman to Szajkowski to hide from the Communists after quitting the Party because he feared they would try to kill him. In reality, we know that the name change preceded quitting the Party, but that later account confirms that Szajkowski long feared the Communists. See William Meyers, "Profiles in Combat," *New York Sun*, October 11, 2007.

30. These include "The Alliance Israélite Universelle in the United States, 1860–1949," *Publications of the American Jewish Historical Society* 39, no. 4 (1950): 389–443; "Conflicts in the Alliance Israélite Universelle and the Founding of the Anglo-Jewish Association, the Vienna Allianz and the Hilfsverein," *Jewish Social Studies* 19 (1957): 29–50; "Jewish Diplomacy: Notes on the Occasion of the Centenary of the Alliance Israélite Universelle," *Jewish Social Studies* 22, no. 3 (1960): 131–58; and "The Schools of the Alliance Israélite Universelle (on the Occasion of the Centenary of the Alliance)," *Historia Judaica* 22 (1960): 3–22.

31. Madame Yvonne Lévyne, interview with the author, November 6, 2007 (Lévyne began work in the library in 1954); letters between Cherniak and Weill, in AIU AM SG019e.

32. Sarah Farmer, *Martyred Village: Commemorating the 1944 Massacre at Oradour-sur-Glane* (Berkeley, CA: University of California Press, 1999).

33. Georges Weill, interview with author, August 28, 2007.

34. Zosa Szajkowski, "Emigration to America or Reconstruction in Europe," *Publications of the American Jewish Historical Society* 42, no. 2 (1952): 160n6.

35. See Honigmann, "Les Archives," 155–57; and Weill, "Le Sort," 166–67. The term "lost forever" is used in Ginsburger's report on the founding of the organization, cited in Honigmann's article.

36. See "Sommaire," *Archives Juives: Cahiers de la Commission française de archives juives*, no. 1 (1965): 1–11.

37. Gilbert Cahen, correspondence with author, 2008–09.

38. Georges Weill, interview with author, August 28, 2007.

39. Georges Weill, interviews with author, August 28, 2007, and February 15, 2008. See also Weill, "Le Sort."

40. See Isaac Schneersohn to Léon Meiss, president of the Paris Consistory, October 27, 1948, and November 2, 1948, in Archives CDJC, Paris, MDXXXVI-11: Personnel of the CDJC; box Isaac Schneersohn Correspondence.

41. The Moch papers are now microfilmed and can be consulted at the Alliance Israélite Universelle library. The papers are a mix of Moch's notes and the original papers of the Consistory in the war. Moch's book was posthumously published

as *L'Etoile et la Francisque: les institutions juives sous Vichy*, ed. Alain Michel and Claire Damon (Paris: Cerf, 1990).

42. See "Lettre au Lecteur," *Archives Juives* 2 (1965–66): 2. On the Consistory archives, I also rely here on my interview with former Consistory archivist Gérard Nahon, February 6, 2008; my correspondence with Philippe Landau, current archivist of the Consistory in Paris, December 5, 2007; and my interview with Landau on December 11, 2007.

43. X. Y. [Pierre Nora], "Les Archives des communautés juives en Algérie au moment de l'Indépendance," *Archives Juives* 2, no. 4 (1965–66): 8–10; information confirmed in author's interview with Pierre Nora, November 26, 2007.

44. On the *Nouvelle Gallia Judaica* and related projects of the CFAJ, see the project description: http://ngj.vjf.cnrs.fr/Administration/presentation.htm.

Chapter 8

1. Hebrew Union College (HUC) merged with the Jewish Institute of Religion (JIR) in New York in 1950. However, the purchases from Szajkowski were done on behalf of the Cincinnati-based HUC library, so in this chapter, I refer only to "HUC."

2. Roger Kohn, *Inventory of the French Jewish Communities Record Group (1648–1946)* (New York: JTS, 1991), 1–2.

3. See "Report of the Administrative Secretary of the HUC library, April 30, 1956," in Klau Library Ms. Collection 20: Hebrew Union College-Jewish Institute of Religion Klau Library, box G-1.

4. As reported in Roger Kohn, *Inventory to the French Consistorial Collection* (New York: Yeshiva University Archives, 1988). The consistory system was established in 1808 as a state-supported network of regional agencies based in the areas of large Jewish populations (e.g., Paris, Bordeaux, Strasbourg, Metz) answering to a Central Consistory based in Paris. The system was responsible for Jewish religious life, including training rabbis, running synagogues, religious education, etc. After 1905, with the separation of church and state, the consistories continued to function even though they no longer received state support. However, since they no longer had a monopoly on French Jewish life, the Eastern European Jewish immigrants tended not to associate with them, instead founding their own institutions. For a good overview of the consistory system's evolution over time, see Paula E. Hyman, *The Jews of Modern France* (Berkeley, CA: University of California Press, 1998).

5. The Alliance Israélite Universelle was founded in 1860 in Paris as an international philanthropic organization dedicated to helping Jews in other countries. It advocated for equal rights for Jews in the countries where they lived and is perhaps best known for the French-language Jewish schools it established for Jews in North Africa and the Middle East. Because it was also devoted to the study of Jews around the world, its founders also created a library and archives.

For a good overview of the organization's work, see Hyman, *The Jews of Modern France*, 77–90.

6. "Brandeis University Library, Waltham, Massachusetts," *Association for Jewish Libraries Bulletin* 5, no. 2 (June 1971): 10–11.

7. Jonathan Rodgers, *Inventory to the French Miscellanea Collection, 19th–20th Centuries* (Cincinnati, OH: HUC, 1979).

8. "Report of the Administrative Secretary," in Klau Library Ms. Collection 20, box G-1.

9. From the Klau Library's *Inventory* to its "Sephardic Jews of France" collection, we learn that the materials in that particular collection were purchased in 1960 from Zosa Szajkowski. Rodgers writes, "At the time of purchase this collection was part of the 'French Collections.' These were subsequently separated and the resulting related collections are now the Consistoire Central, the Alsace-Lorraine, and Small French Collections," 1.

10. Kohn, *Inventory*, 1.

11. Jewish Theological Seminary of America (JTS), ARC 120, folder Arthur Hertzberg, 1956–1987.

12. Correspondence between Nahum Sarna, JTS librarian, and Arthur Hertzberg, describing the purchases of 1960–62, in JTS ARC 120, Hertzberg folder.

13. Judith E. Endelman, "Archives Manual: Library of the Jewish Theological Seminary of America," (1978), 9–10. I thank Judith Endelman for sharing a copy of this document with me.

14. List of taxes due from the Jews of the former community of Metz, December 31, 1814, held in the Central Archives for the History of the Jewish People, Jerusalem (CAHJP), FCMe10.

15. For example, on a letter from folder 1/10 in the French Miscellanea collection, HUC Klau Library; the same Yiddish name stamp can be found on other documents in the same collection, e.g., an 1856 letter in folder 1/7.

16. JTS, French Jewish Communities Record group, box 3/28e.

17. For a discussion of the elaboration of the concept of *respect des fonds* and the struggles it entailed within the national archives system, see Lara Moore, *Restoring Order: the Ecole des Chartes and the Organization of Archives and Libraries in France, 1820–1870* (Duluth, MN: Litwin, 2001), 105–54.

18. Kohn, *Inventory*, 5.

19. In his *Inventory*, Kohn notes that this reorganization took place sometime before he worked with the collection in the late 1980s, but it was not possible to find out when. See 4–5.

20. Jonathan Rodgers, *Inventory of the Alsatian Jewish Inventories, 1738–1805* (Cincinnati, OH: Klau Library, 1979), 3.

21. Zosa Szajkowski, "Alsatian Jewish Inventories in the Hebrew Union College Library," *Studies in Bibliography and Booklore* 4, no. 2 (1959): 96–97.

22. Rodgers, *Inventory of the Alsatian Jewish Inventories*.

23. Leo Lichtenberg, "An Inventory to the Alsace-Lorraine Collection, 1786–1868" (HUC library, 1977).

24. Szajkowski to Marcus, March 18, 1959; Marcus to Szajkowski, March 24, 1969; and Szajkowski to Marcus, April 2, 1959; all in "Correspondence, Zosa Szajkowski," Marcus papers, American Jewish Archives, Cincinnati, OH.

25. Receipt dated March 31, 1957, prepared by Jacob Dienstag for Szajko Frydman, from Yeshiva University Archives, collection S. Frydman, cab. 25, drawer 2.

26. Undated list in CAHJP, Israeli Historical Society (IHS) papers, correspondence of Israel Halperin, ca. June 1954.

27. In letters he wrote her, dated January 18, February 14, and February 23, 1967. Much gratitude to Frances Malino for sharing these, and so many of her memories from the era, with me.

28. See his plans to work for CAHJP (both in Israel and as an emissary in France) as documented in letters to Israel Halperin dated July 1, 1952, and December 1, 1954, CAHJP, IHS papers. See also Hertzberg's attempts to help him land a job at JTS, as documented in a letter from Hertzberg to Nahum Sarna, July 10, 1962, in JTS ARC 120, Arthur Hertzberg file.

29. U.S. Bureau of Labor Statistics, "100 Years of Consumer Spending: 1960–61," 29, http://www.bls.gov/opub/uscs/1960-61.pdf. Information on the apartment's style—it was a "junior four"—was learned when the apartment came on the market in summer 2013.

30. School records of Chana Frydman and Isaac Frydman in Montreal and New York, 1964–1974, in YIVO RG 800, Szajkowski papers.

31. Author's interview with Richard I. Cohen, January 6, 2013.

32. Cynthia Ozick, "Envy; or, Yiddish in America," *Commentary* 48, no. 5 (1969): 33–53.

33. Zosa Szajkowski, *Agricultural Credit and Napoleon's Anti-Jewish Decrees* (New York: Editions historiques franco-juives, 1954), 19.

34. Sajkowski to Malino, February 14, 1967, in personal collection of Frances Malino.

35. Richard I. Cohen, "Zosa Szajkowski z"l," *Zion* 43, no. 3–4 (1978): 369. I thank Cliff and Debbie Miller for their help with this translation.

36. Marked Judaica catalogues (with names of buyers and sellers) of the 1950s and '60s, Rosenthal archive, held privately, London.

37. Interview with Menahem Schmelzer, September 10, 2009.

38. Interviews with Victor Berch, September 25, 2008, and Menahem Schmelzer, September 10, 2009.

39. Elisabeth Kaplan, "We Are What We Collect, We Collect What We Are: Archives and the Construction of Identity," *American Archivist* 63 (2000): 126–51.

40. Harry M. Rabinowicz, *The Jewish Literary Treasures of England and America* (New York: Thomas Yoseloff, 1962), 126.

41. Michael Meyer, *Hebrew Union College-Jewish Institute of Religion: A Centennial History, 1875–1975* (Cincinnati, OH: Hebrew Union College, 1976), 118–20.

42. Rabinowicz, *Literary Treasures*, 126.

43. Alexander Marx, *Bibliographical Studies and Notes on Rare Books and Manuscripts in the Library of the Jewish Theological Seminary of America* (New York: Ktav, 1977), viii.

44. Rabinowicz, *Literary Treasures*, 74.

45. Pamela S. Nadell, *Conservative Judaism in America: A Biographical Dictionary and Sourcebook* (New York: Greenwood Press, 1988): 280–83 and *passim*.

46. Herman Dicker, *Of Learning and Libraries: The Seminary at 100* (New York: JTSA, 1988): 53–59.

47. Nahum Sarna to Menahem Schmelzer, April 25, 1966, in the American Jewish Archives, Cincinnati, OH, Nahum Sarna papers, 19/4.

48. Menahem Schmelzer, "Making a Great Judaica Library: At What Price?" in *Tradition Renewed: A History of the Jewish Theological Seminary*, ed. Jack Wertheimer (New York: JTSA, 1997), 680.

49. Barry D. Cytron, "The Fire of '66," in Dicker, *Of Learning and Libraries*, 79–80. Quotation from Sarna in his letter to Schmelzer, April 25, 1966.

50. Rabinowicz, *Literary Treasures*, 85.

51. Historical Society of Israel, "The Jewish Historical General Archives" (Jerusalem, 1961), 2.

52. Binyamin Lukin, "The Creation of a Documentary Collection on the History of Russian Jewry at the CAHJP," *Slavic and East European Information Resources* 4, no. 2/3 (2003): 17–36; and Denise Rein, "Die Bestände der ehemaligen jüdischen Geminden Deutschlands in den 'CAHJP' in Jerusalem: Ein Uberblick über das schicksal der verschinedenen Gemeindearchive," *Der Archivar* 4 (2002): 318–27.

53. "Jewish Historical General Archives," 4–5; for an earlier discussion of these efforts, see also Daniel J. Cohen, "Jewish Records from Germany in the Jewish General History Archives in Jerusalem," *LBI Year Book* 1, no. 1 (1956): 331–45.

54. "Jewish Historical General Archives," 3.

55. Szajkowski to Halperin, February 5, 1953, in CAHJP, IHS papers, P127, correspondence of I. Halperin. Chrétien de Lamoignon de Malesherbes (1721–1794) was a French statesman and lawyer who, on the eve of the Revolution, gathered information to support his quest to have Jews granted equal rights in France.

56. Copy of letter from Shmeruk to Szajkowski, March 18, 1956, in CAHJP, IHS papers, P127. Translation by Lillian Leavitt and Iosif Lakhman.

57. Author's interview with Mordechai Altshuler, January 11, 2013; and correspondence with Hadassah Assouline, January 17, 2013.

58. See receipts for Szajkowski dated December 10, 15, and 29, 1949, and January 6 and 10, 1950, in CDJC, MDXXXVI-13: Correspondence Internationale, folder Argentina-United States, 1946–1951. An announcement of the purchases from Szajkowski appeared in the CDJC's journal, the *Monde Juif*, in June 1950.

59. See, e.g., Szajkowski, *Autonomy*, 687 n.223; 688 n.227.

60. Zosa Szajkowski, "Pinkassim fun Karpentras, 18tn Y.H.," *YIVO Bleter* 21, no. 3 (1943): 351–55.
61. Simone Mrejen-O'Hana, "Les Pinqassim de Carpentras au regard du Saint-Siège," *Bulletin du Centre de recherche français de Jérusalem* 16 (2005): 47–52.
62. One collector who remembers buying from Szajkowski is Alfred Moldovan, whom I interviewed by telephone on July 15, 2010.

Epilogue

1. Interview with Claire Dienstag, Norman Gechlik, and Leonard Gold, former librarians of the Jewish Division at New York Public Library, October 30, 2008. Szajkowski's final days inspired novelist Jerome Badanes (who frequented YIVO in the late 1970s) to write his book, *The Final Opus of Leon Solomon* (New York: Simon & Schuster, 1985). The account is fictional and many elements are invented whole cloth, but certain elements are recognizable as having been drawn from Szajkowski's life and death.
2. Death certificate for Szajko Frydman, Surrogate's Court of the County of New York, file 5545, 1978.
3. Joel Fishman and Rivka Duker Fishman, Skype interview with author, December 12, 2013.
4. Ezekiel Lifshutz, "Notes about the Writer I Knew: Zosa Szajkowski/Shayke Frydman," unpublished Yiddish manuscript, 1983. Lifshutz papers, CAHJP, Jerusalem, P130.
5. On these scholars and the interests that led them to study the history of Jews in France, see Lisa Leff, "L'Histoire des juifs de France vue des Etats-Unis," *Archives Juives* (March 2010): 126–36.
6. Georges Weill, "Les Archives Juives en France," in *Terres promises: mélanges offerts à André Kaspi* (Paris: Publications de la Sorbonne, 2008), 549–65.

BIBLIOGRAPHY

Scholarly Works by Zosa Szajkowski

Cohen, Richard, and Zosa Szajkowski. "A Jewish Leader in Vichy France, 1940–1943: The Diary of Raymond-Raoul Lambert." *Jewish Social Studies* 43, nos. 3–4 (1981): 291–310.

Fridman, Shayke. *Etyudn tsu der Geshikhte fun ayngevandertn yidishn Yishev in Frankraykh (Ershtn Band)*. Paris: n.p., 1936.

———. "Frantseyzishe apklangen vegn Yidn in Poiln-Rusland fun 15tn biz onhayb 19tn Y.H." In *Yidn in Frankraykh: Shtudyes un Materialn*. Edited by Elias Tcherikower, 1:16–32. New York: YIVO, 1942.

———. *Di Profesionele Bavegung tsvishn di yidishe Arbeter in Frankraykh biz 1914*. Paris: Tsuzamen, 1937.

———. "Di Revolutsye fun 1848 un di inevaynikste Kamfn in frantseyzishn Yidntum." In *Yidn in Frankraykh: Shtudyes un Materialn*. Edited by Elias Tcherikower, 1:205–35. New York: YIVO, 1942.

Szajkowski, Zosa. "150 Yor yidishe Prese in Frankraykh." In *Yidn in Frankraykh: Shtudyes un Materialn*. Edited by Elias Tcherikower, 1:236–308. New York: YIVO, 1942.

———. "1515 Yidishe Mishpokhe in Paris." *Yidishe Ekonomik* 2, nos. 9–10 (1938): 471–80.

———. *Agricultural Credit and Napoleon's Anti-Jewish Decrees*. New York: Editions historiques franco-juives, 1954.

———. "The Alliance Israélite Universelle and East European Jewry: A Postscript." *Jewish Social Studies* 7, no. 2 (1945): 151.

————. "The Alliance Israélite Universelle and East-European Jewry in the '60s." *Jewish Social Studies* 4, no. 2 (1942): 139–60.

————. "The Alliance Israélite Universelle in the United States, 1860–1949." *Publications of the American Jewish Historical Society* 39, no. 4 (1950): 389–443.

————. "Alsatian Jewish Inventories in the Hebrew Union College Library." *Studies in Bibliography and Booklore* 4, no. 2 (1959): 96–97.

————. *Analytical Franco-Jewish Gazetteer, 1939–1945, with an Introduction to Some Problems in Writing the History of the Jews in France during World War II.* New York: S. Frydman, 1966.

————. *Antisemitzm in der Frantseyzisher Arbeter-Bavegung: fun Furierizm bizn sof Drayfus-Afere.* New York: Aroysgegeben fun Mehaber, 1948.

————. "Argo fun yidishe Soldatn in Frankraykh." *Yidishe Shprakh* 2, no. 3 (1942): 89–90.

————. "The Attitude of American Jews to East European Jewish Immigration (1881–1893)." *Publications of the American Jewish Historical Society* 40 (1950): 221–80.

————. "The Attitude of American Jews to Refugees from Germany in the 1930s." *American Jewish Historical Quarterly* 61, no. 2 (December 1971): 101–43.

————. "The Attitude of French Jacobins toward the Jewish Religion." *Historia Judaica* 18 (1956): 107–20.

————. "L'Attività di Armand Lévy in Italia a favore degli ebrei di Rumenia nel 1879." *La Rassegna Mensile di Israel* 22, no. 6 (1956): 243–51.

————. "An Auto-da-Fé against the Jews of Toulouse in 1685." *Jewish Quarterly Review* 49, no. 4 (1959): 278–81.

————. *Autonomy and Communal Jewish Debts during the French Revolution of 1789.* New York: n.p., 1959.

————. "The Baron Hirsch's Attempts in Favor of Russian Jews." *Davke* 2, no. 8 (1951): 401–16.

————. "The Beginning of Jewish Colonization in Argentina." *Argentiner YIVO Schriften* 12 (1957): 31–33.

————. "Bibliografie fun Bicher un Broshurn vegn Varshever Geto." *YIVO Bleter* 30, no. 2 (1947): 280–88.

————. "Bibliography of Jewish Periodicals in Belgium, 1841–1959." *Studies in Bibliography and Booklore* 4, no. 3 (1960): 103–22.

————. "A Bintl Faktn vegn elzaser Yidn in Amerike." *YIVO Bleter* 20, no. 2 (1942): 312–17.

————. "Bordeaux et l'abolition de l'esclavage dans les colonies en 1848." *Revue historique de Bordeaux et du département de la Gironde,* 2ᵉ Série, no. 3 (1954): 113–41.

————. "Budgeting American Jewish Overseas Relief (1919–1939)." *American Jewish Historical Quarterly* 59, no. 1 (September 1969): 83–113.

————. *Catalogue of the Exhibition: Drawings and Paintings by Jewish Children in Eastern Europe 1919–1939.* New York: YIVO, 1974.

———. *Catalogue of the Exhibition: Morris Rosenfeld (1862–1923) and His Time.* New York: YIVO, 1962.

———. *Catalogue of the Exhibition: The Shtetl, 1900–1939.* New York: YIVO, 1959.

———. *Catalogue of the Exhibition: Simon Dubnow (1860–1941): The Life and Work of a Jewish Historian.* New York: YIVO, 1961.

———. "The Comtadin Jews and the Annexation of the Papal Province by France, 1789–1791." *Jewish Quarterly Review* 46, no. 2 (1955): 181–93.

———. "Concord and Discord in American Jewish Overseas Relief, 1914–1924." *YIVO Annual of Jewish Social Science* 14 (1969): 99–158.

———. "Conflicts in the Alliance Israélite Universelle and the Founding of the Anglo-Jewish Association, the Vienna Allianz and the Hilfsverein." *Jewish Social Studies* 19, nos. 1–2 (April 1957): 29–50.

———. "The Consul and the Immigrant: A Case of Bureaucratic Bias." *Jewish Social Studies* 36, no. 1 (1974): 3–18.

———. "The Decline and Fall of Provençal Jewry." *Jewish Social Studies* 6, no. 1 (1944): 31–54.

———. "Demands for Complete Emancipation of Germany during World War I." *Jewish Quarterly Review* 55, no. 4 (1965): 350–64.

———. "The Demographic Aspects of Jewish Emancipation in France during the French Revolution." *Historia Judaica* 21, no. 1 (1959): 7–36.

———. "Deportation of Jewish Immigrants and Returnees before World War I." *American Jewish Historical Quarterly* 67, no. 4 (June 1978): 291–306.

———. "Destruction of Zaromb." Translated by Shulamit Friedman. www.jewishgen.org/Yizkor/Zareby/Zareby.html. Originally published in Yiddish in *Le-zikaron olam: die Zaromber yidn vos zaynen umgekumen al kidesh-hashem,* 7–23. New York: United Zaromber Relief, 1947.

———. "The Discussion and Struggle over Jewish Emancipation in Alsace in the Early Years of the French Revolution." *Historia Judaica* 17 (1955): 121–42.

———. "Dokumentn fun di arbe Kehiles in 18tn Y.H." In *Yidn in Frankraykh: Shtudyes un Materialn.* Edited by Elias Tcherikower, 2:304–16. New York: YIVO, 1942.

———. "Double Jeopardy—the Abrams Case of 1919." *American Jewish Archives* 23 (1971): 1–32.

———. "East European Jewish Workers in Germany during World War I." In *Salo Baron Jubilee Volume, on the Occasion of His Eightieth Birthday.* Edited by Saul Liberman and Arthur Hyman, 887–918. Jerusalem and New York: American Academy for Jewish Research, 1975.

———. *The Economic Status of the Jews in Alsace, Metz and Lorraine (1648–1789).* New York: Editions historiques franco-juives, 1954.

———. "The Emancipation of Jews during the French Revolution: A Bibliography of Books, Pamphlets and Printed Documents, 1789–1800." *Studies in Bibliography and Booklore* 3 (1957): 55–68; 4 (1958): 87–114; 5 (1959): 21–48.

———. "Emigration to America or Reconstruction in Europe." *Publication of the American Jewish Historical Society* 42, no. 2 (1952): 157–88.

————. "Di Erste organizirte Emigratsie fun Mizrakh-Eyrope in di Faraynikte Statn, 1869–1870." *YIVO Bleter* 40 (1956): 224–25.

————. "The European Aspect of the American-Russian Passport Question." *Publication of the American Jewish Historical Society* 46, no. 2 (1956): 86–100.

————. "La Fondazione del comitato del 'Alliance Israélite Universelle' a Roma nel maggio 1873." *La Rassegna Mensile di Israel* 22 (1956): 27–33.

————. *Franco-Judaica: An Analytical Bibliography of Books, Pamphlets, Decrees, Briefs and Other Printed Documents Pertaining to the Jews in France 1500–1788.* New York: American Academy for Jewish Research, 1962.

————. "French 17th–18th Century Sources for Anglo-Jewish History." *Journal of Jewish Studies* 12, nos. 1–2 (1961): 59–66.

————. "French Jewry during the Thermidorian Reaction." *Historia Judaica* 20, no. 2 (1958): 97–108.

————. "French Jews in the Armed Forces during the Revolution of 1789." *Proceedings of the American Academy for Jewish Research* 26 (1957): 139–60.

————. "French Jews during the Revolution of 1830 and the July Monarchy." *Historia Judaica* 22 (1961): 105–30.

————. "Fun Yidishn Arbeter-lebn in Pariz." *Yidishe Ekonomik* 2, nos. 5–6 (1938): 232–49.

————. "The German Appeal to the Jews of Poland, August 1914." *Jewish Quarterly Review* 59, no. 4 (1969): 311–20.

————. "The German Ordinance of 1916 on the Organization of the Jewish Communities of Poland." *Proceedings of the American Academy for Jewish Research* 34 (1966): 111–39.

————. "Gli Ebrei nei club dei giacobini durante la rivoluzione francese del 1789." *La Rassegna Mensile di Israel* 24, no. 7 (1958): 296–304.

————. "Glimpses on the History of Jews in Occupied France." *Yad Vashem Studies on the European Jewish Catastrophe and Resistance* 2 (1958): 133–57.

————. "Goldfadn in Pariz." *YIVO Bleter* 15, no. 4 (1940): 291–95.

————. "Goral ha-tiķim, be-minisṭeryon ha-ḥuts ha-tsarfati ha-nog'im la-'alilat dameseķ." *Zion* 19, nos. 3–4 (1954): 167–70.

————. "Di Grindung fun Parizer 'Alians' (1860)." *YIVO Bleter* 18 (1941): 1–20.

————. "The Growth of the Jewish Population of France (Concluded)." *Jewish Social Studies* 8, no. 4 (1946): 297–318.

————. "The Growth of the Jewish Population of France: Political Aspects of a Demographic Problem." *Jewish Social Studies* 8, no. 3 (1946): 179–96.

————. "Hitnagshuyot ha-Orṭodoķsim Veha-Reformim be-Tsarfat." *Horev* 14–15 (1960): 253–92.

————. "How the Mass Migration to America Began." *Jewish Social Studies* 4, no. 4 (1942): 291–310.

————. *An Illustrated Sourcebook of the Holocaust.* 3 vols. New York: Ktav, 1977–1979.

————. "The Impact of the Beilis Case on Central and Western Europe." *Publications of the American Academy for Jewish Research* 31 (1963): 197–218.

———. "Incident at Compiègne." *Conservative Judaism* 21, no. 2 (1967): 27–33.

———. "Internal Conflicts within the Eighteenth Century Sephardic Communities of France." *Hebrew Union College Annual* 31 (1960): 167–80.

———. "Internal Conflicts in French Jewry at the Time of the Revolution of 1848." *YIVO Annual of Jewish Social Science* 2–3 (1947): 100–117.

———. "Jean Jaurès un di Drayfus-Afere." *Yidisher Kemfer* 29, no. 748 (1948): 44–51.

———. "The Jewish Aspect of Levying Taxes during the French Revolution of 1789." *Journal of Jewish Studies* 11, nos. 1–2 (1960): 35–47.

———. "Jewish Autonomy Debated and Attacked during the French Revolution." *Historia Judaica* 19 (1957): 31–46.

———. "The Jewish Community of Marseilles at the End of the Eighteenth Century." *Revue des Études Juives/Historia Judaica*, 4e série, tome 1 (121), nos. 3–4 (1962): 367–82.

———. "Jewish Diplomacy: Catalogue of the David Mowschowitch Collection in YIVO." *YIVO Bleter* 43 (1968): 183–96.

———. "Jewish Diplomacy: Notes on the Occasion of the Centenary of the Alliance Israélite Universelle." *Jewish Social Studies* 22, no. 3 (1960): 131–58.

———. *Jewish Education in France, 1789–1939*. Edited by Tobey B. Gitelle. Jewish Social Studies Monograph Series, No. 2. New York: Conference on Jewish Social Studies, 1980.

———. "Jewish Emigration from Bordeaux during the Eighteenth and Nineteenth Centuries." *Jewish Social Studies* 18, no. 2 (1956): 118–24.

———. "Jewish Emigration Policy in the Period of the Rumanian 'Exodus' 1899–1903." *Jewish Social Studies* 13, no. 1 (1951): 47–70.

———. "Jewish Émigrés during the French Revolution." *Jewish Social Studies* 16, no. 4 (1954): 319–34.

———. "Jewish Participation in the Sale of National Property during the French Revolution." *Jewish Social Studies* 14, no. 4 (1952): 291–316.

———. "The Jewish Problem in Alsace, Metz, and Lorraine on the Eve of the Revolution of 1789." *Jewish Quarterly Review* 44, no. 3 (1954): 205–43.

———. "Jewish Relief in Eastern Europe, 1914–1917." *Leo Baeck Institute Year Book* 10 (1965): 24–56.

———. "Jewish Religious Observance during the French Revolution of 1789." *YIVO Annual of Jewish Social Science* 12 (1958): 211–34.

———. "The Jewish Saint-Simonians and Socialist Antisemites in France." *Jewish Social Studies* 9, no. 1 (1947): 33–60.

———. "The Jewish Status in Eighteenth-Century France and the 'Droit d'Aubaine.'" *Historia Judaica* 19 (1957): 147–63.

———. "The Jews and New York City's Mayoralty Election of 1917." *Jewish Social Studies* 32, no. 4 (1970): 286–306.

———. "Jews and the Elihu Root Mission to Russia—1917." *Proceedings of the American Academy for Jewish Research* 37 (1969): 57–116.

———. "Jews in the Foreign Legion." *Conservative Judaism* 21, no. 4 (1967): 22–34.

———. *Jews and the French Foreign Legion.* New York: Ktav, 1975.

———. "Jews in the French Foreign Legion, 1939–40." *Jewish Review: A Journal Devoted to the Study and Interpretation of Jewish Life and Thought* 5, nos. 1–4 (1948): 136–43.

———. *Jews and the French Revolutions of 1789, 1830 and 1848.* New York: Ktav, 1970.

———. *Jews, Wars and Communism.* Vol. 1, *The Attitude of American Jews to World War I, the Russian Revolutions of 1917, and Communism (1914–1945).* New York: Ktav, 1972.

———. *Jews, Wars and Communism.* Vol. 2, *The Impact of the Red Scare on American Jewish Life.* New York: Ktav, 1974.

———. *Jews, Wars and Communism.* Vol. 3, *Kolchak, Jews, and the American Intervention in Northern Russia and Siberia, 1918–1920.* New York: self-published, 1977.

———. *Jews, Wars and Communism.* Vol. 4, *The Mirage of American Jewish Aid in Soviet Russia.* New York: self-published, 1977.

———. "Judaica-Napoleonica: A Bibliography of Books, Pamphlets and Printed Documents, 1801–1815." *Studies in Bibliography and Booklore* 2 (1956): 107–52.

———. "Di Kamf fun Yahudism vegn Tsionizm." *Yidisher Kemfer,* no. 821 (September 23, 1949).

———. "Der Kamf kegn Yidish in Frankraykh: 19tn un 20th Y.H." *YIVO Bleter* 14, nos. 1–2 (1939): 46–77.

———. "Di Kamfn arum der Valsistem in di yidishe Kehiles in Frankraykh, 1850–80." *YIVO Bleter* 35 (1951): 139–64.

———. *Katalog fun der oysshtelung yidish lebn in Shankhay: September 1948–Yanuar 1949: Yidisher Visnshaftlekher Institut-YIVO.* New York: YIVO, 1948.

———. "Kevurat yisrael bi-yme ha-mahpekhah ha-tsarfatit mi-shnat 1789." *Horev* 13 (1958): 165–78.

———. "The Komitee fuer den Osten and Zionism." *Herzl Yearbook* 7 (1971): 286–305.

———. *Ha-Komunah ha-Parisa'it Veha-Yehudim.* Tel Aviv: Hotsa'at ha-Kibuts ha-Me'uḥad, 1956.

———. "Der Konflikt fun dem Baron Hirsh un der Terkisher Regirung." *Davke* 16 (1953): 216–24.

———. "A Konflikt tsvishn di Parnosim fun di sfardishe Yidn in Bordo un an ashknazishn Yid." *Davke* 17 (1953): 325–29.

———. "Ha-konsistorya ha-yehudit ha-merkazit b'tsarfat biymei milkhmemet-ha-olam ha-sheah." *Yad Vashem Studies* 3 (1959): 187–202.

———. "Ktav s'tarim shel sofer yehudi bame'ah ha-18." *Yeda'am* 3, nos. 2–3 (1955): 130–31.

———. "La Vita intellectuale profana fra gli ebrei nella Francia del XVIII secolo." *La Rassegna Mensile di Israel* 27, nos. 3–4 (1961): 122–29, 79–91.

———. "Letter to the Editor" [re: Petliura, an important rejoinder in an ongoing debate with Ukranian nationalists]. *Jewish Social Studies* 32, no. 3 (July 1970).

———. "L'Kheker korot yehudei tsarfat bimei ha-kibush ha-natsi." *Yad Vashem Studies* 2 (1957–58): 115–40.

———. *Dos Loshn fun di Yidn in di arbe Kehiles fun Komta-Venesen.* New York: YIVO, 1948.

———. "Louis François De Beaufleury, a Yidisher Fartreter-Deputat beys der Frantseyzisher Revolutzie." *Davke*, no. 20 (1954): 241–48.

———. "The Marranos and Sephardim of France." *Abraham Weiss Jubilee Volume* (1964): 107–27.

———. "Marriages, Mixed Marriages and Conversions among French Jews during the Revolution of 1789." *Historia Judaica* 19 (1957): 33–54.

———. "Materialn un Notitzn: di Geshikhte fun Karpentraser Beit-Haknesses in 18tn Y.-H." *YIVO Bleter* 23 (1944): 149–52.

———. "Materialn vegn der yidisher Emigratsie keyn Amerike." *YIVO Bleter* 19, no. 2 (1942): 275–78.

———. "Mazarinades of Jewish Interest." *Studies in Bibliography and Booklore* 6, no. 1 (Spring 1962): 29–37.

———. "Mekhumot neged yehudim b'Mets b'shnat 1792." *Zion* 22, no. 1 (1957): 76–77.

———. "Michel Berr: The Failure of an Intellectual among the First Generation of Emancipated Jews in France." *Journal of Jewish Studies* 14 (1963): 53–66.

———. "Mishlehotehem shel yehudei bordo 'el va'adat malzerb (1788) ve-'el ha'asefa ha-le'umit (1790)." *Zion* 18, nos. 1–2 (1953): 31–79.

———. "Naye Materialn vegn Altarasn un zayn Kolonizir-plan." *YIVO Bleter* 21 (1943): 47–70.

———. "Naye oysgabes fun Parizer Yidishn Dokumentatzie-Tsenter." *YIVO Bleter* 30, no. 1 (1947): 116–23.

———. "A Note on the American-Jewish Struggle against Nazism and Communism in the 1930s." *American Jewish Historical Quarterly* 59, no. 3 (1970): 272–89.

———. "Notes autobiographiques d'un armateur bordelais, Salomon Lopes Dubec (1743–1837)." *Revue historique de Bordeaux et du département de la Gironde* (1970): 93–110.

———. "Notes on the Demography of Sephardim in France." *Hebrew Union College Annual* 30 (1959).

———. "Notes on the Languages of the Marranos and Sephardim in France." In *For Max Weinreich on His Seventieth Birthday*, 237–44. London: Mouton, 1964.

———. "Notes on the Occupational Status of French Jews, 1800–1880." In *AAJR Jubilee Volume.* Edited by Salo Baron and Isaac E. Barzilay, 531–54. Jerusalem: AAJR, 1980.

———. "Occupational Problems of Jewish Emancipation in France, 1789–1800." *Historia Judaica* 21, no. 2 (1959): 109–32.

———. *One Hundred Years of the Yiddish Press in America, YIVO Exhibition Catalogue.* New York: YIVO, 1970.

————. *Dos Ophitn Yidishkayt beys der Frantseyzisher Revolutsye fun 1789.* New York: YIVO, 1958.

————. "The Organization of the 'UGIF' in Nazi-Occupied France." *Jewish Social Studies* 9, no. 3 (1947): 239–56.

————. "Osafim Peratiyim shel Sifrei-khol Etsel Yehudey Tsarfat ba-Me'ah ha-18." *Kiryat Sefer* 35 (1960): 495–98.

————. "The Pacifism of Judah Magnes." *Conservative Judaism* 22, no. 3 (1968): 36–55.

————. "Parodia shel sefardey Paris neged ha-ashkenzim b'shnat 1780." *Yeda'am* 4, nos. 1–2 (1956): 85–86.

————. "Paul Nathan, Lucien Wolf, Jacob H. Schiff and the Jewish Revolutionary Movement in Eastern Europe, 1903–1918." *Jewish Social Studies* 29, no. 1 (1967): 3–26, 75–91.

————. "Paul Nathan, Lucien Wolf, and the Versailles Treaty." *Proceedings of the American Academy for Jewish Research* 38 (1967): 26–41.

————. "Ha-Pera'ot be-'Elzas be-'et ha-mahapekhot shel 1789, 1830, 1848." *Zion* 20, nos. 1–2 (1955): 82–102.

————. "Pe'ulot ha-sa'ad shel yahadut artsot ha-berit li-yehudei polin 1918–1923." *Zion* 34, nos. 3–4 (1969): 219–60.

————. "Pinkassim fun Karpentras, 18tn Y.H." *YIVO Bleter* 21, no. 3 (1943): 351–55.

————. "Di Pogromen in Elzas in 1848." *Kiyoum*, no. 6 (1948): 394–97.

————. "Population Problems with Marranos and Sephardim in France, from the 16th to the 20th Centuries." *Proceedings of the American Academy for Jewish Research* 27 (1958): 83–105.

————. *Poverty and Social Welfare among French Jews (1800–1880).* New York: Editions historiques franco-juives, 1954.

————. "Private American Jewish Overseas Relief (1919–1938): Problems and Attempted Solutions." *American Jewish Historical Quarterly* 57, no. 3 (March 1968): 285–350.

————. "Private and Organized American Jewish Overseas Relief and Immigration (1914–1938)." *American Jewish Historical Quarterly* 57, no. 2 (1967): 191–253.

————. "Protestants and Jews of France in the Fight for Emancipation." *Proceedings of the American Academy for Jewish Research* 25 (1956): 119–35.

————. "A Reappraisal of Symon Petliura and Ukrainian-Jewish Relations, 1917–1921—a Rebuttal." *Jewish Social Studies* 31, no. 3 (1969): 185–213.

————. "Reconstruction vs. Palliative Relief in American Jewish Overseas Work (1919–1939)." *Jewish Social Studies* 22, nos. 1–2 (1970): 14–42, 111–47.

————. "The Reform of the Etat-Civil of the French Jews during the Revolution of 1789." *Jewish Quarterly Review* 49, no. 1 (1958): 63–75.

————. "Relations among Sephardim, Ashkenazim and Avignonese Jews in France from the 16th to the 20th Centuries." *YIVO Annual of Jewish Social Science* 10 (1955): 165–96.

————. "Relief for German Jewry: Problems of American Involvement." *American Jewish Historical Quarterly* 62, no. 2 (1972): 111–45.

———. "Religious Propaganda against Jews during the French Revolution of 1789." *Proceedings of the American Academy for Jewish Research* 28 (1959): 103–13.

———. "A Reshime Mapes fun Getos, Lagern, un yidishe partizanishe Kamfn." *YIVO Bleter* 30 (1947): 259–79.

———. "The Schools of the Alliance Israélite Universelle (on the Occasion of the Centenary of the Alliance)." *Historia Judaica* 22 (1960): 3–22.

———. "Secular versus Religious Jewish Life in France." In *The Role of Religion in Modern Jewish History: Proceedings of Regional Conferences of the Association for Jewish Studies Held at the University of Pennsylvania and the University of Toronto in March–April 1974.* Edited by Jacob Katz, 109–25. Philadelphia: Association for Jewish Studies, 1974.

———. "The Sephardic Jews of France during the Revolution of 1789." *Proceedings of the American Academy for Jewish Research* 24 (1955): 137–64.

———. "Simon Deutz: Traitor or French Patriot? The Jewish Aspect of the Arrest of the Duchesse de Berry." *Journal of Jewish Studies* 16 (1965): 53–67.

———. "Socialists and Radicals in the Development of Antisemitism in Algeria (1884–1900)." *Jewish Social Studies* 10, no. 3 (1948): 257–80.

———. "The Soldiers France Forgot." *Contemporary Jewish Record* 5 (1942): 589–96.

———. "Ha-Sotsialistim ha-Yehudim Mehayve Mediniyut Vilson bi-Shenot ha-Milhamah 1917–1919." *M'asef* 1 (1971): 57–125.

———. "The Struggle for Jewish Emancipation in Algeria after the French Occupation." *Historia Judaica* 18 (1956): 27–40.

———. "The Struggle for Yiddish during World War I: The Attitude of German Jewry." *Leo Baeck Year Book* 9 (1964): 131–58.

———. "Sufferings of Jewish Emigrants to America in Transit through Germany." *Jewish Social Studies* 39, nos. 1–2 (1977): 105–16.

———. "Synagogues during the French Revolution of 1789–1800." *Jewish Social Studies* 20, no. 4 (1958): 215–31.

———. "Les Synagogues pendant la Révolution." *L'Arche* 3, no. 31 (July 1959): 30–33.

———. "Trade Relations of Marranos in France with the Iberian Peninsula in the 16th and 17th Centuries." *Jewish Quarterly Review* 50, no. 1 (1959): 69–78.

———. "Ha-Tsav mi-yom ha-28 be-september 1791 bi-devar hovot le-malyim yehudim be-tsarfat." *Zion* 17, nos. 1–4 (1952): 84–100.

———. *Tsu der frikher Geshikhte fun YIVO (Catalogue of the Exhibit on the Early History of YIVO in Vilna and New York Documents and Pictures Presented on the Occasion of the 40th Anniversary Conference of YIVO, Apr. 30–May 5, 1966).* New York: YIVO, 1966.

———. "Tsu der Geshikhte fun di frantzeyzishe Yidn." *Davke*, no. 24 (1955): 238–48.

———. *Tsu der Geshikhte fun yidishn Teater in Pariz.* New York: Yidishn Lerer-seminar un Folks-universitet, 1947.

———. "Di Unterhandlungen tsvishn Vatikan un amerikaner un eyropeyishe Yidn in 1915–1916." *Kiyoum (Paris)*, no. 61 (1953): 429–36.

————. "Vegn Forshn dem ekonomishn Matsev fun Frantzeyzishn Yidntum nokh 1789." *Kiyoum*, no. 11 (1948): 643–46.

————. "Vi Azoy dos Opteyln di Kirkh fun der Melkhe in 1905 Hot Bavirkt di Yidishe Kehilos in Frankraykh." *Davke*, no. 21 (1954): 382–92.

————. "Vi Azoy Men Hot Opgeshemdt Tsemakh Karmi in Karpentras." *YIVO Bleter* 24 (1944): 123–30.

————. *Vilna: A Jewish Community in Times of Glory and in Time of Destruction (YIVO Exhibition Catalogue)*. New York: YIVO, 1960.

————. *The Works of Eliyohu Bokher on the Occasion of the 500th Anniversary of His Birth: Exhibition, May–June 1969*. New York: YIVO, 1969.

————. "The Yahudi and the Immigrant: A Reappraisal." *American Jewish Historical Quarterly* 58, no. 1 (1973): 13–44.

————. "Yehudim be-arba he-kehilot shel ha-provintsya ha-apifiorit bid'rom tsarfat: Bibliografia shel s'farim khovrot umismakhim mudpasim mehame'ah ha-17 ad t'hiliat ha-me'ah ha-19." *Kiryat Sefer* 32 (1956–57): 205–10, 349–56.

————. "Yehudim be-tsiva tsarfat." In *Hayalim Yehudim Be-tsiv'ot Eyropa*. Edited by Yehuda Slutzky and Mordechai Kaplan, 30–41. Tel Aviv: Ma'arakhot, 1967.

————. "Yidishe Fakhshuln in 19tn Y.H." *YIVO Bleter* 42 (1962): 81–120.

————. "Di Yidishe Gezelshaftn in Pariz: dos Yidishe Gezelshaftlekhe lebn in Pariz tsum yor 1939." In *Yidn in Frankraykh: Shtudyes un Materialn*. Edited by Elias Tcherikower, 2:205–47. New York: YIVO, 1942.

————. "Yidishe Motivn in der Folkskultur fun Komta-Venesen in 17tn-19tn Y.-H." *YIVO Bleter* 20 (1942): 312–41.

————. *Di Yidishe Prese in Frankraykh*. Paris: Naye Prese, 1938.

————. "Yidisher Teater in Frankraykh." In *Yiddish Theater in Europe between Two World Wars: Soviet Union, Western Europe, Baltic Countries*, 289–321. New York: Yiddish Culture Congress, 1971.

————. "Yidn in Eyrope forshn Zeyer Umkum, 1939–1946." *YIVO Bleter* 30, no. 1 (1947): 94–106.

————. "Yidn un di nokh-Napoleonishe Restavratsie in Frankraykh." In *Yidn in Frankraykh: Shtudyes un Materialn*. Edited by Elias Tcherikower, 1:190–204. New York: YIVO, 1942.

————. "Yidn un di Parizer Komune fun 1871." In *Yidn in Frankraykh: Shtudyes un Materialn*. Edited by Elias Tcherikower, 2:93–154. New York: YIVO, 1942.

————. *YIVO Institute for Jewish Research (New York), Catalogue of the Exhibition: The History of Yiddish Orthography from the Spelling Rules of the Early Sixteenth Century to the Standardized Orthography of 1936*. New York: YIVO, 1966.

————. *YIVO Institute for Jewish Research (New York), Catalogue of an Exhibition: Jewish Mass Settlement in the United States: Documents and Pictures from the YIVO Archives on Eastern European Jewish Immigration in the Past Hundred Years*. New York: YIVO, 1966.

————. "Der YIVO un Zayne Grinders: Katalog fun der Oysshtelung tsum 50-yor-ikn Yovel fun Yidishn Visnshaftlekhn Institut." *YIVO Bleter* 46 (1980): 22–77.

———. "Zamlung Materialn fun 'Ameriker Dzshoint Rikonstrokshn Fond' (in Arkhiv fun YIVO)." *YIVO Bleter* 40 (1956): 225–33.

———. "The Zionist Problem at the Peace Conference." *Shivat Zion* 4 (1956): 240–63.

Tcher-ski, E. [Elias Tcherikower and Zosa Szajkowski]. "Di Drayfus-afere, di Arbeter-emigrantn un di Frantseyzish-yidishe Firers." In *Yidn in Frankraykh: Shtudyes un Materialn.* Edited by Elias Tcherikower, 2:155–92. New York: YIVO, 1942.

General Bibliography

Archival Collections

AMERICAN JEWISH ARCHIVES (CINCINNATI, OHIO)

- Klau Library Papers
- Papers of Herbert Friedman
- Papers of Ernst Lorge
- Papers of J. R. Marcus, Correspondence with Z. Szajkowski, 1958–77
- Papers of Harold Saperstein
- Papers of Nahum Sarna

ARCHIVES DÉPARTEMENTALES DU BAS-RHIN (STRASBOURG, FRANCE)

- 1709 W 75: Jugement contre Szajkowski (Frydmann)
- Archives of the Société d'Histoire des Israélites d'Alsace et de Lorraine

ARCHIVES DE LA VILLE ET DE LA COMMUNAUTÉ URBAINE DE STRASBOURG (STRASBOURG, FRANCE)

- Dossier Frydmann

ARCHIVES NATIONALES DE FRANCE (PARIS AND FONTAINEBLEAU, FRANCE)

- 72 AJ 253: Bibliothèques françaises pendant la seconde guerre mondiale
- F/17/17974–F/17/19996: Commission de Récupération artistique, sous-commission des livres
- Fonds Moscou, Paris Police Préfecture (at the Centre d'Archives Contemporaine, Fontainebleau, France)

ARCHIVES OF THE ALLIANCE ISRAÉLITE UNIVERSELLE (PARIS)

- Fonds Edmond-Maurice Lévy

- Papers of Maurice Moch (Consistoire papers on microfilm held by AIU)
- Centre de Documentation et de Vigilance
- Livres de bord de la bibliothèque de l'Alliance, 1935–75
- Registres des Procès-verbaux du Comité central de l'Alliance, 1936–66
- Secrétaire Général de l'AIU, papers on Szajkowski, AM SG 019

BRANDEIS UNIVERSITY, ROBERT D. FARBER UNIVERSITY ARCHIVES AND SPECIAL
COLLECTIONS (WALTHAM, MASSACHUSETTS)

- Consistoire Central Israélite de France Collection

CENTRAL ARCHIVES FOR THE HISTORY OF THE JEWISH PEOPLE (JERUSALEM)

- Papers of the Historical Society of Israel
- Holdings on French Jews: General, Communities
- Ezekiel Lifshutz Papers

CENTRE DE DOCUMENTATION JUIVE CONTEMPORAINE-MÉMORIAL DE LA SHOAH
(PARIS)

- MDXXXVI-5: Conférence européenne des commissions historiques et des centres de documentation juives, 1947
- MDXXXVI-13: Correspondance du CDJC, internationale
- MDXXXVI-12: Correspondance du CDJC, nationale
- MDXXXVI-11: Personnel du CDJC

JEWISH THEOLOGICAL SEMINARY OF AMERICA (JTSA) LIBRARY, SPECIAL
COLLECTIONS (NEW YORK)

- ARC 7: Alexander Kohut Memorial Foundation
- ARC 9: American Academy for Jewish Research
- ARC 36: French Jewish Communities Record Group
- ARC 111: Papers of Zosa Szajkowski
- ARC 120: Papers of the JTSA Library

KLAU LIBRARY, HEBREW UNION COLLEGE (CINCINNATI, OHIO)

- Alsace-Lorraine Collection
- Alsatian Jewish Inventories
- Consistoire Central des Israélites de France Collection
- French Miscellanea
- Sephardic Jews Collection

LEO BAECK INSTITUTE (NEW YORK)

- Papers of Guido Kisch
- Papers of Saul Sperling

NATIONAL ARCHIVES AND RECORDS ADMINISTRATION OF THE UNITED STATES
(COLLEGE PARK, MARYLAND)

- RG 260: Administrative records of Offenbach Archival Depot, Munich collecting point, Wiesbaden collecting point

UNITED STATES HOLOCAUST MEMORIAL MUSEUM (WASHINGTON, D.C.)

- LM 0017: Art Looting and Nazi Germany (Ardelia Hall Collection)
- Shoah Foundation Testimonies, Myriam Mitastein and Michelle Haydenblit

YESHIVA UNIVERSITY ARCHIVES (NEW YORK)

- French Consistorial Collection

YIVO ARCHIVES (NEW YORK)

- RG 81: Elias Tcherikower Papers
- RG 100A: YIVO–New York, folder 69, Aspirantur program
- RG 116: France 1 and France 2: France Territorial Collection
- RG 128: Rabbinical and Historical Manuscripts
- RG 210: UGIF Collection
- RG 245: HIAS-HICEM Papers
- RG 356: Jacob Shatzky Papers
- RG 406: Alliance Israélite Universelle Papers
- RG 584: Max Weinreich Papers
- RG 719: Moshe Kligsberg Papers
- RG 800: Zosa Szajkowski Papers

PERIODICALS

Archives Juives
Association for Jewish Libraries Bulletin
Historia Judaica
JTS Register
Jewish Quarterly Review
Jewish Social Studies
Le Monde Juif
Naye Prese

Proceedings of the American Academy of Jewish Research
Revue des Études Juives
Yedies fun YIVO
YIVO Bleter

Selected books and articles

Afoumado, Diane. "1946–2006: 60 ans dans l'histoire d'une revue." *Revue de l'histoire de la Shoah*, no. 185 (July–December 2006): 485–518.

Albert, Phyllis Cohen. "The Archives of the Consistoire Israélite de Bordeaux—1809–1905." *Revue des Études Juives* 131, nos. 1–2 (1972): 171–80.

Alford, Kenneth D. *The Spoils of World War II: The American Military's Role in the Stealing of Europe's Treasures*. New York: Birch Lane, 1994.

American Association of Museums. *Vitalizing Memory: International Perspectives on Provenance Research*. Washington, DC: American Association of Museums, 2005.

Amit, Gish. " 'The Largest Jewish Library in the World': The Books of Holocaust Victims and Their Redistribution Following World War II." *Dapim: Studies in the Holocaust* 27, no. 2 (2013): 107–28.

Anchel, Robert. *Les Juifs de France*. Paris: J. B. Janin, 1946.

Association des archivistes français. *Manuel d'archivistique: Théorie et pratique des archives publiques en France*. Paris: S.E.V.P.E.N., 1970.

Auslander, Leora. "Coming Home? Jews in Postwar Paris." *Journal of Contemporary History* 40, no. 2 (2005): 237–59.

Badanes, Jerome. *The Final Opus of Leon Solomon*. New York: Simon & Schuster, 1985.

Baker, Zachary M. "Getting in on the Ground Floor: Confessions of a Yiddish Impersonator." In *Rosaline and Myer Feinstein Lecture Series*. Association of Jewish Libraries: http://databases.jewishlibraries.org/node/17513.

Baron, Salo. "Communal Responsibility for Jewish Social Research." *Jewish Social Studies* 17, no. 3 (1955): 242–45.

———. "The Journal and the Conference of Jewish Social Studies." In *Emancipation and Counter-Emancipation: Selected Essays from Jewish Social Studies*. Edited by Abraham G. Duker and Meir Ben-Horin, 1–11. New York: Ktav, 1974.

———. "The Spiritual Reconstruction of European Jewry." *Commentary* (November 1945): 4–12.

Bastian, Jeannette Allis. *Owning Memory: How a Caribbean Community Lost Its Archives and Found Its History*. Westport, CT: Libraries Unlimited, 2003.

Benhayon, Yael. *Communauté israélite de Strasbourg, inventaire des archives, années 1930–1950*. Strasbourg, France: n.p., 1999.

Berlin, Charles. *Harvard Judaica: A History and Description of the Judaica Collection in the Harvard College Library*. Cambridge, MA: Harvard College Library, 2004.

Billig, Joseph. *Alfred Rosenberg dans l'action idéologique, politique et administrative du reich hitlérien: inventaire commenté de la collection de documents conservés au C.D.J.C. provenant des archives du Reichsleiter et Ministre A. Rosenberg.* Paris: Editions du Centre, 1963.

Blair, Ann, and Jennifer Milligan. "Introduction." *Archival Science* 7 (2007): 289–96.

Blouin, Francis X., and William G. Rosenberg, eds. *Archives, Documentation and the Institutions of Social Memory: Essays from the Sawyer Seminar.* Ann Arbor: University of Michigan Press, 2006.

Blumenkranz, Bernhard. *Documents modernes sur les Juifs, XVIe–XXe siècles.* Vol. 1, *Dépôts parisiens.* Paris: Privat, 1979.

———. "Les Juifs de France: petite histoire de leurs historiens." In *Les Juifs en France: écrits dispersés,* 13–16. Paris: Commission française des archives juives, 1989.

———. *Les Juifs et la révolution française.* Paris: Franco-Judaïca, 1976.

Blumenkranz, Bernhard, and Monique Lévy. *Bibliographie des Juifs en France.* Toulouse, France: Edouard Privat, 1974.

Boyarin, Jonathan. *Polish Jews in Paris: The Ethnography of Memory.* Bloomington: Indiana University Press, 1991.

Brombert, Victor. *Trains of Thought: Memories of a Stateless Youth.* New York: W. W. Norton, 2002.

Budnitskii, Oleg. *Russian Jews between the Reds and the Whites, 1917–1920.* Translated by Timothy J. Portice. Philadelphia: University of Pennsylvania Press, 2011.

Burton, Antoinette, ed. *Archive Stories: Facts, Fictions, and the Writing of History.* Durham, NC: Duke University Press, 2005.

Cahen, Gilbert. "La Commission française des archives juives—historique." *Archives Juives* 1 (1965): 1–2.

———. "Les Archives des institutions juives en France." *Archives Juives* 1 (1965): 6–10.

———. "Les Archives des institutions juives en France depuis la révolution française." *La Gazette des Archives,* nouvelle série 39 (1962): 177–82.

———. "Les Juifs et la vie économique des campagnes (1648–1870)." *Revue d'Alsace* 97 (1958): 143–58.

Cardin, Nina Beth, and David Wolf Silverman, eds. *The Seminary at 100: Reflections on the Jewish Theological Seminary and the Conservative Movement.* New York: JTSA, 1987.

Carlebach, Elisheva, John M. Efron, and David N. Myers, eds. *Jewish History and Jewish Memory: Essays in Honor of Yosef Hayim Yerushalmi.* Hanover, N.H.: Brandeis University Press, 1998.

Cassou, Jean, ed. *Le Pillage par les Allemands des oeuvres d'art et des bibliothèques appartenant à des Juifs en France.* Paris: Editions du Centre, 1947.

Coeuré, Sophie. *La Mémoire spoliée: les archives des français: butin de guerre nazi puis soviétique.* Paris: Payot, 2007.

Coeuré, Sophie, and Vincent Duclert. *Les Archives.* Paris: La Découverte, 2001.

Cohen, Beth B. *Case Closed: Holocaust Survivors in Postwar America*. New Brunswick, NJ: Rutgers University Press, 2007.

Cohen, Daniel J. "Jewish Records from Germany in the Jewish General History Archives in Jerusalem." *LBI Year Book* 1, no. 1 (1956): 331–45.

Cohen, Richard I. *The Burden of Conscience: French Jewry's Response to the Holocaust*. Bloomington: Indiana University Press, 1987.

———. "The Fate of French Jewry in World War II in Historical Writing (1944–1983): Interim Conclusions." In *The Historiography of the Holocaust Period: Proceedings of the Fifth International Yad Vashem Conference*. Edited by Yisrael Gutman and Gideon Grief, 155–86. Jerusalem: Yad Vashem, 1988.

———. "French Jewry's Dilemma on the Orientation of Its Leadership, from Polemics to Conciliation, 1942–1944." *Yad Vashem Studies* 14 (1981): 167–204.

———. "Zosa Szajkowski z"l." *Zion* 43, nos. 3–4 (1978): 367–69.

Colla, Elliott. *Conflicted Antiquities: Egyptology, Egyptomania, Egyptian Modernity*. Durham, NC: Duke University Press, 2007.

Combe, Sonia. *Archives intérdites: l'histoire confisquée*. Paris: La Découverte, 2001.

Commission on European Cultural Reconstruction, Research Staff. "Tentative List of Jewish Cultural Treasures in Axis-Occupied Countries." *Supplement to Jewish Social Studies* 8, no. 1 (1946).

———. "Tentative List of Jewish Educational Institutions in Axis-Occupied Countries." *Supplement to Jewish Social Studies* 8, no. 3 (1946).

Dawidowicz, Lucy S. *From That Place and Time: A Memoir, 1938–1947*. New York: W. W. Norton, 1989.

Dean, Martin, Constantin Goschler, and Phillip Ther, eds. *Robbery and Restitution: The Conflict over Jewish Property in Europe*. New York: Berghan, 2007.

Delmas, Bruno. *La Société sans mémoire: propos dissidents sur la politique des archives en France*. Paris: Bourin, 2006.

Delmas, Bruno, and Christine Nougaret, eds. *Archives et nations dans l'Europe du XIXe siècle: actes du colloque organisé par l'Ecole des Chartes (Paris, 27–28 avril 2001)*. Paris: Ecole des Chartes, 2004.

Delsaux, Jenny. *La Sous-Commission des Livres à la Récuperation Artistique, 1944–1950*. Paris: n.p., 1976.

Derrida, Jacques. *Archive Fever: A Freudian Impression*. Translated by Eric Prenowitz. Chicago: University of Chicago Press, 1996.

Dicker, Herman, ed. *Of Learning and Libraries: The Seminary Library at One Hundred*. New York: JTSA, 1988.

Dobbs, Michael. "Epilogue: Books Looted during Holocaust Might Now Be in Library of Congress." *Washington Post*, January 7, 2000.

Dobin, M. "Di Profesies fun di Yidishe Emigrantn in Pariz." *YIVO Bleter* 4, no. 1 (1932): 22–42.

———. "Yidishe Emigrantn-arbeter in Pariz." *YIVO Bleter* 3, nos. 4–5 (1932): 385–403.

Dobroszycki, Lucjan. "YIVO in Interwar Poland: Work in the Historical Sciences." In *The Jews of Poland between Two World Wars*. Edited by Yisrael Gutman, Ezra

Mendelsohn, Jehuda Reinharz, and Chone Shmeruk, 494–518. Hanover, NH: Brandeis University Press, 1989.

Douglas, Lawrence. *The Memory of Judgment: Making Law and History in the Trials of the Holocaust.* New Haven, CT: Yale University Press, 2001.

Dreyfus, Jean-Marc, and Sarah Gensburger. *Des camps dans Paris: Austerlitz, Lévitan, Bassano. juillet 1943–août 1944.* Paris: Fayard, 2003.

Dubnow-Ehrlich, Sophie. *The Life and Work of S. M. Dubnow: Diaspora Nationalism and Jewish History.* Translated by Judith Vowles. Bloomington: Indiana University Press, 1950.

Eckert, Astrid M. *The Struggle for the Files: The Western Allies and the Return of German Archives after the Second World War.* Translated by Donna Geyer. New York: Cambridge University Press, 2012.

Edsel, Robert. *The Monuments Men: Allied Heroes, Nazi Thieves, and the Greatest Treasure Hunt in History.* New York: Center Street, 2009.

Eisenbach, Artur. "Jewish Historiography in Interwar Poland." In *The Jews of Poland between Two World Wars.* Edited by Yisrael Gutman, Ezra Mendelsohn, Jehuda Reinharz, and Chone Shmeruk, 453–93. Hanover, NH: Brandeis University Press, 1989.

Ettinghausen, Maurice L. *Rare Books and Royal Collectors: Memoirs of an Antiquarian Bookseller.* New York: Simon & Schuster, 1966.

Farmer, Sarah. *Martyred Village: Commemorating the 1944 Massacre at Oradour-sur-Glane.* Berkeley: University of California Press, 1999.

Favier, Jean, and Danièle Neirinck. "Les Archives." In *L'histoire et le métier d'historien en France, 1945–1995.* Edited by François Bédarida, 89–100. Paris: Editions de la Maison des sciences de l'homme, 1995.

Feuerwerker, David. "Robert Anchel." *Revue des Études Juives* (1953): 53–66.

Fishman, David E. *Embers Plucked from the Fire: The Rescue of Jewish Cultural Treasures in Vilna.* New York: YIVO, 1996.

———. *The Rise of Modern Yiddish Culture.* Pittsburgh: University of Pittsburgh Press, 2005.

Foote, Kenneth E. "To Remember and to Forget: Archives, Memory and Culture." *American Archivist* 53 (1990): 378–92.

Frankel, Jonathan, ed. *Reshaping the Past: Jewish History and the Historians.* Vol. 10, *Studies in Contemporary Jewry: An Annual.* New York: Oxford University Press, 1994.

Fredricksen, Oliver J. *The American Military Occupation of Germany, 1945–1953.* U.S. Army HQ, Europe: Historical Division, 1953.

Friedman, Hebert A. *Roots of the Future.* Jerusalem: Gefen, 1990.

Fritzsche, Peter. "The Archive." *History and Memory* 17, nos. 1–2 (2005): 15–44.

———. *Stranded in the Present: Modern Time and the Melancholy of History.* Cambridge, MA: Harvard University Press, 2004.

Garbarini, Alexandra. *Numbered Days: Jewish Diaries and the Holocaust.* New Haven, CT: Yale University Press, 2006.

Gartner, Lloyd P. "In Memoriam: Abraham G. Duker, 1907–1987." *Jewish Social Studies* 49 (Summer/Fall 1987): 189–94.

Gerber, Noah S. "The Cultural Discovery of Yemenite Jewry: Between Ethnography and Philology." Ph.D. diss., Hebrew University, Jerusalem, 2009.

Gerson, Stéphane, and Laura Lee Downs. *Why France? American Historians Reflect on an Enduring Fascination.* Ithaca, NY: Cornell University Press, 2007.

Giles, Geoffrey J. "Archives and Historians: An Introduction." In *Archivists and Historians: The Crucial Partnership.* Edited by Geoffrey J. Giles, 5–13. Washington, DC: German Historical Institute, 1996.

Goldberg, Sylvie Anne. "Paradigmatic Times: An-Sky's Two Worlds." In *The Worlds of S. An-Sky: A Russian Jewish Intellectual at the Turn of the Century.* Edited by Gabriella Safran and Steven Zipperstein, 44–52. Stanford, Calif.: Stanford University Press, 2006.

Goldsztejn, Isabelle. "Le Rôle de l'American Joint dans la reconstruction de la communauté." *Archives Juives* 28, no. 1 (1995): 23–37.

Grafton, Anthony. *The Footnote: A Curious History.* Cambridge, MA: Harvard University Press, 1997.

Green, Nancy L. *The Pletzl of Paris: Jewish Immigrant Workers in the Belle Epoque.* New York: Homes & Meier, 1986.

———. "La Révolution dans l'imaginaire des immigrants juifs." In *Histoire politique des Juifs de France: entre universalisme et particularisme.* Edited by Pierre Birnbaum, 153–62. Paris: Fondation nationale des sciences politiques, 1990.

Grimsted, Patricia Kennedy. "The Road to Minsk for Western 'Trophy' Books: Twice Plundered but Not Yet 'Home from the War.'" *Libraries and Culture* 39, no. 4 (2004): 351–404.

———. "Road to Ratibor: Library and Archival Plunder by the Einsatzstab Reichsleiter Rosenberg." *Holocaust and Genocide Studies* 19, no. 3 (2005): 390–458.

———. *Trophies of War and Empire: The Archival Heritage of Ukraine, World War II, and the International Politics of Restitution.* Harvard Papers in Ukrainian Studies. Cambridge, MA: Harvard University Press, 2001.

Grimsted, Patricia Kennedy, F. J. Hoogewoud, and Eric Ketelaar, eds. *Returned from Russia: Nazi Archival Plunder in Western Europe and Recent Restitution Issues.* Builth Wells, UK: Institute of Art and Law, 2007.

Gross, Henri. *Gallia Judaica: dictionnaire géographique de la France d'après les sources rabbiniques.* Translated from German by Moïse Bloch. Paris: Cerf, 1897.

Grossmann, Atina. *Jews, Germans, and Allies: Close Encounters in Occupied Germany.* Princeton, NJ: Princeton University Press, 2007.

Grunberger, Michael. "Special Challenges in Dealing with Holocaust-Era Looted Assets." Paper presented at the Vilnius International Forum on Holocaust-Era Looted Assets, October 3–5, 2000.

Grynberg, Anne. "Une Découverte récente; le fonds d'archives de la commission des camps (1941–1943)." *Le Monde Juif*, no. 131 (1988): 108–18.

Harris, Verne. "A Shaft of Darkness: Derrida in the Archive." In *Refiguring the Archive.* Edited by Carolyn Hamilton, Verne Harris, Jane Taylor, Michele Pickover, Graeme Reid, and Razia Saleh, 61–81. Dordrecht, Netherlands: Kluwer, 2002.

Hazan, Katy. "La Politique antijuive de Vichy dans les procès de l'épuration." *Archives Juives* 28, no. 1 (1995): 38–51.

Heald, Carolyn. "Is There Room for Archives in the Postmodern World?" *American Archivist* 59 (1996): 88–101.

Heller, Bernard. "Displaced Books and Displaced Persons." *Liberal Judaism* (March 1951): 18–22.

———. "The Homecoming." *Liberal Judaism* (September 1950): 24–28.

———. "Invisible Spectators." *Liberal Judaism* (June 1951): 34–37.

———. "Operation Salvage." *Jewish Horizon* 6 (February 1950): 12–14.

Herman, Dana. "Hashavat Avedah: A History of Jewish Cultural Reconstruction, Inc." Ph.D. diss., McGill University, Montréal, 2008.

Hertzberg, Arthur. *The French Enlightenment and the Jews: The Origins of Modern Anti-Semitism.* New York: Columbia University Press, 1968.

Hildesheimer, Françoise. *Les Archives de France: mémoire de l'histoire.* Paris: Honoré Champion, 1997.

———. *Les Juifs dans les Bouches-du-Rhône: catalogue des documents conservés dans les dépôts publics (Moyen âge, époques moderne et contemporaine).* Paris: Cahiers de la Commission française des archives juives, 1998.

Hinsley, Curtis M., Jr. "Digging for Identity: Reflections on the Cultural Background of Collecting." In *Repatriation Reader: Who Owns American Indian Remains?* Edited by Devon A. Mihesuah, 37–55. Lincoln: University of Nebraska Press, 2000.

Hoffman, Adina, and Peter Cole. *Sacred Trash: The Lost and Found World of the Cairo Geniza.* New York: Nextbook, 2011.

Honigmann, Peter. "Das Projekt von Rabbiner Dr. Bernhard Brilling zur Errichtung eines Jüdischen Zentralarchivs im Nachkriegsdeutschland." In *Historisches Bewusstsein im Jüdischen Kontext: Strategien-Aspekte-Diskurse.* Edited by Klaus Hödl, 223–41. Innsbruck, Austria: Studien Verlag, 2004.

———. "Die Akten des Exils: Betrachtungen zu den mehr als Hunderjährigen Behüngen um die Inventarisierung von Quellen zur Geschichte der Juden in Deutschland." *Der Archivar* 54, no. 1 (2001): 23–31.

———. "Les Archives de la société d'histoire des israélites d'Alsace et de Lorraine au cours de la première moitié du XXe siècle." Paper presented at the XXIIIe Colloque de la Société d'histoire des israélites d'Alsace et de Lorraine, Strasbourg, France, 2001.

Honigmann, Peter, and Yael Benhayon. *Consistoire Israélite du Bas-Rhin, inventaire des Archives, 1808–1930.* Strasbourg, France: 2001.

Hyman, Paula E. *From Dreyfus to Vichy: The Remaking of French Jewry, 1906–1939.* New York: Columbia University Press, 1979.

————. "French Jewish Historiography since 1870." In *The Jews in Modern France*. Edited by Frances Malino and Bernard Wasserstein, 327–46. Hanover, NH: Brandeis University Press, 1985.

————. "The Ideological Transformation of Modern Jewish Historiography." In *The State of Jewish Studies*. Edited by Shaye J. D. Cohen and Edward L. Greenstein, 143–57. Detroit, MI: Wayne State University Press, 1990.

————. *The Jews of Modern France*. Berkeley: University of California Press, 1998.

Jacoubovitch, Jules. *Rue Amelot*. Translated from Yiddish into French by Gabrielle Jacoubovitch-Bouhana. http://archive.is/kn3Y.

Jewish Theological Seminary of America, Library, Archives. *Preliminary List of Holdings*. New York: JTSA, 1978.

Job, Françoise. *Juifs en Lorraine: Inventaire de documents concernant les juifs conservés aux Archives Départementales de Meurthe-et-Moselle, suivi de Elisabeth Couteau, "Inventaire des Archives de la Communauté Israélite de Lorraine."* Paris: Cahiers de la Commission française des archives juives, 1998.

Jockusch, Laura. *Collect and Record! Jewish Holocaust Documentation in Early Postwar Europe*. New York: Oxford University Press, 2012.

Jordan, James, Lisa Leff, and Joachim Schlör. "Jewish Migration and the Archive: Introduction." *Jewish History and Culture* 15, nos. 1–2 (2014): 1–5.

Kafka, Ben. *The Demon of Writing: Powers and Failures of Paperwork*. New York: Zone, 2012.

Kagan, Berl. *Leksikon fun Yidish-Shraybers: mit Hesofes un Tikunim tsum Leksikon fun der nayer Yidisher Literatur, un 5,800 Psevdonimen*. New York: Aroysgegebn fun Raya Ilman-Kohen, 1986.

Kalman, Jason, and Jacqueline S. du Toit. *Canada's Big Biblical Bargain: How McGill University Bought the Dead Sea Scrolls*. Montréal: McGill-Queen's University Press, 2010.

Kaplan, Elisabeth. "We Are What We Collect, We Collect What We Are: Archives and the Construction of Identity." *American Archivist* 63 (2000): 126–51.

Karff, Samuel E., ed. *Hebrew Union College–Jewish Institute of Religion at One Hundred Years*. Cincinnati, OH: Hebrew Union College Press, 1976.

Karlip, Joshua M. "At the Crossroads between War and Genocide." *Jewish Social Studies* 11, no. 2 (2005): 170–201.

————. "Between Martyrology and Historiography: Elias Tcherikower and the Making of a Pogrom Historian." *East European Jewish Affairs* 38, no. 3 (2008): 257–80.

————. *The Tragedy of a Generation: The Rise and Fall of Jewish Nationalism in Eastern Europe*. Cambridge, MA: Harvard University Press, 2013.

Karlsgodt, Elizabeth Campbell. *Defending National Treasures: French Art and Heritage under Vichy*. Stanford, CA: Stanford University Press, 2011.

Kassow, Samuel D. *Who Will Write Our History? Emanuel Ringelblum, the Warsaw Ghetto and the Oyneg Shabes Archive*. Bloomington: Indiana University Press, 2007.

Kerner, Samuel. *La Communauté juive d'Odratzheim au XVIIIe et au XIXe siècles.* Paris: n.p., 1983.

Kirchhoff, Markus. "Looted Texts: Restituting Jewish Libraries." In *Restitution and Memory: Material Restoration in Europe.* Edited by Dan Diner and Gotthart Wunberg, 161–88. New York: Berghan, 2007.

Klausner, Abraham. *A Letter to My Children: From the Edge of the Holocaust.* San Francisco: Holocaust Center of Northern California, 2002.

Kohn, Roger. *An Inventory to the French Jewish Communities Record Group (1648–1946).* New York: Jewish Theological Seminary of America, 1991.

———. *An Inventory to the Mordechai Bernstein Collection, 1605–1965.* New York: Yeshiva University Archives, 1987.

———. *Répertoire numérique des archives du Consistoire Israélite de Bordeaux.* Bordeaux, France: n.p., 1977.

Kornhendler, Yekheskel. *Alt Pariz.* Paris: Oyfgang, 1936.

———. *Briv fun Lektur: Fir Yor Natsi-Hershaft in Frankraykh.* Paris: Oyfgang, 1947.

Kovnitz, Milton. "YIVO Comes to Morningside: America Gains a New Institute of Learning." *Commentary* 4 (1947): 48–54.

Kruk, Herman. *The Last Days of the Jerusalem of Lithuania: Chronicles from the Vilna Ghetto and the Camps, 1939–1944.* Edited by Benjamin Harshav; translated by Barbara Harshav. New Haven, CT: Yale University Press, 2002.

Kugelmass, Jack. "The Father of Jewish Ethnography?" In *The Worlds of S. An-Sky: A Russian Jewish Intellectual at the Turn of the Century.* Edited by Gabriella Safran and Steven Zipperstein, 346–59. Stanford, CA: Stanford University Press, 2006.

Kühlmann, Marie. "Les Bibliothèques dans la tourmente." In *Histoire des bibliothèques françaises: les bibliothèques au XXe siècle, 1914–1990.* Edited by Martine Poulain, 222–47. Paris: Promodis, 1992.

Kuperminc, Jean-Claude. "La Bibliothèque de l'Alliance Israélite Universelle." In *Histoire des bibliothèques françaises: les bibliothèques au XXe siècle, 1914–1990.* Edited by Martine Poulain, 238. Paris: Promodis, 1992.

———. "La Reconstruction de la Bibliothèque de l'Alliance Israélite Universelle, 1945–1955." *Archives Juives* 34, no. 1 (2001): 98–113.

———. "The Return of Looted French Archives: The Case of the Library of the Alliance Israélite Universelle." In *Returned from Russia: Nazi Archival Plunder in Western Europe and Recent Restitution Issues.* Edited by Patricia Kennedy Grimsted, F. J. Hoogewoud, and Eric Ketelaar, 135–47. Builth Wells, UK: Institute of Art and Law, 2007.

Kuperminc, Jean-Claude, and Rafaële Arditti, eds. *Preserving Jewish Archives as Part of the European Cultural Heritage: Proceedings of the Conference on Judaica Archives in Europe, for Archivists and Librarians, Potsdam, 1999, 11–13 July.* Paris: Les Editions du Nadir de l'Alliance Israélite Universelle, 2001.

Kurtz, Michael. *America and the Return of Nazi Contraband: The Recovery of Europe's Cultural Treasures.* New York: Cambridge University Press, 2006.

Kuznitz, Cecile. *YIVO and the Making of Modern Jewish Culture: Scholarship for the Yiddish Nation.* Cambridge, UK: Cambridge University Press, 2013.

———. "An-Sky's Legacy: The Vilna Historic-Ethnographic Society and the Shaping of Modern Jewish Culture." In *The Worlds of S. An-Sky: A Russian Jewish Intellectual at the Turn of the Century.* Edited by Gabriella Safran and Steven Zipperstein, 320–45. Stanford, CA: Stanford University Press, 2006.

Laffitte, Michel. *Un engrenage fatal: L'UGIF face aux réalités de la Shoah.* Paris: Liana Levi, 2003.

———. *Juif dans la France allemande: institutions, dirigeants et communautés au temps de la Shoah.* Paris: Tallandier, 2006.

Laffitte, Michel, and Annette Wieviorka. *A l'intérieur du camp de Drancy.* Paris: Perrin, 2012.

Landau, Philippe-E., and Jean-Claude Kuperminc. "Les Archives Juives." In *Les Religions et leurs archives: enjeux d'aujourd'hui, journée d'études de la direction des archives de France, Paris, Collège de France, 11–12 Mars 1999.* Paris: Direction des Archives de France, 2001.

Lansky, Aaron. *Outwitting History: The Amazing Adventures of a Man Who Rescued a Million Yiddish Books.* Chapel Hill, NC: Algonquin, 2005.

Laurent, Sébastien, ed. *Archives "secrètes," secrets d'archives?: l'historien et l'archiviste face aux archives sensibles.* Paris: CNRS, 2003.

Leff, Lisa Moses. "L'Histoire des juifs de France vue des Etats-Unis." *Archives Juives* (March 2010): 126–36.

———. "Post-Holocaust Book Restitutions: How One State Agency Helped Revive Republican Franco-Judaism." In *Post-Holocaust France and the Jews, 1945–55.* Edited by Seán Hand and Steven T. Katz. New York: New York University Press, forthcoming 2015.

———. *Sacred Bonds of Solidarity: The Rise of Jewish Internationalism in Nineteenth Century France.* Stanford, CA: Stanford University Press, 2006.

Liberles, Robert. "Postemancipation Historiography and the Jewish Historical Societies of America and England." In *Reshaping the Past: Jewish History and Historians.* Edited by Jonathan Frankel, 45–65. New York: Oxford University Press, 1994.

———. *Salo Wittmayer Baron: Architect of Jewish History.* New York: New York University Press, 1995.

Loeser, Hans F. *Hans's Story.* New York: iUniverse, 2007.

Loveland, Kristen. "The Association for Jewish Studies: A Brief History." Report Prepared for the Association for Jewish Studies 40th Annual Conference, December 21–23, 2008.

Lowenthal, David. *The Heritage Crusade and the Spoils of History.* Cambridge, UK: Cambridge University Press, 1998.

Lukin, Binyamin. "The Creation of a Documentary Collection on the History of Russian Jewry at the CAHJP." *Slavic and East European Information Resources* 4, nos. 2–3 (2003): 17–36.

Malinovich, Nadia. *French and Jewish: Culture and the Politics of Identity in Early Twentieth-Century France.* Oxford: Littman, 2008.

Mandel, Maud S. *In the Aftermath of Genocide: Armenians and Jews in Twentieth-Century France.* Durham, NC: Duke University Press, 2003.

———. "Philanthropy or Cultural Imperialism? The Impact of American Jewish Aid in Post-Holocaust France." *Jewish Social Studies* 9, no. 1 (2002): 53–94.

Mankowitz, Zeev W. *Life between Memory and Hope: The Survivors of the Holocaust in Occupied Germany.* Cambridge, UK: Cambridge University Press, 2002.

Marx, Alexander. *Bibliographical Studies and Notes on Rare Books and Manuscripts in the Library of the Jewish Theological Seminary of America.* New York: Ktav, 1977.

Mayorek, Yoram. "Zosa Szajkowski and the Transfer of French-Jewish Archives to the U.S." *Arkhiyyon*, nos. 10–11 (1999).

Mbembe, Achille. "The Power of the Archive and Its Limits." In *Refiguring the Archive.* Edited by Carolyn Hamilton, Verne Harris, Jane Taylor, Michele Pickover, Graeme Reid, and Razia Saleh, 19–26. Dordrecht, Netherlands: Kluwer, 2002.

McDade, Travis. *Thieves of Book Row: New York's Most Notorious Rare Book Ring and the Man Who Stopped It.* New York: Oxford University Press, 2013.

Melamed, Efim. "'Immortalizing the Crime in History. . . ': The Archives of the Ostjüdisches Historisches Archiv (Kiev-Berlin-Paris, 1920–1940)." In *The Russian Jewish Diaspora and European Culture.* Edited by P. Wagstaff, J. Schulte, and O. Tabachnikova, 373–86. Leiden, Netherlands: Brill, 2012.

Menes, A. "Di Yidn in Frankraykh." *YIVO Bleter* 11, no. 5 (1937): 329–55.

Meyer, Michael A. *Hebrew Union College, Jewish Institute of Religion, a Centennial History, 1875–1975.* Cincinnati, OH: Hebrew Union College, 1992.

Meyer, Pierre-André. *Histoire des Juifs de Lorraine, bibliographie, en complément à la bibliographie des Juifs en France, collection "Franco-Judaïca," Privat, 1974, travaux parus de 1973–1999.* Paris: Cahiers de la Commission française des archives juives, 1999.

Milligan, Jennifer S. "Making a Modern Archive: The Archives Nationales of France." Ph.D. diss., Rutgers University, New Brunswick, NJ, 2002.

Milton, Sybil H. "Lost, Stolen and Strayed: The Archival Heritage of German-Jewish History." In *The Jewish Response to German Culture: From the Enlightenment to the Second World War.* Edited by Jehuda Reinharz and Walter Schatzberg, 317–35. Hanover, NH: Brandeis University Press, 1985.

Miron, Guy. *The Waning of Emancipation: Jewish History, Memory and the Rise of Fascism in Germany, France and Hungary.* Detroit, MI: Wayne State University Press, 2011.

Moch, Maurice. *L'Etoile et la francisque: les institutions juives sous Vichy.* Edited by Alain Michel and Claire Darmon. Paris: Cerf, 1990.

Mohrer, Fruma, and Marek Web, eds. *Guide to the YIVO Archives.* New York: YIVO Institute for Jewish Research, 1998.

Moore, Lara Jennifer. *Restoring Order: The Ecole des Chartes and the Organization of Archives and Libraries in France, 1820–1870.* Duluth, Minn.: Litwin, 2001.

Mrejen-O'Hana, Simone. "Les Pinqassim de Carpentras au regard du Saint-Siège." *Bulletin du Centre de recherche français de Jérusalem* 16 (2005): 45–75.

Myers, David N. "The Fall and Rise of Jewish Historicism: The Evolution of the Akademie für die Wissenschaft des Judentums (1919–1934)." *Hebrew Union College Annual* 63 (1992): 107–44.

———. *Re-Inventing the Jewish Past: European Jewish Intellectuals and the Zionist Return to History*. New York: Oxford University Press, 1995.

Myers, David N., and David B. Ruderman, eds. *The Jewish Past Revisited: Reflections on Modern Jewish Historians*. New Haven, CT: Yale University Press, 1998.

Nadell, Pamela S. *Conservative Judaism in America: A Biographical Dictionary and Sourcebook*. New York: Greenwood, 1988.

Nesmith, Brian. "Seeing Archives: Postmodernism and the Changing Intellectual Place of Archives." *American Archivist* 65 (2002): 24–41.

Netter, Nathan. *Vingt siècles d'histoire d'une communauté juive (Metz et son grand passé)*. Paris: Librairie Lipschutz, 1938.

Nicholas, Lynn H. *The Rape of Europa: The Fate of Europe's Treasures in the Third Reich and the Second World War*. New York: Vintage, 1994.

Nora, Pierre. "Ben Bella: Pourquoi Cette Crise?" *France Observateur*, August 2, 1962, 8–9.

———. "Between History and Memory: General Introduction." In *Realms of Memory*. Edited by Pierre Nora, 1–20. New York: Columbia University Press, 1996.

———. "La Guerre du Souvenir." *Le Nouvel Observateur*, February 1976.

Norich, Anita. *Discovering Exile: Yiddish and Jewish American Culture during the Holocaust*. Stanford, CA: Stanford University Press, 2007.

Offenbach Archival Depot. *Photographic History [of the books, ceremonial and art objects confiscated by the Nazis and collected at the Offenbach Archival Depot]*. Offenbach, Germany: OMGUS, 1946.

Osborne, Thomas. "The Ordinariness of the Archive." *History of the Human Sciences* 12, no. 2 (1999): 51–64.

O'Toole, James. "The Symbolic Significance of Archives." *American Archivist* 56 (1993): 234–55.

Ozick, Cynthia. "Envy; or, Yiddish in America." *Commentary* 48, no. 5 (1969): 33–53.

Panitch, Judith M. "Liberty, Equality, Posterity? Some Archival Lessons from the Case of the French Revolution." *American Archivist* 59 (1996): 30–47.

Parfitt, Tudor. "'The Year of the Pride of Israel': Montefiore and the Damascus Blood Libel of 1840." In *The Century of Moses Montefiore*. Edited by Sonia and V. D. Lipman, 131–48. London: Littman, 1985.

Patt, Avinoam J., and Michael Berkovitz, eds. *"We Are Here": New Approaches to Jewish Displaced Persons in Postwar Germany*. Detroit, MI: Wayne State University Press, 2010.

Peiss, Kathy. "Cultural Policy in a Time of War: The American Response to Endangered Books in World War II." *Library Trends* 55, no. 3 (2007): 370–86.

Perego, Simon. "Commémorations." In *Dictionnaire du Judaïsme français depuis 1944*. Edited by Jean Leselbaum, 175–77. Paris: Armand Colin, 2013.

———. "Libération." In *Dictionnaire du Judaïsme français depuis 1944*. Edited by Jean Leselbaum, 544–48. Paris: Armand Colin, 2013.

———. "Les commémorations de la destruction des Juifs d'Europe au Mémorial du martyr juif inconnu du milieu des années cinquante à la fin des années soixante." *Revue d'histoire de la Shoah*, no. 193 (2010): 471–507.

———. "Jurys d'honneur: The Stakes, Modes, and Limits of the Purges among the Jews in Post-Liberation France." In *Jewish Honor Courts: Revenge, Retribution and Reconciliation in Europe and Israel after the Holocaust*. Edited by Gabriel Finder and Laura Jockusch. Detroit, MI: Wayne State University Press, forthcoming 2015.

Poliakov, Léon. *L'Auberge des musiciens: mémoires*. Paris: Mazarine, 1981.

Pollack, Emmanuelle. "A la Fondation CASJP-Cojasor. Retrouvées, classées, enfin accessbiles: les archives du Comité de Bienfaisance Israélite de Paris (CBIP)." *Archives Juives* 36, no. 2 (2003): 131–38.

Pomian, Krzysztof. "Les Archives: du Trésor des Chartes au Caran." In *Les Lieux de mémoire*. Edited by Pierre Nora, 163–233. Paris: Gallimard, 1992.

Pomrenze, Seymour J. "The Restitution of Jewish Cultural Treasures after the Holocaust: The Offenbach Archival Depot's Role in the Fulfillment of U.S. International and Moral Obligations (a First Hand Account)." Feinstein Lecture, National Foundation for Jewish Culture, 2002.

Poovey, Mary. *A History of the Modern Fact: Problems of Knowledge in the Sciences of Wealth and Society*. Chicago: University of Chicago Press, 1998.

Posner, Ernst. "Some Aspects of Archival Development since the French Revolution." In *Archives and the Public Interest: Selected Essays by Ernst Posner*. Edited by Ken Munden. Washington, DC: Public Affairs, 1967.

Poste, Leslie. "The Development of U.S. Protection of Libraries and Archives in Europe during World War II." Ph.D. diss., University of Chicago, 1958.

Poulin, Martine. *Livres pillés, lectures surveillées: les bibliothèques françaises sous l'occupation*. Paris: Gallimard, 2008.

Poznanski, Renée. "La Création du Centre de Documentation Juive Contemporaine en France (avril 1943)." *Vingtième siècle. Revue d'histoire* 63 (1999): 51–63.

———. *Jews in France during World War II*. Translated by Nathan Bracher. Hanover, NH: Brandeis University Press, 2001.

———. *Propagandes et persécutions. La Résistance et le "problème juif."* Paris: Fayard, 2008.

Prager, Leonard. "In Memory of Zosa Shaykovski (Szajkowski) né Shayke Fridman (Frydman)." *The Mendele Review: Yiddish Literature and Language* 2.035 (1998).

Rabinowicz, Harry M. *The Jewish Literary Treasures of England and America*. New York: Thomas Yoseloff, 1962.

Raphaël, Freddy, and Robert Weyl. *Juifs en Alsace: culture, société, histoire*. Paris: Privat, 1977.

Rayski, Adam. *The Choice of the Jews under Vichy: Between Submission and Resistance.* Translated by Will Sayers. Notre Dame, IN: University of Notre Dame Press, 2005.

Rein, Denise. "Die Bestände der ehemalingen jüdischen Gemeinden Deutschlands in den 'Central Archives for the History of the Jewish People' in Jerusalem. Ein Überblick über das Schicksal der verschiedenen Gemeinderarchive." *Der Archivar* 55, no. 4 (2002): 318–27.

Reymes, Nicholas. "Le Pillages des archives appartenant à des juifs pendant l'occupation: les livres dans la tourmente." *Le Monde juif*, no. 168 (2000): 31–56.

Rigg, Bryan Mark. *Rescued from the Reich: How One of Hitler's Soldiers Saved the Lubavitcher Rebbe.* New Haven, CT: Yale University Press, 2004.

Rodrigue, Aron. "Léon Halévy and Modern French Jewish Historiography." In *Jewish History and Jewish Memory: Essays in Honor of Yosef Hayim Yerushalmi.* Edited by Elisheva Carlebach, John M. Efron, and David N. Myers, 413–27. Hanover, NH: Brandeis University Press, 1998.

Rose, Jonathan, ed. *The Holocaust and the Book: Destruction and Preservation.* Amherst: University of Massachusetts Press, 2001.

Rosenberg, Pnina. "The World of Yiddish Theater in France." http://www.jewish-theatre.com/visitor/article_display.aspx?articleID=2288.

Roskies, David G. *Against the Apocalypse: Responses to Catastrophe in Modern Jewish Culture.* Cambridge, MA: Harvard University Press, 1984.

Roth, Cecil. "The Restoration of Jewish Libraries, Archives and Museums." *Contemporary Jewish Record* 7, no. 3 (1944): 253–57.

Roth, Irene. *Cecil Roth: Historian without Tears.* New York: Sepher-Hermon, 1982.

Rousso, Henry. *The Vichy Syndrome: History and Memory in France since 1944.* Translated by Arthur Goldhammer. Cambridge, MA: Harvard University Press, 1991.

Sachar, Abram L. *Brandeis University: A Host at Last.* Hanover, NH: Brandeis University Press, 1995.

Sarna, Jonathan D. "Recalling Arthur Hertzberg: Public Intellectual." *Jewish Week*, April 21, 2006.

Schidorsky, Dov. "The Salvaging of Jewish Books in Europe after the Holocaust." In *Jüdischer Buchbesitz als Raubgut: Zweites Hannoversches Symposium.* Edited by Regine Dehnel, 197–212. Frankfurt, Germany: Klostermann, 2006.

Schmelzer, Menahem. "Making a Great Judaica Library: At What Price?" In *Tradition Renewed: A History of the Jewish Theological Seminary.* Edited by Jack Wertheimer, 677–715. New York: JTSA, 1997.

Schwab, Moise, and Zosa Szajkowski. *Index of Articles Relative to Jewish History and Literature Published in Periodicals, from 1665 to 1900, Augmented Edition, with an Introduction and Edited List of Abbreviations, by Zosa Szajkowski.* New York: Ktav, 1971.

Schwartz, Joan M., and Terry Cook. "Archives, Records and Power: The Making of Modern Memory." *Archival Science* 2 (2002): 1–19.

Schwartz, Shuly Rubin. "The Schechter Faculty: The Seminary and 'Wissenschaft des Judentums' in America." In *Tradition Renewed: A History of the Jewish Theological Seminary*. Edited by Jack Wertheimer, 293–325. New York: JTSA, 1997.

Schwarzfuchs, Simon. "Les Archives religieuses juives d'Europe." *Archivum* (1955): 165–68.

———. "Les Consistoires: La reconstruction dans l'immédiat après-guerre." *Le Monde Juif* 52, no. 158 (1998): 90–103.

———. "L'UGIF et l'histoire." *Les Nouveaux cahiers* 83 (1985–86): 48–55.

Segall, Aryeh. *Guide to Jewish Archives*. Jerusalem and New York: World Council on Jewish Archives, 1981.

Shandler, Jeffrey. *Awakening Lives: Autobiographies of Jewish Youth in Poland before the Holocaust*. New Haven, CT: Yale University Press, 2002.

Simon-Nahum, Perrine. "Entre Vajda et Levinas: les études juives en France après 1945." *Les Cahiers du judaïsme* 3 (1998): 27–35.

Simpson, Elizabeth, ed. *The Spoils of War: World War II and Its Aftermath: The Loss, Reappearance, and Recovery of Cultural Property*. New York: Harry N. Abrams, 1997.

Smith, Bonnie G. *The Gender of History: Men, Women, and Historical Practice*. Cambridge, Mass.: Harvard University Press, 1998.

Smith, Laurajane. *Uses of Heritage*. London: Routledge, 2006.

Stoler, Ann Laura. *Along the Archival Grain*. Princeton, NJ: Princeton University Press, 2009.

———. "Colonial Archives and the Arts of Governance: On the Content in the Form." In *Refiguring the Archive*. Edited by Carolyn Hamilton, Verne Harris, Jane Taylor, Michele Pickover, Graeme Reid, and Razia Saleh, 83–100. Dordrect, Netherlands: Kluwer, 2002.

Szapiro, Elie. "Les Fonds judeo-français de Hebrew Union College." *Archives Juives* 9, no. 1 (1972–73): 11–13.

Tcherikower, Elias, ed. *Historishe Shriftn*. Vilna, Poland: YIVO, 1937–39.

———. *Yidn in Frankraykh: Shtudyes un Materialn*. 2 vols. New York: YIVO–Section of History, 1942.

Thomas, Marcel. "Détournements, vols, destructions." In *Histoire des bibliothèques françaises: les bibliothèques de la révolution et du XIXe siècle*. Edited by Dominique Varry, 263–71. Paris: Promodis, 1991.

Trouillot, Michel-Rolph. *Silencing the Past: Power and the Production of History*. Boston: Beacon, 1995.

Valland, Rose. *Le Front de l'art: défense des collections françaises, 1939–1945*. Paris: Réunion des musées nationaux, 1997.

Varry, Dominique. "D'un Siècle à l'autre." In *Histoire des bibliothèques françaises: les bibliothèques de la révolution et du XIXe siècle*. Edited by Dominique Varry, 625–31. Paris: Promodis, 1991.

Volkoff, Anne. "La Bibliothèque Tourgueniev." In *Histoire des bibliothèques françaises: les bibliothèques au XXe siècle, 1914–1990.* Edited by Martine Poulain, 28–29. Paris: Promodis, 1992.

Waite, Robert G. "Returning Jewish Cultural Property: The Handling of Books Looted by the Nazis in the American Zone of Occupation, 1945–1952." *Libraries and Culture* 37, no. 3 (2002): 213–28.

Web, Marek. "Between New York and Moscow: The Bund Archives." In *Jewish Politics in Eastern Europe: The Bund at 100.* Edited by Jack Jacobs, 243–54. New York: New York University Press, 2001.

Weill, Georges. "Les Archives Juives en France." In *Terres promises: mélanges offerts à André Kaspi.* Edited by Hélène Harter, Antoine Marès, Pierre Melandri, and Catherine Nicault, 549–65. Paris: Publications de la Sorbonne, 2008.

———. "Les Archives Juives d'Alsace: un patrimoine à préserver." Paper presented at the XXe Colloque de la Société d'histoire des Israélites d'Alsace et de Lorraine, Strasbourg, France, 1998.

———. "Les Bibliothèques Juives en Europe." In *European Jewry, a Handbook/ Communautés Juives d'Europe, Receuil.* Edited by Ernest Stock, 155–63. Ramat Gan, Israel: Turtledove, 1982.

———. "Compte-rendu de l'assemblée générale de la Société des études juives et de la Revue des études juives/Collection de la revue des études juives." *Revue des Études Juives* 165, nos. 3–4 (2006): 605–18.

———. "Le Sort des archives de la Société d'histoire des israélites d'Alsace et de Lorraine: quelques observations à propos de la communication du Dr. Honigmann." Paper presented at the XXIIIe Colloque de la Société d'Histoire des Israélites d'Alsace et de Lorraine, Strasbourg, France, 2001.

Weill, Georges, Samuel Kerner, and Richard Ayoun. *Alliance Israélite Universelle, Catalogue des manuscrits de la bibliothèque.* Paris: Alliance Israélite Universelle, 1979.

Weinberg, David. *A Community on Trial: The Jews of Paris in the 1930s.* Chicago: University of Chicago Press, 1977.

———. "The French Jewish Community after World War II: The Struggle for Survival and Self-Definition." *Forum* 45 (1982): 45–54.

Weinberg, Gerhard L. "German Documents in the United States." *Central European History* 41 (2008): 555–67.

Weinreich, Max. *Hitler's Professors: The Part of Scholarship in Germany's Crimes against the Jewish People.* New York: YIVO, 1946.

Wieviorka, Annette. "Du Centre de Documentation Juive Contemporaine au Mémorial de la Shoah." *Revue de l'histoire de la Shoah*, no. 181 (2004): 10–36.

———. "La Construction de la mémoire du génocide en France." *Revue de l'histoire de la Shoah*, no. 149 (1993): 23–38.

———. *Déportation et génocide: entre la mémoire et l'oubli.* Paris: Plon, 1992.

———. "Despoliation, Reparation, Compensation." In *Starting the Twenty-First Century: Sociological Reflections and Challenges.* Edited by Ernest Krausz and Gitta Tulea, 201–22. New Brunswick, NJ: Transaction, 2002.

———. "Les Juifs en France au lendemain de la guerre: état des lieux." *Archives Juives* 28, no. 1 (1995): 4–22.

Wieviorka, Annette, and Floriane Azoulay. *Mission d'étude sur la spoliation des juifs de France: le pillage des appartements et son indemnisation.* Paris: La Documentation française, 2000.

Yerushalmi, Yoself Hayim. *Zakhor: Jewish History and Jewish Memory.* New York: Schocken, 1989.

Zaagsma, Gerben. "A Fresh Outburst of the Old Terror? Jewish Volunteers in the Spanish Civil War." Ph.D. diss., European University Institute, Florence, Italy, 2008.

———. "The Local and the International—Jewish Communists in Paris between the Wars." *Simon Dubnow Institute Yearbook* 8 (2009): 345–63.

———. " 'Red Devils': The Botwin Company in the Spanish Civil War." *East European Jewish Affairs* 33 (2003): 83–99.

INDEX

THE OXFORD SERIES ON HISTORY AND ARCHIVES

General Editors
Francis X. Blouin Jr. and William G. Rosenberg,
University of Michigan

Processing the Past: Changing Authorities in History and the Archives
Francis X. Blouin Jr. and William G. Rosenberg

"Collect and Record!": Jewish Holocaust Documentation
in Postwar Europe
Laura Jockusch